D1031807

THE VALUES OF CHANGE IN SOCIAL WORK

Current changes in social work practice pose moral and political dilemmas which are relevant to practitioners, students, social work educators and policy makers alike. The contributors to this book, all highly experienced and respected social work practitioners and theoreticians, analyse social work values in relation to these changes in practice. This uniquely practical approach makes the difficult and complex arguments surrounding values accessible to both students and practitioners.

The contributions examine major developments in social work from a moral, philosophical and political perspective, and place them in relation to each other. Some describe theoretical and practical difficulties faced by social workers in changing forms of practice, while others deal with a particular change and examine it in detail.

With its emphasis on the ethical dimensions of practice, *The Values of Change in Social Work* represents a major contribution to the debate about the nature of social work. In addition, it has a direct bearing on current social work practice and will be an invaluable source of practical help for social work practitioners at all levels, as well as a useful tool for students attempting to come to terms with complex value concepts.

The Editor
Steven Shardlow is Lecturer in Social Work Studies at the University of Sheffield.

TAVISTOCK LIBRARY OF SOCIAL WORK PRACTICE

General Editor: M. Rolf Olsen

THE VALUES OF CHANGE IN SOCIAL WORK

Edited by
STEVEN SHARDLOW

TAVISTOCK/ROUTLEDGE
London and New York

First published 1989 by Routledge
11 New Fetter Lane, London EC4P 4EE
29 West 35th Street, New York, NY 10001

© 1989 Steven Shardlow

Typeset by J&L Composition Ltd, Filey, North Yorkshire
Printed and bound in Great Britain by
Biddles Ltd, Guildford and King's Lynn

British Library Cataloguing in Publication Data

The Values of change in social work.——
(Tavistock library of social work practice).
1. Great Britain. Welfare work. Values
I. Shardlow, Steven
361.3'01'3

ISBN 0–415–01837–4
ISBN 0–415–01838–2 *Pbk*

Library of Congress Cataloging-in-Publication Data

The Values of change in social work.
(Tavistock library of social work practice)
Bibliography: p.
Includes indexes.
1. Social service—Great Britain. 2. Social
values. 3. Social service—Philosophy. I. Shardlow,
Steven, 1952–   . II. Series.
HV245.V35 1989   361.3'0941   88–32533
ISBN 0–415–01837–4
ISBN 0–415–01838–2 (pbk.)

FOR POLLY

CONTENTS

Acknowledgements   ix

General Editor's Foreword   x

List of Contributors   xiv

1 CHANGING SOCIAL WORK VALUES:
  AN INTRODUCTION   1
  Steven Shardlow

        PART ONE: SETTING THE SCENE

2 SOCIAL WORK VALUES: CONTEXT AND
  CONTRIBUTION   11
  Noel Timms

3 VALUES IN ACTION   24
  Juliet Cheetham

        PART TWO: CHANGING VALUES

4 VALUES IN LOCALLY BASED WORK   45
  Michael Bayley

5 HOLISTIC HEALTH CARE AND
  PROFESSIONAL VALUES   61
  Mike Simpkin

CONTENTS

6 RESIDENTIAL SOCIAL WORK WITHOUT
  RESIDENCE   82
  Steven Shardlow

7 PARTICIPATION AND PATERNALISM   98
  Eric Sainsbury

8 OPEN RECORDS AND SHARED DECISIONS
  WITH CLIENTS   114
  Malcolm Payne

9 DISCRETION AND MANAGERIALISM   135
  Terry Bamford

10 TAKEN FROM HOME   155
   Olive Stevenson

11 THE MORALITY OF PRIVATE SOCIAL
   CARE: PRIVATIZATION IN SOCIAL WORK   180
   Stuart Etherington

   References   198

   Name index   211

   Subject index   215

ACKNOWLEDGEMENTS

Many people have been involved in the preparation of this book. It is not possible or practical to mention them all; my thanks go to all those who have helped in any way whatsoever. I offer particular thanks for the support and advice given by Simon Holdaway and Huw Edwards in the early stages of developing the concept behind the book, and to Rolf Olsen and Eric Sainsbury for their encouragement and help. Many departmental secretaries have been involved in typing several drafts of this book: I would like to express my gratitude to them all. Finally, mention must be made of the partners and children of the contributors, who bore the direct consequences of the writing of this, and other books, by giving the authors time to work.

GENERAL EDITOR'S FOREWORD

In recent years the question of social work has become the centre of controversy and debate. The anti-social work critique has fostered some improbable alliances between groups of social administrators, sociologists, doctors, and certain newspapers. The criticisms vary in content and emphasis, and are often contradictory in their conclusions. Baroness Wooton was of the view that at a professional level social workers remain over-dominated by therapeutic concerns and the significance of the relationship, and inflict on their clients a watered-down psychoanalysis, under the guise of casework, in place of a proper concern for their social rights.

An opposing view criticises social work for assuming a political role, and expounding radical ideas which raise clients' dissatisfaction with their disadvantaged position, in the process failing to consider psychological explanations for motivation and actions. Others suggest that social workers are no more than agents of control, maintaining the status quo, enforcing the views of the ruling establishment, constituting a threat to individual freedom and rights. Contrary opinion argues that social workers sanction and provide pious excuses for social transgression and lawlessness, and encourage a cult of social and personal irresponsibility.

The reasons for these denouncements can be considered in a number of ways; not least, in the light of the particular position and role of social work in society and the values which govern its practice. Social work is deeply concerned with social well-being of the individual, with socially and economically disadvantaged groups, to represent people who do not fulfil or respect normal social expectations, to advocate on their behalf and ensure the adequacy of the systems and social institutions which affect them. Charlotte Towle once characterised social work as 'the profession which embodies and expresses the social conscience of society' (*The Learner in Education for the Professions*, 1954). This conception places immense responsibility on the profession, which is asked to implement a set of values to which society may give contradictory or only partial support. This role requires the social worker to adopt a particular moral and political stance which may be publicly unpopular. It also serves to remind society of its failures. Rapoport (*Social Work*, 1962) concludes that these roles give social workers the attributes of a minority group, which is at best ambivalently tolerated. Bisno asserts that 'the minority position is an additional insecurity to be added to the burden of daily professional tensions and frustrations' (*Social Work*, 1956).

Professor R. A. Hinde, FRS, a biologist, in a letter to *The Times* argued

> The problems confronting the social sciences are more
> difficult than that of landing a man on the moon or
> unravelling the structure of complex molecules, and involve
> issues at several levels of complexity. They are also more
> important. If one takes only the area of social psychology, the
> development of personality, the nature of interpersonal
> relationships and the dynamics of groups are issues that affect
> us all.
>   (Hinde, 22 February 1982)

This book shows that the complexity of the problem does not mean that it can be ignored. Rather it demands a remorseless teasing apart of the interacting issues by parallel examinations in the diverse social situations in which social workers are expected to practice, reach decisions, and to take actions.

It has been written by a distinguished group of practitioners and academics, most of whom are 'household names' in the field of social work, and some of whom have been in the heat of the public arena during the media debates relating to social work values.

This book is one of a series in the Tavistock Library of Social Work Practice, designed to represent the collaborative effort of social work academics, practitioners, and managers. In addition to considering the theoretical and philosophical debate surrounding the topics under consideration, the texts are firmly rooted in practice issues and the problems associated with the organisation of the services. Therefore the series will be of particular value to undergraduate and postgraduate students of social work and social administration.

The Tavistock Library of Social Work Practice series was prompted by the growth and increasing importance of the social services in our society. Until recently there has been a general approbation of social work, reflected in benedictory increase in manpower and resources, which has led to an unprecedented expansion of the personal social services, a proliferation of the statutory duties placed upon them, and major reorganisation. The result has been the emergence of a profession faced with the immense responsibility of promoting individual and social betterment, and bearing a primary responsibility to advocate on behalf of individuals and groups who do not always fulfil or respect normal social expectations of behaviour. In spite of the growth in services these tasks are often carried out with in-adequate resources, an uncertain knowledge base, and as yet unresolved difficulties associated with the reorganisation of the personal social services in 1970. In recent years these difficulties have been compounded by a level of criticism unprecedented since that attracted by the Poor Law, united in its belief that social work has failed in its general obligation to 'provide services to the people', and in its particular duty to socialise the deliquent, restrain parents who abuse their children, prevent old people from dying alone, and provide a satisfactory level of community care for the sick, the chronically handicapped, and the mentally disabled.

These developments highlight three major issues that deserve particular attention: first, the need to construct a methodology for analysing social and personal situations, and prescribing action; second, the necessity to apply techniques that measure the performance of the individual worker and the profession as a whole in meeting stated objectives; third, and outstanding, the requirement to develop a knowledge base against which the needs of clients are understood and decisions about their care are taken. Overall, the volumes in this series make explicit and clarify these issues; contribute to the search for the distinctive knowledge base of social work; increase our understanding of the aetiology and care of personal, familial, and social problems; describe and explore new techniques and practice skills; aim to raise our commitment towards low status groups which suffer public, political, and professional neglect; and promote the enactment of comprehensive and socially just policies. Above all, these volumes aim to promote an understanding which interprets the needs of individuals, groups, and communities in terms of the synthesis between inner needs and the social realities that impinge upon them, and which aspire to develop informed and skilled practice.

M. Rolf Olsen, 1988

CONTRIBUTORS

Terry Bamford read law at Oxford and Social Administration at LSE. He has worked as a probation officer and a senior probation officer with responsibility for training. For some four years he was the Assistant General Secretary for BASW before becoming an Assistant Controller (Development) with Harrow Social Services Department. He is currently the Director of Social Services for the Southern Health and Social Services Board. He was the Chair of BASW from 1982–1984.

Michael Bayley has undertaken research into what passed for 'community care' for the mentally handicapped; this resulted in the publication of *Mental Handicap and Community Care* in 1973. Subsequently he undertook research into locally based social work at Dinnington, near Sheffield. He was a lecturer in social administration at the University of Sheffield from 1973 until 1987, when he took early retirement. He is now working half-time with the Sheffield Health Authority Mental Handicap Services on ways of developing links with the community for people leaving hospitals and hostels.

Juliet Cheetham read English and History and Social Studies at St Andrews and Oxford Universities. After working as a probation officer in London she became Lecturer in Applied Social Studies and Fellow of Green College at Oxford University. She has researched and written books on race relations, social work with ethnic minorities, and unwanted pregnancy. She has served on a number of public bodies, including the Commission for Racial Equality and the Social Security Advisory Committee. She is now Professor and Director of the Social Work Research Centre at Stirling University.

Stuart Etherington received a BSc in Politics from Brunel University and an MA in Social Service Planning from Essex University. He has been at various times a social worker, a researcher, a policy analyst, and a director of a voluntary organization. He is currently Director of Advocacy and Information at the Royal National Institute for the Deaf. He is the Chair of the Health Policy Group of the Social and Liberal Democrats and fought for the constituency of Tottenham in the 1987 general election.

Malcolm Payne is Head of Applied Community Studies at Manchester Polytechnic. He has previously worked in probation, in social services, in local and national voluntary organizations, and as a lecturer in social work at Bristol University. He chaired the BASW project group on case recording and is the author of many articles on social work practice, educational management, and policy. His latest book is *Social Care in the Community* (1986).

Eric Sainsbury worked as a school teacher, probation officer, family caseworker, and student unit supervisor. He was Professor of Social Administration and Director of Applied Social Studies at the University of Sheffield until his retirement in 1987. His research has been mainly concerned with service users' and social workers' views of social work processes, and his publications include *Social Diagnosis in Casework* (1970), *Social Work with Families* (1975), *The Personal Social Services* (1977), *Social Work in Focus* (1982), and *Mental Health Social Work Observed* (1983). He has served at various times on committees of CCETSW, the Joint University Council, and ATSWE, and of various local services and organizations in South Yorkshire, where he is also a magistrate.

Steven Shardlow read PPE and Applied Social Studies at Oxford University. He has worked as a residential and field social worker, and also as a social work manager. Currently he is a lecturer in social work studies at the University of Sheffield, where he teaches a course on social work and social values. He is in part-time practice in a locally based social services project for Sheffield Family and Community Services Department.

Mike Simpkin studied at the Universities of Oxford and Nottingham. He has almost twenty years of experience as a field social worker, initially in Surrey and then in Sheffield, where he has been attached both to a psychiatric team and to a general practice. He now works for the Leeds City Council Health Unit. He is the author of *Trapped Within Welfare* (1983) (second edition).

Olive Stevenson is Professor of Social Work Studies at Nottingham University, having previously held chairs at Keele and Liverpool. She was before that Reader in Applied Social Studies at Oxford University and Professorial Fellow of St Anne's College. Her career in social work started in child care, but over the years her interests have widened and her main academic and research interests have been in the personal social services generally, with specialist interest in child welfare and the social care of frail elderly people. She teaches the ethics sequence for the social work students. She was a member of the Maria Colwell Inquiry in 1974 and is currently a member of the Social Security Advisory Committee and of the Registered Homes Tribunal. Published works include *Specialization in Social Work Teams* (1981), *Child Abuse: aspects of professional co-operation* (with Hallet) (1980), and *Age and Vulnerability: a guide to better practice* (1989).

Noel Timms is the Director of the School of Social Work, Leicester University, and Chairman, Centre for the Study of Individual and Social Values. Previously he has held chairs at Bradford and Newcastle Universities. Recent publications include *Social Work Values: an enquiry* (1983) and *Intervention in Marriage* (with Annette Blampied) (1987).

Chapter One

CHANGING SOCIAL WORK VALUES: AN INTRODUCTION

STEVEN SHARDLOW

We may believe in an intuitive way that values are a vital component of social work, yet give little thought to why they are important or to the characteristics of the relationship between values and social work practice, or indeed to the nature of values themselves. As R. Huws Jones wrote in 1970, 'A man's values are like his kidneys: he rarely knows he has any until they are upset' (Timms 1983:16). In the hurly-burly of current social work practice it is all too possible to respond to immediate pressures without giving much thought to the values implicit in our actions.

Why then are values so important? At least part of the answer may be sought in the complex network of relationships between the social worker and the public. They are first and foremost fellow human beings and citizens of a common state. These two sets of relationships imply the existence of mutual rights and duties. (For example, members of a given state have a mutual obligation, in most circumstances, to obey the law of the land.) The very existence of society and the state is predicated upon such a reciprocal system. In common with other groups, e.g. lawyers, doctors, and teachers, social workers have additional sets of rights and duties. At least three such sets can be identified: those relating to people served by social workers, those relating to their employers, and those relating to the wider profession. Two broad issues arise. First, any additional rights and duties accruing to social workers need to be exercised or carried out according to some widely accepted set of principles. Second, these rights and duties open the very real possibility of conflict between social workers and members of the public, or

1

indeed their employers or the wider profession. Even where such conflict is absent and a social worker's actions are sanctioned by the client's permission, there is need for some guidance about how to act: just because an act is sanctioned by a client it is not necessarily right to perform that act. Social workers are morally accountable for any reasonably foreseeable consequences of their actions, and in that respect they are no different from anyone else, but there are additional responsibilities imposed on them by virtue of their being social workers, and so they must exercise additional caution when performing professional duties.

There is a direct link between values and action. When we perform an action we, and the act itself, may be judged according to values expressed through that action. Questions of value run through all our actions as social workers. Guidance is necessary because of the very nature of social work, involving as it does work with people: 'competence in the art of working with values is competence in an art [the social worker] will practise for the length of his working days' (Leighton, Stalley, and Watson 1982:2).

We cannot escape dealing in the stuff of values because of the very nature of social work practice. The very fact of undertaking work with people involves complex decisions and dilemmas of a moral nature which are not reducible to technocratic solutions. That is why the Central Council for the Education and Training of Social Workers (CCETSW) has stated that an essential minimum requirement of social workers at the point of qualification should be the 'capacity to apply a system of professional values' (CCETSW 1988:15). Similarly the British Association of Social Workers (BASW) states as the first item in its code of ethics: 'Social work is a professional activity. Implicit in its practice are ethical principles which prescribe the professional responsibility of the social worker' (BASW 1975). Similar statements expressing the idea that social work practice is based on values of one sort or another are to be found in ethical codes adopted by other social work bodies (SCA 1986; NASW 1980). There is then considerable agreement that social work needs a value system, and there is evidence of attempts to formulate this in the various codes of practice.

Questions about values do not only affect individual relationships between social workers and their clients, they permeate the whole context of social work practice. We can identify with some confidence the loci of potential disputes about values. Downie and Loudfoot (1978) have attempted this, enumerating the following areas:

> In the first place, the very idea of having some form of social work system embodies value judgements, for it presupposes that there are certain categories of people who ought to be given help of certain kinds, and that there ought to be special occupations to provide this kind of help. How best to provide this help, in terms of both general policy and specific instance, poses a second set of value-problems. Third, complex value judgements are generated by the questions of whether there are special skills which it is possible for a social worker to acquire, and if so, in what manner it is permissible or desirable for him to exercise them. Finally, there are questions of value raised by the direction in which social work is or ought to be evolving, and, in particular, whether it ought to become more or less 'professionalized' or 'institutionalized'.
>
> (Downie and Loudfoot 1978:111)

Now all of these questions are susceptible to answers of a sort, based upon value judgements. Following the work of Hare (1981), any value judgement as an answer to any of these questions should have the quality of being prescriptive and universalizable and should have the quality of 'overridingness'. In other words, it should tell us what to do, it must apply in all similar sets of circumstances, and it should override other sorts of answers precisely because it is a value judgement. It tells us what *ought* to be the case. Even so, the answer given by any one individual is quite likely to be different from that given by another. There are at least two reasons for this. First, any answer will be grounded in belief and will rest upon the ethical and political views of the individual. Beliefs about fundamental principles vary according to personal taste or professional opinion. Second, there may be agreement about fundamental principles but disagreement over their application to a particular case. It is important to come to some understanding about the reasons for such disagreements.

This is no small point. We need to understand the grounds on which different individuals make their value judgements: it is not so much the answers but more the process by which those answers are derived that will further our understanding about 'values' in social work. For Leighton, Stalley, and Watson (1982) this is the hallmark of philosophical discussion. It requires that two tasks be undertaken: 'discussion aimed at clarification of the value judgement ... critical evaluation of the logical relation between grounds offered and the judgement made' (Leighton *et al.* 1982:3). How then are we to go about such tasks in order to increase our understanding of values in social work? By so doing we shall not discover definitive answers, but we may understand the questions a little better.

But we are rushing ahead. In our haste to establish a method of approach we have omitted to ask what we mean by the term 'values'. Much to do with values is obscure or confusing, not least the very concept of 'values'. When we see calm, reassuring phrases written about social work values we should be on our mettle immediately. Take the expression 'the value base of social work', often bandied about by practitioner and academic alike. This comforting phrase seems to imply that there is something solid and firm upon which the enterprise of social work is erected. The inclusion of the definite article implies the existence of one such solid support for the whole of social work practice. Yet on closer examination we find something of a paradox: the lack of a clear consensus about the nature of social work values, yet an apparent belief that such a consensus exists. As we have seen, there is wide-scale, although not universal, assent for the notion that social work needs a value system. There is much less agreement about the content of any such system. Indeed, the CCETSW (1976) working party set up to examine values in social work abandoned any attempt to define simply and succinctly the concept of 'values'. The reason for so doing is not hard to find; it was admirably summed up by Noel Timms:

> Almost any kind of belief and obligation, anything preferred for any reason or for no apparent reason at all, any objective in the short or long run, any ideal or rule, is heaped into a large pantechnicon carrying the device 'Social Work Values – will travel anywhere'.
>
> (Timms 1983:2)

We expect much of the word 'value': it has become a ubiquitous synonym for a variety of other concepts – *inter alia*, professional ethics, political beliefs, and personal morality. It is difficult to reach agreement about the content of social work values when the notion of values is itself so extensive and vague; erecting such a complex activity as social work on such a weak foundation seems well-nigh impossible.

It is hardly surprising that many social workers would prefer to ignore the difficulties and to take refuge in old certainties. It is far easier to subscribe to the idea that there is indeed a finite number of values specific to social work, such as is found in Biestek's list of seven 'principles': individualization, purposeful expression of feelings, controlled emotional involvement, acceptance, non-judgemental attitude, client self-determination, and confidentiality (Biestek 1961:17). Those who adopt this viewpoint only delude themselves by reducing the complex to the simple. However, recognizing the lack of agreement about the constituents of 'values' in social work, or reaffirming their importance, does little enough to advance our real understanding, except perhaps in so far as it makes us aware of the complexity of value questions in social work, and for that matter generally.

We can now return to our question 'How ought we to broaden our understanding of value questions in social work?'. For the busy practitioner or student, abstract discussions about values at a theoretical level can be both dry and uninformative. Rather than try to develop an understanding about the place of values in contemporary social work by applying abstract concepts to practice, this book examines areas of social work where change is a significant element, and it considers value problems that daily confront practitioners. An analysis of values taking as its starting-point current areas of practice in social work should make debates more accessible to, and more relevant to the needs of, the practitioner. By examining a series of current changes it is possible to identify current themes across a range of normally discrete and diverse elements of practice. Are there, for example, common and current moral dilemmas that arise out of new forms of practice? Are social workers in these various fields facing similar value problems?

This book, then, adopts a distinctive approach in an attempt to illuminate value questions through the medium of change. By analysing values in relation to changes in practice we are able to reveal a rich seam. Change is often a challenge to existing structures and traditions. Changing practice sharpens our naturally somewhat blunted concern for value questions. In the process of change we are more likely to seek to ensure that existing values are preserved, and therefore more able to describe and recognize what these are and how they operate. Alternatively, as change in social work practice may be generated for a variety of reasons – managerial fiat, worker initiative, or public pressure – it is possible that new or evolving values may themselves be the engine of change. We are most likely to see present 'values' changing, adapting, being transmuted into different forms, or indeed we may even see the emergence of new 'values'. Where change is taking place it is likely that discussion about value issues will be at its sharpest. For some, innovation may be a source of challenge and refreshment; for others it may be the cause of stress and disaffection; for all it will be a source of debate.

In recent years there have been substantial changes both in the nature of social work practice and in the broader context in which social work operates. These two factors must be related: social work does not operate in a vacuum, isolated from society. It is not the purpose of this book to provide a detailed analysis of changes in social work practice or of the relationship of social change to developments in social work; it is rather to enable us better to understand some aspects of social work values in order to aid the development of ethically sound practice. Obviously, it is not possible in one volume to examine more than a few changes taking place in social work practice. Those selected are intended to represent significant developments which will have, and indeed are having, an important effect on the way social work is practised. Of course with the benefit of hindsight other developments may come to be seen to have more significance or be more durable.

In the last twenty-five years many major developments in social work have occurred: new models of practice have emerged, a host of organizational structures have evolved, and child sexual abuse has been 'discovered', to mention but a few. Moreover, social work is being conducted against a backcloth of social change of increasing ferocity for many service uses (Wicks 1987). The post-war consensus about the nature and function of the state has broken down. An enterprise culture is being vigorously promoted by government, fostered by the growth in dominance of the 'New Right' ideology. There is no longer broad agreement about the scope of the welfare state, as those at the margins of society increase in number and compassion seems to falter. This has tremendous implications for the future of social work practice. An increasingly important debate for social workers will be the extent to which social work can fit into the enterprise culture – indeed how far it should attempt to do so; and how does ethically competent practice relate to these wider changes?

A persistent theme for social workers has been the nature of their relationship to the people who receive social work help. New practice models are being developed which attempt to relate social work more to the needs of people in local communities, whether the help comes from neighbourhood offices, resource centres, or health centres. These models challenge traditional concepts of health care and social work. We need to understand the ethical implications of some of these developments to enable us to work better with people in local communities and create effective working relationships with colleagues, especially as part of multidisciplinary teams. Without an understanding of the values implicit in these developments we shall be unable to translate them into effective models of service delivery.

Another important theme has been the demand for the greater involvement and participation of clients in the social work process, both through access to records about themselves and for greater control over the decisions made by public bodies which affect the lives of individuals. Social work has attempted to respond to this pressure, which reflects a growth of consumerism in society as a whole. These developments cannot be seen in isolation. The trends towards making social work more relevant to local communities and towards involving people in decisions about their lives interact with each other and lead to the need to examine changes which have taken place in the relationships between social workers and their clients.

Equally, it should not be forgotten that social workers are

usually part of large organizations, and undertake their practice in that context. The challenge to managers and social workers alike is to define models of professional practice which allow managers to manage and social workers to conduct their practice effectively and ethically, yet which can accommodate changes which are evident in practice. Also, there is now considerable media pressure on social workers, especially in child abuse cases. Often the social worker is put into an untenable position, criticized for over-hasty action when children are removed from their parents, yet pilloried if abused children are left at home and subsequently killed or seriously injured by parents. We need to understand more about the values involved when social workers remove people from the community – not just children but other groups as well.

This book examines these themes through consideration of particular changes with a view to:–

a) understanding the philosophical principles and the moral or political values implicit in these developments
b) identifying recurring moral dilemmas and value questions that arise as a result of new forms of practice, to explore the implications for practitioners
c) discovering whether there are common themes emerging across the range of new developments.

The book is divided into two parts. The first section describes some current value difficulties facing social workers, both from a theoretical examination of some difficulties in the way we think and talk about values and through an account of value problems of the type which regularly occur in practice and of the ways in which social workers attempt to deal with these difficulties. The second part of the book examines particular changes in detail.

© Steven Shardlow

Part One

SETTING THE SCENE

Chapter Two

SOCIAL WORK VALUES: CONTEXT AND CONTRIBUTION

NOEL TIMMS

INTRODUCTION

This book focuses on particular difficulties, those described as moral dilemmas, in the contemporary practice of social work, and on specific value issues implicit in new forms or particular aspects of that practice. It centres on the work of social workers, on facing and resolving problems at the level of the individual practitioner, the team, and the agency. This chapter contributes indirectly to the particular consideration and the concrete instance through a critical discussion of value-talk in social work. Such talk has to be set in a context wider than that provided by social work and its practice. This produces difficulty, since the notion of values in general use, as well as in sociology, philosophy, and so on, supplies no ready-made nostrums or even rules that can be applied to social work. In other words, if simple and quick solutions are envisaged (what the original Lady Bountiful in Farquhar's play called 'receipts'), the news of this chapter is not good. Social work has for too long blessed itself, as it were, with values, without enquiring at all closely into their ingredients. The enquiry which I am proposing is no curtsey in the direction of academic respectability. It is a necessary requirement for making more intelligible the project of this book.

A sample from what is already contained in this chapter may help to illustrate the general approach to be adopted. Take the sentence at the start of this introduction. Those familiar with social work writing probably glanced over it without pausing. A re-consideration suggests certain problems requiring attention before we can be sure that the point of the sentence has been grasped. Not all difficulties may be described as moral, nor are all moral difficulties dilemmas. What relationship, if any, can be

11

discerned between moral dilemmas and 'value issues'? How is 'moral' to be understood? These may appear obfuscating questions, particularly in view of the ease and frequency with which the adjective 'moral' appears in social work writings. We seem satisfied with 'moral panic' and 'moral career' as explanations of some kind, no matter what. We are pleased to detect signs of (regrettable) life in the 'moral' categories of deserving and undeserving; we praise the avoidance of moral judgement, failing to distinguish it from judgements of a moralistic kind. Yet the force and function of 'moral' in these and other instances remains blandly unclear. Is it, for instance, the same aspect or aspects of careers, panics, categories, and judgements that make them 'moral'? Finally, the idea of the explicit expression of a value-position may be relatively easily grasped, particularly in the case of social work. Social work, to judge from its literature, engages in self-conscious refrains around 'values' more than any other profession. Yet the notion of values implied in a practice requires unravelling. By what means, for example, can we come to an agreement with another practitioner or outside observer that such and such are indeed the values inescapably caught up in the practice under consideration?

Questions like these require answers if value-talk in social work is to provide the medium for any sustained conversation on topics and problems of evident importance. Answers, however, are not 'out there', waiting to be found, either in society at large or in the disciplines that could be expected to have developed special knowledge and skill in relation to 'values'. Philosophy, it might be supposed, should be able to render immediate help in relation to the difficulties just raised concerning the meaning of 'moral'. Yet the meaning is so highly controversial in contemporary philosophy that Wollheim has recently commented, 'Just what moral scrutiny is or what makes a form of scrutiny moral, I take to be one of the obscurest issues in human culture, and we should not close our minds to the thought that there is no one such thing' (1984:197). This kind of difficulty (evident also in the treatment of values in anthropology and sociology) is fundamental, but it should not act as a deterrent in the search for and use of a wide context for the elucidation of value-talk in social work. This is for two main reasons. First, the wider context is simply a requirement for

12

understanding and undertaking such talk: we cannot adequately grasp self-determination, individualism, fraternity, and so on, within the confines of social work. Second, as we work towards making social work value-talk more robust and more discriminating, it is possible to envisage a social work contribution to the wider debate. We may be able to offer with increased confidence significant examples of sharp conflict and poignant difficulty, and in their delineation escape the present confines of the anecdotal and parochial. As Blum (1973:3) has put it: 'much useful moral philosophy could be done just by trying to describe fully, accurately, and realistically certain *typical* [italics supplied] moral situations and attempting to face the problems inherent in this task without one's philosophical presuppositions about what counts as a morally relevant consideration and what does not.' This attention to a story-telling that is not unending and the avoidance of premature casuistry (cf Halmos 1949) constitutes a good base from which to explore relationships between a notion of care and the point of morality: 'if human beings did not care about one another there could not be what we speak of as morality, for the reason that morality is a manifestation of that caring' (Beehler 1978:1).

The main sections of this chapter will consider the extent to which social work value-talk, in its present condition, is able to give robust help to practitioners facing particular problems, and how newly defined problems and changes in practice may be approached.

VALUE-TALK IN SOCIAL WORK

A Canon of Unevenly Developed Fragments

It appears that once the new form of CCETSW training has been introduced any problems in value-talk will be more or less a thing of the past. CCETSW Paper 20:6 confidently expects that social workers in the 1990s will be able (as they will be required) to articulate a value system that is coherent, to show they can recognize a value system other than their own when they see one, and to demonstrate an understanding of that coherent value system which governs their professional actions and attitudes. Such expectations exaggerate the confidence we may

13

presently place on the current state of value-talk in social work and in general. Value-talk in social work is in actuality a rather halting affair. Asking the question 'What are social work values?' tends to evoke a slightly impatient response. 'Well, they are things like self-determination, acceptance, confidentiality, respect for the individual and so on.' Such a response normally acts as a conversation stopper, but it at least outlines the belief in a clutch of important ideas taken as somehow canonical in a broad church of social work. The ideas, however, remain at different stages of development, and it is not immediately apparent how they go together as 'like', nor what indeed they are like; and the 'and so on' is not without problems.

Notions of self-determination have been analysed in relation to social work at least to the extent that its complexities both in meaning and in operation have become apparent. This has come about partly because elucidation of self-determination in social work relies on the treatment of liberty in the wider context of the literature of political and moral philosophy (McDermott 1975). A similar stage of development has been reached, for much the same reason, in relation to the idea of respect for the individual (Plant 1970; Clark 1985). In contrast, other items remain in a primitive state, and their meaning accordingly lacks security. Take, for example, acceptance. The words 'I accepted this' occur frequently in the records of social workers but they refer to one or more of the following – at least:

I made no response
I took the information at face value
I did not challenge the statement, though this was expected
I explicitly made known I had grasped the point of the statement
I implicitly made known I had grasped the point
I explicitly/implicitly avoided blaming someone
I showed that a statement or a person was being taken seriously
... and so on.

What calls for systematic study is the point of acceptance, as well as what the term means. Is 'acceptance' a calm recognition of reality or the conveyance of a judgement that a particular reality should flourish? Are we to see acceptance as a synonym for toleration, a forgotten but familiar virtue, and, if this is the case, are there conditions or characters that cannot or should not be tolerated? Acceptance, in short, looks like a rather low-key matter, until it is placed in context – a context other than that supplied by the current loose-leaf catechism of social work values. Take, for example, the crucial role given to acceptance in Wollheim's recent moral psychology (1984). Acceptance is placed at the core of friendship, and involves 'the overcoming of confusion, the abatement of intolerance, and the relinquishing of certain controlling attitudes' (p. 280).

Finally, we must consider 'acceptance' in the light of the emphasis some practitioners, and CCETSW, now place on ideas of challenge and confrontation. Such notions, akin to the current trend towards equating behaviour which any person finds 'offensive' with behaviour which *ipso facto* others ought not to display, seem strangely aristocratic. In any case, they sit somewhat awkwardly with some of the items in the ordinary list of social work values.

The Canon as a Whole

Questions such as those raised above are posed by any serious attempt to understand the list as it were item by item, but we also need to grasp the list as a whole, and current value-talk raises certain difficulties in this regard. First, value-talk in social work – and more generally – has what might be described as a tandem quality. Typically, 'values' are found coupled explicitly with 'ethics', 'attitude', and 'beliefs', and implicitly with rules (or norms) or ideals (or justifications). These are different notions but related, and they each and all require defining in relation to each other before we can be sure that any sort of coherence has been grasped and articulated. Second, the current manner of value-talk seems to encourage an assumption that the list of values is already complete. It is difficult to consider either adding to or deleting from a list without a clear idea of how the listing was carried out in the first place and of what the identity of the items *as* items consists, i.e., are we listing attitudes, or beliefs, or rules, or aspects of each?

Third, values, again in social work and more generally, are commonly linked with the notion of system. It is almost as if one cannot be mentioned without the other. I believe that our ordinary usage of 'system' does emphasize the connection between 'values', but we should be sceptical that the best description of the connection is one referring to 'system'. Such reference must address at least three problems: what it is that is considered as linked (or how do we define values); issues of choice between 'goods'; the way values may be construed by those engaged in any social practice.

Some social work writers seem to believe that a system of values refers simply to a set of preferences which happen to go together. Such a focus on preferences collapses the rich and complex notions covered by our idea of values into rather meaningless tokens. As Baier (1985:265) has noted, 'We are simply to throw the sacred values into the hopper along with every other preference, ignore differences of level among the "preferences" or "tastes" we are taking into account, and measure all of them by the amount of money the preferrer will pay to get her way, ignoring the different sort of *expression* values of different sorts typically get and simply trying to thwart as few people as possible as little as possible.' 'Preference' is quite incapable of carrying unaided the weight of 'values'.

We use 'values' to refer to ordering and orientating ideas of the life to be led by the individual and of the worthwhile way of life for any particular society. If this is even an approximation of what we mean by 'values', then the connection between values as constituents of an individual's course of life and values as constituents of a way of social life cannot be captured by 'system'. The course of a life is lived, a way of life is followed; the connection of either with, say, a system of propositions is obscure.

Talk of 'systems' is likely also to discount the crucial problem of the choice to be made between ends or objectives, each of which may be viewed as 'good'. Griffin (1986:91) has pictured this problem in the following manner: 'What needs defending is not a mere plurality of values but a certain picture of how they are related – that they clash, that they all matter, that they all have their day, that there are no permanent orderings or rankings among them, that life depressingly often ties gain in one value to terrible loss in another, that persons may go in very different directions and still lead equally valuable lives.'

Finally, it is fruitful to consider how what to an 'outsider' may appear 'a system' is actually experienced by the 'insider'. Flathman (1976) on the idea of a social practice is useful here. A social practice consists of a patterning of characteristic actions emanating from a willing acceptance by participants of different kinds of rules. Such rules apply to commendations, obligations, and to the whole class of what Austin (1975) christened 'verdictives'. What is crucial from the viewpoint of 'systems' is both an exhaustive grouping of the subjects of the rules (for without this one would not know what is being 'systematically' linked), and also Flathman's insistence that these rules neither result from nor create the sorts of natural, physical, or logical necessity that would characterize systems.

SOCIAL WORK VALUE-TALK RESPONDS TO CHANGE

It is appropriate in view of the focus of this book to attempt to advance on the present state of value-talk in social work, which has been outlined, to consider how values might be treated in relation to the main current changes in social work. These changes may be loosely described as political: new groupings press for recognition (for example, 'blacks' and 'gays'); new ways of working aim at increasing the power of various 'communities'; notions of liberation and solidarity are increasingly used, and some traditional notions, such as rights, become much more dominant. In the face of these changes, how can value-talk in social work best be pursued? Our approach should be governed, I shall suggest, by the following arguments: the present set of social work values should not simply be discarded; the terms used to structure judgement and conception – terms like 'rights', 'interests', 'dilemmas' – should be used with more care, though not with undue reverence; we should explore more imaginatively the commonality of voice and sense to be found in the rich notion of citizenship. As these arguments are developed it is important to recall the intention of the present chapter, which was encapsulated in the title as 'context' and 'contribution'. Pursuing the arguments may help us generally, and not just in social work, to increase our grasp on the elusive phenomena we presently call 'values'. Rescher's observation describes the current general position: 'It is no exaggeration to say that we do not have available even a suitable terminology in which to record an individual's or group's values, let alone precise instruments for ascertaining what they are or what changes they are undergoing, and we are in a still worse position with regard to determining the soundness of values' (1969:v).

Against Simple Dismissal

The case against the currently acknowledged values of social work arises from different sources. Value-talk in relation to any activity faces, sooner or later, the unmasking challenge. In social work the suspicion that value-talk derives significance more from what it hides than from what it expresses received reinforcement from the various theoretical schemes that have from time to time influenced social work training. At least three of these (learning theory, and Marxist and Freudian ideas) indicate a particular way of understanding values. The first points towards the sovereignty of survival values, whilst the remaining two suggest that values are to be understood as secondary manifestations of the primary processes of production or of individuation respectively. Later developments indicating the possibility of relative autonomy for either ideology or the ego serve only to express the same problem in a different way. The appearance of values is granted to be more than 'mere', but their point is still to conceal what actually are the determinants of action, and these, so the arguments go, are in the grim reality of economic relations or in what is taken to be simple self-interest. It is clear that ideas of value, or of anything else, cannot be treated as if they arose, flourished, and died in contextless worlds, but the relationship between ideas and history constitutes a problem that cannot be solved by the simple device of collapsing one category into the other. Similarly, it should not be lightly assumed that every instance of altruism merely conceals self-interest.

We should be wary of the wholesale dismissal of currently appreciated values on the grounds that they are empty vessels standing idle until they are filled with suspicious, usually bureaucratic, substances. Nor should we accept that the currently acknowledged values are nothing more than the expression of a particular, very abstracted kind of individualism. The connectedness of the individual to society can receive acknowledgement in our treatment of self-determination, self-respect, and so on, without any necessary reference to the obscure Marxist view that the individual is directly the social being.

18

Attend To Structural Terms

It is sadly undeniable that both the substantive areas with which 'values' are concerned and also the terms in which 'values issues' are treated are of great complexity. I refer to such structural terms as rights, interests, dilemmas, preferences, and so on. I have elsewhere (Timms, 1986) attempted to show the importance of one particular classification of rights (Hohfeld's four-fold division into liberties, claims, immunities, and powers) for understanding a notion like self-determination. This illuminates classification problems; other, more serious, problems remain (Griffin 1986). And I have already referred briefly to some of the difficulties of relying exclusively on 'preferences' as a quick way through all the complexities. Consequently, I shall be mainly concerned in this section with interests and dilemmas.

'Interests' have not received as much attention in the social work literature as 'needs' and 'wants': they have not had the attention they deserve. Current discussion of 'interests' is in danger of dominance by questions concerning the degree to which knowledge of one's true interests may be attained and the means of attaining it. Danger lies in the possibility that we may rush into controversy before ensuring that our grasp on 'interests' is sufficiently firm. In pursuing 'values' it is, for instance, important to know in what relationship 'interests' stand to 'principles'. Reeve and Ware (1983), in a useful examination of the concept of interests in political theory, contrast two positions:

> The first holds that to say something is in a person's interest
> provides an initial reason for somebody's doing something,
> but it is merely an *initial* reason in the sense that it can be
> overriden, especially by reasons derived from (moral)
> principles. The second position allows moral principles to
> enter into the interest-statement, so such statements carry
> more normative weight. The one conception of interests is
> limited, and in some versions contrasts interest-statements
> with principles; the second is more all-embracing, because in a
> sense it includes principles in interests. (pp. 379–80)

It is also crucial to settle if and on what grounds statements of interest are defensible. Can someone be significantly mistaken not simply about whether or not something will in fact promote his or her well-being over the course of time but about the constituents of that well-being? Who knows when someone is mistaken about his or her interests, and how, if at all, may they accordingly act towards the person who has made this mistake?

The main points to be made in relation to 'moral dilemmas' revolve around the importance of distinguishing kinds of 'moral' difficulty: a moral dilemma is a moral difficulty of a particular kind.

Some difficulties are at the systemic level. They arise because we assume that morality is morality is morality: morality is one single kind of thing and the thing it is has only one base. So, it is proposed that the basis of morality is deontological (the force of morality derives from the recognition of duty and duty constitutes the sole reason for action); or the basis is viewed as some kind of teleology (what I should do is that which is directed towards achieving the future purpose of liberation or of total self-expression); or we look to an axiological base (aspects of character or situation are good because of my approval). Clearly, people operating from such different viewpoints would find it difficult to agree in general, and in the particular case, about the facts to be considered relevant to moral judgement, and about treating these facts. However, Emmet (1979) has argued that morality should be viewed as widely based, encompassing each of the three positions outlined, and that each position should be seen as contestable: 'One starts, therefore, with moral conflict as central; not just conflict between duty and inclination, which can be practically pressing but otherwise not very interesting. More interesting is conflict between different factors within morality, and conflicts between moral theories with different priorities' (p. 14).

Other difficulties spring from disagreements between two or more actors about which states of affairs should be considered relevant to moral judgement and whether such states of affairs actually obtain. Milo (1986), in a recent discussion of radical moral disagreements, has outlined three kinds of reason why moral disagreement might persist even when two or more actors agree about the facts of a particular case and, more generally, about which factual considerations are relevant to moral judgement. So, people may agree on basic moral standards but disagree on their judgement when these standards come into conflict. Thus, suggests Milo, two people may be in agreement that lying is wrong and that mental anguish should be reduced, relieved, and so on, but when these two considerations clash, the two people weigh them differently. Similarly, argues Milo, we can envisage situations in which disagreement between people who are agreed in so much else persists either because of disagreement about exceptions and limitations, or about applicability.

The arguments of Emmet and Milo, and of others, raise many questions for those trying to make sense of 'values', either generally or in social work in particular. They are introduced here mainly to advance the idea that in order to grasp moral dilemmas we require some kind of taxonomy of moral difficulties. 'Dilemmas' possess a certain specificity: they impinge within a moral view, rather than at a point between moral views; they press on an individual caught in a situation which demands that he or she does ill. A dilemma is a special kind of conflict.

Citizenship Re-visited

Social work is changing (it was, as a matter of fact, always so). Social workers adopt, for various reasons, different modes of organizing work – the patch system, the residential 'place' as a resource. They are pressed by emerging pressure groups – a gay person should have the same 'rights' as anyone to offer a foster/ adoptive home to a child, no 'black' child should be placed with a 'white' family. In addition social workers and social work educators criticize the 'received practice wisdom' (more remarkable, it must be said, for the extent of its reception than for the depth of its wisdom).

This is a demanding and highly critical situation. The danger is the loss of nerve and the creation and maintenance of exclusive enclaves, without the benefit even of Lateran treaties. This possibility arises from a way of understanding our present 'western' condition and an acceptance of the powerfulness of 'the new groups'. I shall briefly illustrate these two, related themes.

First, it appears increasingly misleading to assume that we live currently by a single, explicit set of acknowledged moral rules. Today, as MacIntyre (1967) has argued, we are the recipients of 'the inheritance of not only one, but of a number of

21

well-integrated moralities [italics added]. Aristotelianism, primitive Christian simplicity, the Puritan ethic, the aristocratic ethic of consumption, and the traditions of democracy and socialism have all left their mark on our moral vocabulary. . . . Between the adherents of rival moralities and between the adherents of one morality and the adherents of none there exists no court of appeal, no impersonal neutral standard. . . . We cannot expect to find in our society a single set of moral concepts, a shared interpretation of the vocabulary' (pp. 266–8). Unless collective work is undertaken to integrate the fragmented notions belonging to different traditions our condition will continue to be one of incoherence rather than pluralism.

We are prone, partly because of the situation, to recognize independent sub-sovereignties of various kinds. One example would be the reluctance to test different kinds of knowledge-claims made by or on behalf of newly emerging groups. Only blacks, it is argued, really know or know about 'the black experience'; only women can fully appreciate a woman's experience. Such epistemological apartheid is based partly at least on failure to distinguish 'knowing' from 'knowing better than', and 'perfect knowledge' from 'knowledge adequate for certain circumscribed purposes'.

The problems I have outlined – and only outlined – are of considerable complexity, and solutions have to be worked for. I believe that a return to, and a reworking of, a notion influential at the time when modern social work was created would constitute at least a start. The notion is that of citizenship, incorporating, as it does, a lively sense of the common and also a recognition of the importance of its expression. Considering and acting on 'citizenship' represents the most helpful way forward from what would otherwise be the entrapment of moral subjectivism and moral relativism. As Beiner (1983) has emphasized in his important study of the judgement which is, in my view, at the centre of social work, namely, political judgement:

It is through rational dialogue, and especially through political dialogue, that we clarify, even to ourselves, who we are and what we want. It is mistaken to assume that we necessarily enter into dialogue with an already consolidated view of where we stand and what we are after. . . . On the contrary, communication between subjects joined in a community of rational dialogue may entail a process of moral self-discovery that will lead us to a better insight into our own ends. ... Here politics functions as a normative concept describing what collective agency should be like. ... The political expression of this ideal is the republican tradition. (p. 152)

This notion of collective agency illustrates the specific virtues to be attained through extended use of the idea of citizenship. Take, for example, the notion of contract, which is enjoying something of a vogue in social work circles. This can be treated as if the most important point was the clarity of objectives agreed between two individuals each seeking the condition of 'being clear'. More rewardingly we may hear in 'contract' something of the overtones of the social contract of political theory. In such a context the contract is seen as a participation in the common sense of how things are and should be: two citizens come to an understanding. Coming to an understanding highlights a shared social process that acknowledges certain difficulties (coming *to*) and also the product of that process (an understanding acknowledged on the basis of shared social arrangements as both cognitive and pragmatic).

© 1989 Noel Timms

Chapter Three

VALUES IN ACTION

JULIET CHEETHAM

Social workers have to endure criticism as an inevitable component of their jobs. They use various defences as protection: insufficient resources; inadequate management or training, and so on. These constraints are indeed endemic but if social workers were well managed, excellently resourced, thoroughly and continuously trained, would they be immune from the attacks, fierce and sober, thoughtful and thoughtless, which are commonplace in public discourse? The answer must be no. Social workers are peculiarly vulnerable to criticism, more than many other professional groups, because they work daily with moral and political conundrums of dreadful complexity.

The case studies which follow, drawn from everyday practice, illustrate choices which have to be made between the conflicting interests of different family members, between the consumers of social work and other citizens; they also illustrate the penalties imposed by social workers on people for behaviour which is, in part, the consequence of forces beyond their control. These case studies also show the limits of social workers' worthy espousal of the primacy of the individual and of the centrality of self-determination as guidelines in their practice. All the various ethical and practical implications of these values are often inadequately considered, at least in the rhetoric of social work, if not in its practice.

In attempts to resolve the dilemmas of social work, conflicting opinions about morality and politics are more likely than agreement about the proper course of action, but, understandably, social workers are disinclined to display the morals and politics which, at least in part, guide their decisions. They play down the

24

moral aspect of decision-making because they have lived long in the shadow of an embarrassing history of alleged superiority and certainty. In the nineteenth and the early part of this century this often reflected the unquestioning, punishing morality of the times. Social workers knew, or thought they knew, how people should behave, and told them so; and taking this advice could be the price of practical help. Less explicitly these practices remain today, often concealed in the more democratic context of social skills training, behaviourism, and contract. There can, and this chapter will argue that there should be, no escape from a degree of moral arbitration but there are many strategies which can be used, with varying degrees of legitimacy, to dilute or disguise it.

First, there is the hope that from the collection of more and better information the correct resolution of a dilemma will plainly emerge. Thus there are hopes that information about the past histories of individuals and events will clarify rights and obligations and predict the likely future. There is information too of a more general nature, perhaps derived from research, which may also be used to justify actions by predicting outcomes. Incarceration in institutions may hasten death (Booth 1985); encourage criminality (Morris 1963); foster delinquency and truancy (Polsky 1966; Giller and Rutter 1983; Millham *et al.* 1975); hinder development (Bowlby 1953). Resort to institutional care should thus be avoided on the assumption, often untested, that various forms of community care will avoid these hazards and promote a better quality of life. The search for causal mechanisms must be commended as intrinsic to rational life but their status is usually highly questionable. The 'scientific' claims made by the Victorians about the rehabilitative, reformative, and altruistic characteristics of institutional care now seem hollow. Contemporary claims about the benefits of community care may seem to future generations equally mistaken. Retreat from known ills does not guarantee the benefits of the alternatives. The facts of history and careful, properly informed weighing of the greater and (usually) lesser certainties of research illuminate the complexities of the dilemmas of social workers and their clientele. Only rarely do they resolve them.

Waters are further muddied when 'value talk' is disguised in allegedly factual discourse. 'Infants thrive best when cared for by their mother' and 'welfare benefits foster dependence' are both statements which purport to be grounded in fact but which can be shown to be misusing or ignoring empirical evidence. Put thus the moral assertions 'mothers should care for their infants' and 'welfare benefits should be reduced to the minimum' are less explicit. Making distinctions between facts and values should be a crucial component of ethical decision-making. It will not resolve dilemmas but it can expose more clearly those decisions which can be justified empirically and those which may be supported or disputed by competing moral standpoints.

Second, facts, assumptions, and untested hypotheses may merge as theories used to justify decisions and actions. Changing rationales about unmarried mothers and their children's needs have been used in the last half-century to justify their separation and their life together. Historically these theories reflected prevailing moral and political values, and economic priorities, which were strengthened by empirical observations whose selection and interpretation may also have been influenced by the values of the beholder and the propounder (Cheetham 1976).

The third strategy used to solve dilemmas without open resort to moral justification is to call in aid statutory, authority, or agency policy. Acts of Parliament determine to a large extent the priorities of social work agencies. The demands of so-called 'statutory work', the protection of children and the supervision of offenders (themselves reflections of society's moral priorities), may rule out many or any services for other groups, their moral claims being thus diminished or ignored. Again, agency policies on the procedures to be followed in the exercise of statutory authority may protect social workers from moral quandary in every case while leaving them pondering on the morality of local authority powers to decide on the greater and lesser rights of different social groups, and on their obligations to their employers.

The remaining strategies for resolving dilemmas espouse more openly moral or political assumptions and, probably for this reason, are rarely resorted to explicitly. Unusually in Britain, but more commonly in countries where there are recognized professional disciplinary procedures and a case law based on earlier judgements and interpretations, social workers may use their professional ethical codes to justify or defend their actions.

26

It has been argued elsewhere that the values propounded in these codes are by no means the exclusive property of social work (Downie and Telfer 1969; Rhodes 1986); and that their qualifications and codicils can either render them meaningless or give exceptions the status of the principle. But whatever the flexibilities of interpretation social workers may still, *inter alia*, argue strongly that the rule of confidentiality should protect their clients' identity and whereabouts from the intrusions of other authorities.

Very rarely in social workers' case papers or reports, but more commonly in private discussion, will overt moral and political justifications emerge. They are more likely to be explicit in committee papers, where they may be the butt of accusations that services are being turned into a political football. The most common of these rationales are likely to be assertions of utilitarianism, humanism, socialism, and liberalism; and in any one case these value systems may run together and against each other. Consistency is unusual; perhaps impossible. In the following case studies, although political and moral preferences are rarely explicit, we shall see social workers and their managers struggling to promote the greatest happiness, or perhaps the least misery, for the greatest number of people; to distribute the meagre resources available to them to strengthen the weakest and the most impoverished while trying to resist the sacrifice of some individual's happiness or welfare which this may mean – a sacrifice which denies the humanistic roots of social work in its respect for all persons.

MISS SAD, MISS SMALL, AND JANE

Miss Small is eighteen and Jane is her illegitimate daughter. Since she became pregnant Miss Small has had no contact with Jane's father or with her own parents. She has spent most of her life in children's homes. She has never had a regular job and although of average intelligence is barely literate. Miss Sad, a social worker, has known Miss Small for two years.

Throughout her pregnancy Miss Small was adamant that she wanted the baby, would care for her herself, and would not contemplate either abortion or adoption. This is still her attitude although she has never looked after Jane herself for more than a few weeks. She discharged herself from hospital and left the baby there. Shortly after, she was reunited with Jane and given a room in a hostel for mothers with babies. After a month she disappeared, again leaving Jane behind. Jane was placed in a short-term foster home. When Miss Small discovered this some weeks later she was incensed and distressed. She begged Miss Sad to help her live 'like an ordinary mother' with Jane. Recalling her own troubled and arid childhood, she had a dream of the existence she would like for Jane and herself, a life which would give Jane the security she had never had and herself more than a stringing together of meaningless days. Articulate and clear-sighted about her past, Miss Small moved her social worker, who was well aware of the poor social work she and her parents had received over the years. Her file was thin and the decisions taken and their rationale missing or unclear. Apparently Miss Small had been taken into care voluntarily when her mother's marriage broke up. She lived in a small nursery for two or three years. Her mother seems to have visited but probably with difficulty as the nursery was in the country, far from her mother's home. Miss Small's mother appears then to have married a man who had two children. The couple had two more. Miss Small went back to her mother briefly but could not fit into the new household. She returned to the nursery and shortly afterwards an attempt was made to foster her near her own mother, perhaps with a view to preparing her for a return home; on this the file is silent. What is clear is that there were many disruptions and much distress in the foster home. Miss Small was said to be difficult and unresponsive in the home, attention-seeking and aggressive at school. Her mother's sporadic visits to the foster home and Miss Small's visits to her seem to have been scenes of disaster and disruption. Peace was bought by Miss Small's removal to a children's home; her mother faded from the picture and from the file. This quiet, commonplace tragedy reveals all the child-care failures, muddles, and malpractices graphically described by Rowe and Lambert (1973), Aldgate (1980), and Fisher *et al.* (1986).

Miss Sad was determined that this history of passing, unplanned time and no decisions should not be repeated; but also she felt responsible, on behalf of the department, for its earlier failures and thought that its legacy for Miss Small could not be dismissed. Everything that had happened to her had probably loaded the dice against her making a reasonable life as a young single mother; and she was not responsible for what had been inflicted on her. The social services department, and she as its agent, had to try to give Miss Small the chance to fulfil her wishes and to support her in the way her mother had never been. To this her superiors agreed.

Miss Small and her social worker found a small flat and Jane, now one year old, was given a day nursery place, partly to help Miss Small learn how to care for her and partly to allow her to take literacy classes. There were attempts to help Miss Small manage on her meagre income but she quickly became destitute and failed to pay the bills or to feed herself or Jane properly. She did not go to the day nursery as planned and, amidst mounting anxiety, eventually asked that Jane should be placed with foster parents while she 'set herself up'. Miss Sad agreed to the placement but began to think of permanent care for Jane away from her mother. Miss Small visited Jane sporadically and when she did seemed devoted to her.

Miss Sad began the painful discussions with Miss Small about Jane's long-term future. Inevitably perhaps this complicated the relationship between them. Miss Small piteously described her baby as 'the only thing in the world that is mine'. Although encouraged and helped to visit Jane she rarely turned up at the planned time. As the months went on she disappeared and reappeared. By now Miss Sad thought that the local authority should assume parental rights and make arrangements for Jane's adoption, if necessary without her mother's consent. With this plan to the fore active efforts to help Miss Small re-establish herself with her child ceased. Her absence from important meetings and her failure to visit Jane were taken by some as indicating that she really thought Jane should be adopted, although she could not bear to give consent herself. There were other voices that pointed out how intolerably painful it must be for a mother who felt she had failed, and who the world thought would fail again, to stay in touch with her child and to confront the successful foster parents and the representatives of a department now apparently turned against her. Nevertheless they agreed that the best that the social services department could provide could not make an adequate life for Miss Small and Jane and that legislation and morality required that they should give 'first consideration to the need to safeguard and protect the welfare of the child throughout her childhood' (Child Care Act, 1980, Sect 18 (1)). Miss Small finally disappeared, and when Jane was three she was adopted.

Services for single mothers and their children illustrate well the entanglement of political and moral precepts with alleged theoretical justifications for prevailing policies. Until the mid-nineteenth century women who had illegitimate children were subjected, not without compassionate interest for their own welfare, to punishment and reform. Their welfare and future were given priority. Without her child, the living proof of the woman's immorality, there was some chance she could reinstate herself in respectable society. Huge infant mortality rates, especially for illegitimate children, and the bleak future for any such child who survived, encouraged a realistic but depressed fatalism that it would be better for them to die, or at least not to strive hard to provide for their future.

Later in the nineteenth century, in some charitable institutions, there emerged the idea that the mother could be rehabilitated through her child. This was later to develop into the principle that the welfare of the mother and child were inevitably bound up together, a principle encouraged by an emerging welfare state which would provide at least the minimum material infrastructure to make it a practical reality. Economics and welfare intertwined then as now. Providing for large numbers of illegitimate children in institutional care would be hugely expensive. There was also great disillusionment with large institutions for children, a disillusionment encouraged by public enquiries of the 1940s and given scientific status by the research of Bowlby (1953) and others, who demonstrated the harmful consequences of such care for children and the vital necessity for their emotional development of a warm, continuous relationship with a mother or mother-substitute.

This convenient integration of rationality and morality is given further support by psychological theories, albeit developed on an inadequate base, about the motives and needs of unmarried mothers, of which Leontine Young (1954) is the clearest exponent. Having an illegitimate baby was seen as closely associated with family or individual problems, an attempt to break free of maternal bonds, a revenge against the male sex, the acquisition of someone to love who would love in return. Despite this problematic aetiology, save in the most exceptional circumstances it was argued there could be a mutuality of interest between mother and child. Separation would only mean replacing the lost infant with another. Thus was behaviour, still subject to considerable moral opprobrium, given purpose and meaning, and social workers, parents, courts, and society were spared the anguish of making choices between the interests of mother and child. Miss Sad had certainly hoped, although without much confidence, and probably not much influenced by such theories, that there could be a mutuality of interest between Miss Small and Jane.

These assumptions did not go long unchallenged. Research confirmed what disadvantaged people and their social workers knew all too well: the welfare state was not the munificent benefactor some had expected, and single mothers faced gross hardships (Wimperis 1960; Wynn 1964; Marsden 1969). These hardships influenced the lives of their children. In nearly every respect illegitimate children fared worse in their physical, emotional, and intellectual development than legitimate children and those who had been adopted (Crellin *et al.* 1971). Miss Sad would certainly have been anxious about such disadvantages, despite the changed demography of the 1980s.

Although Holman (1975) and others argued convincingly that illegitimate children's poor development should not be construed as evidence of inadequate and blameworthy parents but of the great economic and social difficulties which make such parenthood such an overwhelming task, focusing on the interests of the child came more and more to mean arranging permanent substitute homes, preferably via adoption. The development of adoption practices and new legislation encouraged this; and empirical evidence pointed to the superiority of substitute homes for children whose parents were unable to manage their own and their children's lives.

Decision-making could never be so simple. There were, of course, other considerations. First, the available research concerned children born several years earlier. Conditions for younger children may be less bleak and their disadvantage thus diminished. Certainly attitudes towards illegitimacy have mellowed.

How right, therefore, is it to rest decisions on gloomy, deterministic assumptions? Second, research describes the conditions of groups within which there are large differences. Crellin's data could not predict precisely which illegitimate children would be particularly vulnerable to disadvantage, or how serious such disadvantage might be. How proper is it to base decisions about individuals on generalizations about groups? Third, as divorce increases and more children, now one in six, experience some part of their childhood in a single-parent family, how right is it to make distinctions between illegitimate children and others living with single parents? To these proper questions about the strength of the evidential basis for decisions must be added the old questions of justice. As Mandell (1973) pointed out, and Miss Sad acknowledged, it is easier to create child removal services than the conditions which truly support family life. Should social workers collude with this process? Should they give less weight to contemporary realities and the likely future of an individual child than to political considerations?

What strategies did Miss Sad employ in the attempts to tackle practical and moral dilemmas imposed by Miss Small and Jane? She was certainly influenced by research about the likely careers of children who remain in care without definite decisions being made for their future. Miss Sad was rightly haunted by the similarities between Miss Small's life in care and the numerous accounts of poor child-care practice. She wanted therefore to provide Miss Small with a better chance of succeeding than her mother had been given.

Miss Small's family and emotional history made it likely that she would find it particularly difficult to cope with the inevitable struggles of single parenthood on the breadline, but there could be no absolute certainty about this and, in so far as this history had been the responsibility of earlier social workers, it seemed to Miss Sad and her colleagues particularly unjust not to make extra allowances and attempt some reparation. History was used to illuminate rights and obligations. No doubt more help could have been given to reduce Miss Small's isolation and her domestic responsibilities. Although Miss Small's behaviour was unpredictable it was, in comparison to that of many parents in touch with social services departments, surprisingly free of problems: she was not delinquent; she did not abuse drugs or alcohol; she was not caught up in a circle of disturbed and damaging friends. But by the standards of Miss Sad's department and most other departments at the time Miss Small had a reasonably good standard of social work service. It did not achieve Miss Sad's goals and adoption, with its advantages for Jane (Crellin *et al.* 1971; Tizard 1977), increasingly seemed the option most consistent with the local authority's responsibility to give 'first consideration' to the welfare of the child. This statutory obligation in the end gravely limited Miss Small's self-determination and parental rights.

Miss Sad and her colleagues were well aware of the great deficiencies in housing, income, and social support for women like Miss Small and their children. They decided, perhaps implicitly, that in their work battles to reduce structural inequalities could not be an alternative to making decisions about the victims of these disadvantages. Miss Small and Jane were both victims and, in giving priority to Jane, Miss Sad and her colleagues acted in some respects unjustly. On behalf of the child in care, already the victim of her natural parents' inability to provide adequately for her, frequently because they were themselves ill advised and unsupported, decisions are made which are cruel to parents.

Questions of social justice remain. Morality may be influenced by pragmatism: it does not depend on it. Human happiness does not have to be measured only in terms of health, wealth, and attainment. Sacrifice of maternal instinct and freedom of decision may be too great a price to pay in the uncertain search for a child's welfare. Perhaps few would argue this strongly if they knew the precise details of Miss Small's circumstances and behaviour, but contemporary emphasis on parents' freedoms and responsibility in the education and control of their children is closely connected with the persisting view that parents should be the arbiters of their children's fate and future.

Poverty, often chronic and severe, the common fate of single parents, is strongly associated with their children's poor development. Given this, a juster method of underwriting the satisfactory development of the Janes of this world will be to provide a better standard of living for single-parent families, not to punish them twice over by allowing poverty and then removing their children. But constrained by notions of desert, the morality of supporting irregular family relationships, and by economic stringencies, all post-war governments have failed to tackle effectively the deprivations of single-parent families; and there are certainly no signs in the next decade of a brighter future. So despite a social worker's best efforts to manipulate the most social services could offer, despite counselling sensitive to a mother's sorrows and aspirations, despite the most deft handling of foster care, Miss Sad's decisions about justice for individual clients were shadowed by the injustices of social arrangements over which no army of social workers has control. Resort to history, theory, research, and statutory authority cannot disguise the moral and political dilemmas which rest heavy, albeit rarely openly acknowledged, on the shoulders of social workers.

MISS ERNEST, SAM, AND THE INTERMEDIATE TREATMENT PROJECT

Miss Ernest, a probation officer, is reviewing her caseload to decide on the priorities which should guide the allocation of her time. For two years she has worked with Sam, aged sixty-five, who has spent long periods in prison. He is a heavy drinker and frequently homeless. All other social workers in the area find him impossible to work with, but he has a good relationship with Miss Ernest. He goes to see her two or three times a week, sometimes for help with countless practical problems, a bed for the night, a letter for the supplementary benefits office, and so on, and sometimes for a talk and company. He appears to have no other friend in the world. It seems highly unlikely that this way of life will change, although Miss Ernest believes that without her help he might become a complete vagrant and that his health, already poor, would deteriorate. She estimates that her work with Sam takes three hours a week.

Miss Ernest's other colleagues are keen to establish an inter-mediate treatment (IT) project for children on the local housing estate. There are few facilities for them, and there is a high rate of court appearances and reception into care. The IT project is designed to reduce both. Because of her special training and experience Miss Ernest's commitment to it is essential if it is to flourish. Miss Ernest's senior believes that she cannot take on this new work and continue her contact with Sam. Miss Ernest, left to make the choice herself, has decided to tell Sam that he will have to go to a voluntary organization or the Duty Office if he is in difficulties. She commits herself to the IT project.

Miss Ernest and her colleagues are unusual in making such a choice. More commonly social workers would try, probably at cost to their work and themselves, to continue with both responsibilities. Both Sam and the young people on the housing estate are in conflict with themselves and with authority because of their anti-social behaviour. Miss Ernest has been trying to reduce this conflict for the good of vulnerable individuals and also of the wider society. The services and human contact Miss Ernest gives Sam, and would give the young people, would at least marginally improve the quality of their lives. They are also designed to reduce behaviour which can be unpleasant and which could, in the end, attract severe penalties: prison for Sam; juvenile court appearances, youth custody, and detention centre for the young people, at considerable financial cost, and highly unlikely to produce positive outcomes.

The arguments for continued work with both Sam and the young people are therefore strong. What is the case for giving priority to the IT group? First, the numbers of people affected will be larger, and so simple utilitarianism may be a defence. The greater hopes, and perhaps the greater duties, of influencing younger rather than older people, especially those with Sam's history, provide a further justification. It would also be possible to argue, although not without contention, that intermediate treatment can affect the recidivist behaviour of young people or, if carefully organized, at least halt or slow down the custodial histories of the more serious offenders. But intermediate treatment is not necessarily an unmitigated blessing. It may be seen as unfairly rewarding delinquent young people at the expense of those with less chequered histories. Perhaps more seriously, it may draw into the net of social services children who then become the object of attention in ways which are unhelpful if they carry with them stigma; or hasten progress through the tariff system of juvenile courts; or result in court disposals out of proportion to the offence but designed to match the needs of the young person whose circumstances are regarded as problematic or pathological (Morris 1981, 1983; Thorpe and

Paley 1974; Tutt 1974). In choosing intermediate treatment Miss Ernest is not exchanging work with little positive tangible outcomes for work with certain effectiveness. Resort to theory cannot here provide a reasoned justification for abandoning Sam.

Even if Miss Ernest had this defence the immediate objection must be the sacrifice of Sam's interest as an individual whose humanity is diminished through the lack of attention to his needs or priority accorded to his rights as a citizen. But since he does not figure as a person for whom any agency or individual has statutory obligations he is low or non-existent in agencies' hierarchies of priorities.

Traditionally, voluntary societies are the only or the last refuge for the Sams of this world, and the very quality of their work, and the less pressure on them to demonstrate effectiveness in conventional ways, value for money, and so on, may discourage statutory agencies from offering parallel or complementary services. It does not have to be so. In recent years some probation services have developed day centres which cater for drifting, isolated people who may seriously abuse alcohol or drugs. There are arrangements with the police and courts for their diversion from arrest or prosecution, if they are willing, to the centres, which may provide social activities, classes, groups, meals, companionship, advice, counselling, or simply shelter. The people who in the past were given fifty pence to go away by probation officers now figure legitimately in their caseloads. This is not, however, a simple matter. Such centres demand specialization. As Miss Ernest's experience shows, this work is not easily combined with other statutory responsibilities. There is also often pressure on the centres to justify their activities by holding a proportion of probation orders, thus demonstrating a firm involvement with statutory work and, in accordance with the Statement of National Objectives for Probation, preoccupation with 'offending behaviour'. Once again statutory authority is called in aid to justify priorities.

The defence of Miss Ernest's abandonment of Sam by resort to statutory obligation, although logical given the nature of contemporary social welfare, is ultimately unsatisfactory. Wilkes (1981) argues strongly against a preoccupation in social work with activities which appear to deny respect for persons and individuals' worth by limiting or withholding services when no positive response can be expected. Thus are social workers' official responsibilities emphasized rather than their shared humanity with other clients. That part of the British Association of Social Workers code of ethics which recognizes 'the value of dignity of every human being, irrespective of origin, status, sex, sexual orientation, age, belief or contribution to society' strongly endorses Wilkes' argument, but the political and economic context of statutory social services makes it hard, if not impossible, for such a principle to be put fully into practice. Voluntarism and charity, noble though often despised institutions, are for Sam, not the statutory social services. Thus can value judgements made about the worth of various citizens be disguised by reference to theory, research, and legislation.

NASEEM AND MRS HASTY

The last dilemma illustrates the clash between ideals which trip easily and inconsistently off the tongue: religious and cultural tolerance, the virtues of a pluralist society, family loyalties, parental rights, and adolescent self-determination. Clashes of the intensity experienced by this Asian family are rare. Most reach happy resolutions between individual choice and parental wisdom and wishes, but when there is severe conflict social workers are often involved.

Naseem, who is seventeen, and her family came from Pakistan and have lived in Britain for twelve years. After some years of great hardship the family is now reasonably prosperous and well established in the local Moslem community. Naseem has done well at school and plans to go to the local polytechnic. Her success has pleased her family but this has not prevented friction over her growing western orientation in clothes and friendships, and over her view of the world and her place in it. Despite all this, to her school friends and teachers Naseem appears conservative and homebound.

Recently, to Naseem's increasing unease, her parents began to plan her wedding. She continued her friendships with white young men and women and hinted that she would resist both an early marriage and one arranged without her approval. Supported by her teacher and by her parents she proceeded with

37

plans for a career as a pharmacist. Suddenly Naseem's parents announced that a marriage had been arranged with a boy who had recently arrived from Pakistan. The pressure grew for Naseem not to associate informally with boys or go out unescorted: marriage, not a career, was to be her priority. Several bitter family rows ensued. Naseem was at times locked in the house. Once, on her return after a brief escape, she was hit by her father and brothers. As the weeks passed Naseem became more desperate and depressed. Eventually she confided in a social worker, Mrs Hasty, who tried but failed to modify her parents' views and plans. This was not done with great subtlety because Mrs Hasty assumed, as most white social workers would, that Naseem's self-determination in her choice of marriage partner must be the supreme consideration. Mrs Hasty also assumed, incorrectly, that Moslem views on this matter were homogeneous, rigid, and unyielding to compromise. She failed to realize that within Moslem society, as within any religious community, there are divided views, the possibility of flexible interpretation of rules, of inconsistency and compromise. Feeling threatened, Naseem's parents presented a united and apparently immovable front. Communications consisted of attack and counter-attack about alleged prevailing values in Moslem and non-Moslem societies. Before long Mrs Hasty encouraged Naseem to leave home and live in a hostel. She made arrangements for this and refused to tell Naseem's furious family her whereabouts.

It is common in a society in the wake of an imperial history to equate minority differences with inferiority and to highlight racial and cultural conflict. Mrs Hasty appears to have defined the situation thus and in so doing has failed to recognize tensions which often exist in the life of families in all cultures. These are the conflicts of interest between different family members, between older and younger generations. Differences of view over the rights and wrongs of the marriage of young people are common. If Naseem had been a white girl of seventeen planning her own marriage against the wishes of her parents would Mrs Hasty have sided so strongly with her? It is possible she might have trusted more, or at least accorded more respect to, parental judgement and have seen in a more equivocal light the exercise of Naseem's self-determination.

What are the best grounds for defending Mrs Hasty's actions? If we consider Naseem's long-term interests it would be hard to persuade her parents, given the rate of family breakdown in the west, that marriages of free choice and love are more satisfactory than those that have been arranged. We must also wonder how far a girl who has lived all her life in a family of strong cultural traditions, which she at least partly supports, can survive on her own, probably with no help from her relatives and with few other real friends. For young Asian girls life in such circumstances is particularly grim.

To those reared in the individualistic culture of the affluent western world Naseem's own wishes, her rights to be a self-determining young woman, are sufficient justification for Mrs Hasty's intervention; but this must entail a diminution of minorities' rights to conduct their family and religious affairs as they think fit. Thus pluralism is inevitably tempered by the values of the majority. And there are some paradoxes. The most enthusiastic supporters of ethnic minorities' right to toleration are often also those committed to sexual equality and young people's self-determination; and the most articulate advocates of black minorities' duty to adapt to the norms of the white majority often extol most strongly the values of family loyalty and parental responsibility for children's upbringing. Mrs Hasty's decision is thus not simply about the supposed best conditions for Naseem's welfare but also about the politics of race and family life.

This case in particular highlights conflicting moral and political viewpoints in a most naked form. Even the partial resolution of conflicts cannot be attempted by reference to the findings of research, which is silent on the outcomes of arranged or free-choice marriages. Espousing a liberal persuasion which emphasizes a pluralistic society means confronting the conflicts implicit in pluralism. Utilitarian values also offer no escape because it is impossible here to make judgements about the best interests of the greatest number of people. The ethical code of the British Association of Social Workers, a product of late twentieth-century Western European culture, provides some defence in the importance it attaches to individuals' self-determination. But what precedence should be given to such values in a multi-racial, multi-cultural society?

Following Timms in the preceding chapter, these case studies have attempted to offer 'significant examples of sharp conflict and poignant difficulty' (p. 13), and to take some first steps in moral philosophy simply by describing, as Blum (1973) suggested, 'fully, accurately, and realistically certain typical moral situations'. They have also tried to show that social workers' resistance to moral arbitration cannot be the whole truth. Through the law, the obligations of local authorities, and the discretionary powers of social services, society now delegates to social workers fearsome moral decisions for which no better system or resolution has yet been invented.

A graffito at Loughborough University is said to proclaim that 'God is dead but His place has been taken by fifty thousand social workers.' It certainly does not seem so to Miss Sad, Miss Ernest, and Mrs Hasty, who are acutely aware that they possess neither His omniscience nor His omnipotence. They do, however, have the privilege of witnessing the interactions between morality and the frequent vicissitudes of hard-pressed people. From this standpoint they could contribute to the moral and political life of society by sharing more openly the conflicting principles which must so often underly their decisions. They could record the moral and political as well as the factual and technical considerations in decision-making. This could clarify the minds of the writers and their supervisors and, given the increasing availability of records, demonstrate the complexity of issues which political expediency often demands should be simple. In published reports and anonymized case studies, in evidence to Government committees and in the, as yet rare, disciplinary proceedings, social workers, their professional associations, and their unions could, as doctors have done reasonably successfully, hold before us the dilemmas which, although thrust upon them, are the property of society. Argument would not abate but it would be argument about those influences on decisions which, because of their moral or political roots, can command respect if not consensus. In this way social workers would be advancing the rational, political dialogue, argued for by Timms in the previous chapter and by Beiner (1983), which, in attempting to clarify who we are and what we want, may entail moral self-discovery.

All this will certainly not protect social workers from criticism but it will demonstrate that there is no certainty within the community that employs them about the proper fate of Jane, Sam, and Naseem. It will show us too the inevitability and the interest of living, as Browning saw it, 'on the dangerous edge of things'. If we avoid instant judgements and moral absolutes much may be learnt from those who struggle to keep in equilibrium of Browning's 'giddy line midway'.

©1989 Juliet Cheetham

Part Two

CHANGING VALUES

Chapter Four

VALUES IN LOCALLY BASED WORK

MICHAEL BAYLEY

THE DEVELOPMENT AND RATIONALE OF LOCALLY BASED WORK

Many reasons can be given for the development of locally based work, but if we are looking for the fundamental belief which underlies its many different forms, it is the notion that the community itself is the main provider of care. Anything that the formal health and welfare services do is only an aid and support to that care. Formal care is not and cannot be a substitute for informal care. This acknowledgement of the prime importance of the whole complex of informal care, and recognition of the essentially subsidiary role played by the formal services, have considerable implications for the way in which formal services are viewed.

The question ceases to be how the services can be managed most effectively in purely internal managerial terms and becomes a question of how the services can be best organized to fit in with and support informal care. From this perspective the services are not autonomous units which can be organized to suit their own internal requirements and aims, but rather they are supplementary organizations whose central purpose lies outside the organizations themselves.

Such an approach does not assume that informal care is invariably strong and that formal care should be kept to a minimum, but it does assume that informal care must always be taken seriously and that great care needs to be taken to ensure that the practitioners and the service are aware of, and sensitive to, the strengths and weaknesses of informal care in any particular case and any particular area. Central to the locally based

45

approach is a profound respect for the integrity of the culture of those amongst whom the practitioner is working. This is probably most obvious when working with people from a different ethnic background but, though it is not as obvious, it is just as important when middle-class practitioners are working in a working-class area where the culture and assumptions may be very different from their own.

Nothing that has been said so far, apart from use of the phrase 'locally based work', has implied that it will necessarily be based locally. The reasons for arguing that social services need, generally, to be based locally stem from the belief that the community at large is the main provider of welfare and that it is the duty of the services to fit in with it. This is true not just for social services but for all the services concerned with health and welfare. If the services are going to be able to fit in with informal care, they need to know about it in detail. In practice this means that they need to know what happens in particular localities. It is difficult for workers to gain their knowledge by any means other than being based locally. But that is only half the story. It is not just a matter of the workers knowing about local people: it is also a matter of local people knowing about the workers. This means that they must be accessible, and, especially for many of the people who will want the services of social workers, this means that they must be based in the locality.

It is the community orientation that is prior, not the local base, which is only the means to an end. There would be wide agreement that it is desirable that a service should be 'community oriented'. It is a difficult notion with which to disagree. But it should be recognized that such a development could (and ideally should) involve a major change in the service's understanding of its mandate. A centralized, hierarchically controlled, statutory service will tend to see its mandate resting upon statute, and thus upon the state's need. The legislation requires the services to perform certain control functions; it also requires the services to meet the needs of a wide range of people; but these functions are performed, and these needs met, very much on the services' own terms. If a service, or a part of it, acquires a genuine community orientation, this may well change, and the workers in the services may come to see their mandate resting much more on society's needs rather than the state's, and in particular on the needs of the local society or community. This should not be exaggerated, because the locally based statutory service still depends by definition upon statutes; nevertheless, a community orientation may lead to a rather different perception of their role by the workers. At the practical level, instead of their seeing their primary point of reference as the department which employs them, their primary point of reference may become the needs of the people in the area and the local opportunities to develop the work. Thus the priorities of locally based teams and their managements may differ. This may lead to conflict.

It has been argued that the community orientation is prior, and the local base only the means to an end; but that does not mean that it is not important. As we look at other reasons behind locally based work this will become apparent.

The deveolpment of locally based work did not take place in a vacuum. The 1970s saw a growth in the size of the administrative units of social services. The Seebohm reorganization led to the creation of new social services departments which were much larger than the previous children's, welfare, and mental health departments. The scale of welfare administration was increased further by the reorganization of local authorities (and health authorities) in 1974. The larger organizations tended to be more centralized, impersonal, and remote. The setting made it more likely that clients would be considered and treated out of their social context – a tendency to which much social work practice was liable anyway. Black et al. (1983) have described social work teams in three contrasting areas (North Wales, Norfolk, and Central Birmingham) which had precisely this characteristic.

The development of locally based work was a strong reaction against this and a reassertion that the so-called personal social services should indeed be personal. If this was to be achieved, it was argued, then the scale on which the services were organized should be personal, which in turn meant small-scale and therefore local. Kushlick and Blunden (1974), in their seminal paper proposing an integrated locally based health and welfare service for elderly people based on a population of 10,000, point to the importance of the area being sufficiently small for all the health and welfare staff to know one another by name. What is more, a small-scale locally based service means that workers can be

47

known to their clients, the local people, by name. This is not a trivial point. It is a vital aspect of the service being personal and therefore more accessible to vulnerable people, who may shy away from a large-scale, impersonal, and therefore frightening organization.

The Importance of Non-professional Workers

A common, though not invariable, feature of locally based schemes has been a recognition of the key role played by staff such as home helps and wardens. This is consistent with the importance placed on ordinary caring activities carried out by family, friends, and neighbours. Ordinary caring activities are essentially what home helps and wardens are carrying out. In locally based work the importance of this work is recognized, and the workers involved are treated as colleagues by the professional workers. The importance of such workers is enhanced in the locally based approach, as it is likely that many home helps and wardens will live in the locality, unlike the professional staff. They are thus in a position to perform an intermediary function between the professional workers and the informal networks of the locality, of which many of them will be part.

The emphasis placed by some projects on home helps and similar staff (for example Hadley and McGrath 1984:157) has sometimes been seen as an attack on professionalism. There is within the locally based approach a wariness about the tendency of the services to professionalize ordinary caring activities and a desire to put a high value on those who carry them out, whether they be family, friends, and neighbours or home helps or wardens. Such valuing of this work is, however, perfectly consistent with a proper recognition of the professional work of social workers, as Bennett (1983) has shown. The locally based approach does, however, have a particular contribution to make in the emphasis it places on the value and validity of ordinary people doing ordinary tasks.

The Whole-person Approach

The locally based approach is concerned to consider the whole person in their full social context. There are several aspects to this. First a client is not just seen as a client but as a person who

48

lives in a particular house in a particular road and is part of a particular network of family, friends, neighbours, acquaintances, and workmates. Thus the client is seen in his or her social context. Furthermore, though clients may be in need of help when they are first seen, they are not seen as just receivers of services but also as people who may well have something to give. Reciprocity is an essential part of healthy and fulfilling human existence. Healthy social relationships depend on all concerned being able both to give and to receive. If this is true of normal social relationships it is true too of the health and welfare services if they wish to pay more than lip-service to the whole-person approach. The structure of the services and the way they are run needs to be able not just to provide help and services when needed, but also to provide people with the opportunity to give. This will be considered further in the section on participation.

If people are seen in this way it is abundantly obvious that it is impossible to separate off the social services component from the health component or the education component. If the person is to be seen as a whole person, the services need to be able to respond as an integrated whole.

The logic of this is slowly being recognized by, for example, Islington's combined locally based social services, housing, and environmental health offices. However, close collaboration with the health services seems particularly difficult to achieve. What the locally based approach underlines is that what is at stake is not just how the services co-operate with one another but the more fundamental question of 'if we see people as whole people what implications does this have for the services?'.

SOME KEY AREAS OF DEBATE

Participation

If the recognition that informal care is the base on which formal care depends is the starting point for the locally based approach, then recognition of the importance of participation is its centre. Perhaps the major criticism that can be made of those involved in the development of locally based or 'patch' work is their failure to give adequate attention to enabling local people to participate as fully as possible in the planning and running of locally based services. The schemes in Normanton (Hadley and McGrath 1984), East Sussex (e.g. Young 1982; Hadley *et al.* 1984), and Dinnington (Bayley *et al.* 1989) all turned out, whatever the intent, more as ways of delivering services in a different way than as ways of enabling local people to exercise some real control over the services themselves. Beresford and Croft have been particularly critical of this tendency (Beresford 1984; Beresford and Croft 1986).

The participation of local people was seen as a central objective in the Dinnington project. The underlying belief of the project was

> that well-being, welfare and health are not technical matters for the experts but are rooted in the life, experience and competence of ordinary people and that responsibility for them is something to be shared in a partnership with professionals, not handed over to them. Indeed the extent to which it is possible to achieve a genuine partnership is likely to be the acid test of any such project.
>
> (Bayley *et al.* 1989)

Despite this hope the project failed to secure substantial participation by local people in the planning and running of the project. There were many reasons for this but the experience is common. It seems to be exceedingly difficult for statutorily based welfare organizations to devolve power in such a way that local people can play anything more than a nominal part in the running of a project. A major attempt was made in Canada in the province of Quebec, based on legislation which was passed in 1970. Local Centres for Community Services were set up and by 1986 there were 126 centres in the province which each provided services for an average population of 40,000. Great emphasis was placed on 'encouraging the participation of the citizens in the institutions so as to make them more responsive to local needs' (Guay 1986:2). Despite this,

> As for the objective of common control, it is generally considered to be a failure; there was a very low turn-out for the election of users' representatives; those who were elected were professionals for the most part. Furthermore

unfamiliarity with the language and the ways and modes of ...
administration estranged many users' representatives.
Government went as far as to hire community organizers to
encourage participation, but they were accused of provoking
political unrest, and their role was recast. ... Citizens from
local communities did not have much participation or control,
professionals and institutions augmented their privileges and
bureaucratic rationality made state technocrats the real
decision-makers.

(Guay 1986:4)

The notion of participation has been an important ideological
driving force behind the development of locally based work.
This has been true of many fields apart from social services.
Indeed social services have entered the field relatively late. The
Skeffington Report on *Participation in Planning* was published as
long ago as 1969. However, although the idea has been important, the implementation of effective participation by local
people has met with very limited success.

Responsibilities and Rights

The locally based approach places considerable emphasis on the
appropriate involvement of local people in both the planning
and the delivery of services. Such an approach always has to
walk the tightrope between the proper involvement of local
people in performing various helping and supportive caring
activities which they *want* to carry out, and inappropriate attempts
to persuade volunteers to carry out jobs which are properly the
responsibility of paid workers. The fact that there have been
inappropriate attempts to use volunteers in the second way
should not be allowed to divert attention from the great potential of a sensitive interweaving of formal and informal care.

However, the moment one starts considering this sort of
approach the question of rights and duties is raised in an acute
form. An issue which confronts all workers is how far the family
is responsible and how far the worker, the agency, the state are
responsible. In the case of children under the age of sixteen, the
legal position is quite clear. The parents have a duty to provide
care for the child and strong reasons have to be given before

51

they can be deprived of that responsibility. The moment a person reaches the age of sixteen, and especially when they reach their majority at the age of eighteen, the picture becomes much more complex. An aspect of this which is of particular relevance is how far adult children, especially daughters, have a duty to look after their aged parents. As Bruce (1968:34) says:

> The Poor Law Act of 1930 re-asserted the long established liability in explicit terms: 'It shall be the duty of the father, grandfather, mother, grandmother, husband or child of a poor, blind, lame or impotent person ... if possessed of sufficient means to relieve and maintain that person.'

The Poor Law embodied in financial terms the belief that the prime responsibility for supporting people in need rested with the wider family, and the state would only come in if there was no-one else or the wider family's resources were exhausted. Furthermore the help that was given was minimal and punitive. The household means test was not abolished until the Determination of Needs Act passed in 1941. It was a significant step in social policy. Direct financial responsibility was limited to spouses and dependent children.

However, it has not proved as easy to pass the equivalent of the Determination of Needs Act as far as the provision of care is concerned. There is certainly a strong expectation on the part of society in general and the health and welfare services in particular that families will continue to provide large amounts of demanding care for dependent relatives which they are under no legal obligation to provide. But are they under a moral obligation to provide it? Beresford and Croft (1986: 134) write:

> A key premise of the patch and community social work approach is that most caring is carried out informally. But as Finch and others have argued, it would be wrong to assume that women want or choose to care for their relatives because that is what they are doing (Finch 1985:125) .... Patch may be confusing choice with necessity.

There are questions at two levels here. First, do those providing informal care have a *right* to expect help and relief? Second, even if such help and relief is provided do they nevertheless still have a right not to care in the sense of care *for* the dependent

52

person, that is providing the practical services needed to maintain a reasonable standard of life? It is not possible to legislate that people should care in the sense of loving and caring *about* someone. It is important to make the distinction between caring *for* and caring *about*. The fact that a daughter cares *about* her elderly mother does not imply that she will or should necessarily care *for* her, not does the fact that she cares *for* her mother necessarily imply that she will care *about* her. Indeed one of the arguments about the burdens that fall on those providing care is that they may be so great that tiredness and frustration lead to love drying up.

However, the question does not stop there. The question has been discussed so far implicitly in terms of the family's obligations. A community oriented approach would often go beyond the family and seek to involve friends and neighbours as well. Allan (1983) has shown how attempts to involve friends and neighbours in caring *for* are often misconceived, because that is not what friends and neighbours generally do: they generally care *about* people. That is not to say that some friends and neighbours do not also care *for* people, nor is it to deny the value of a friend calling round for a chat, but, as a rule, Allen's warning is sound. Nevertheless, the same general ethical question arises as has been discussed with reference to members of the family – do we as members of society have a duty to care *for* and/or *about* our fellow citizens to whom we are not related?

Clearly it is not a duty that can be enforced by some gigantic extension of community service orders, but the ethical question cannot be dismissed as easily as that. In twentieth-century Britain it is not in the state's power (yet) to compel unrelated neighbours to care; it is also virtually impossible for the state to compel relatives who are determined not to care for a close relative to do so. But though this may be true in individual cases, nevertheless the policy of community care in general, and the community oriented approach in particular, are based on the assumption that such care will be given in the vast majority of cases. It assumes that moral pressure will be sufficient to ensure that the number of relatives who will refuse to care will be sufficiently small to enable present policies to go forward more or less on their present lines.

It is this logic which leads Finch (1984:16) to argue that,

because the present situation is so inherently exploitative of women, 'On balance, it seems to me that the residential route *is* the only one which ultimately will offer us a way out of the impasse of caring'; women can then have a genuine choice over whether they care *for* their relatives or not. This is not a conclusion with which the author would agree, nor is it one which Finch reaches with any enthusiasm, but anyone who is advocating a community oriented approach must be able to suggest, if not an answer, at least an approach which recognizes these issues and gives some hope of resolving them. The present economic and political situation imposes severe limitations and it would be unrealistic not to recognize them; but it should be possible to indicate lines of development which offer hope for the future. This will be considered in the final section.

So far this section has concentrated mostly on duties, but little mention has been made of rights. This must be made good, however briefly, as the two are inseparable. The duties that parents owe toward their children are matched by corresponding rights in relation to them. If society is expecting families to care for their elders, to be responsible for them, what corresponding rights do the members of the family have? If friends and neighbours are similarly involved, do they have rights too? If this is a general policy which affects whole communities, is it adequate to consider this just at the individual level? Is it not necessary to consider this to some extent at a corporate level, in particular at the local level?

At both of these levels – family, friends, and neighbours on the one hand, and the local community (recognizing the necessary vagueness of that term) on the other – the question must be asked not just what responsibilities they have but also what rights; and, in particular, whether they should have some rights over the allocation of the resources needed to discharge their responsibilities.

Sharing Responsibilities

Doubts are sometimes expressed about whether it is practicable for a locally based worker to exercise a control function effectively. Is it possible for your friendly neighbourhood social worker to adopt an authority role and take out a place of safety order on a child?

Like a number of problems that are raised about locally based practice, this appears to be a problem more in theory than in practice. Behind the doubt that has been expressed, there seems to be an assumption that the community at large is against anything that smacks of control. If anything, surely the exact opposite is true. On the whole the public is likely to press for strong action and to recognize that there is a control function in society that has to be exercised. This is not to say that taking a child into care is likely to be any less traumatic if the worker is based locally than if he or she is working to a more traditional model, but there does not appear to be any evidence that it is *more* difficult.

The major strength of locally based work comes before that stage is reached, in preventive work. Evidence from Dinnington showed how the workers were able to keep in close touch with families through a variety of channels where there was concern about children.

One of the social workers illustrated this through her contacts with the complex and interacting relationships of five families. For example:

> MRS C is friendly with and supportive to MRS B, she will join in discussions when I visit the B FAMILY and offer material help. MRS B (not a gossip) is aware of my concern for the A FAMILY children and manages to imply whenever the situation needs further care.
>
> (Seyd *et al.* 1984: 54f)

A vital part of working this way is for the worker to be aware of the constantly changing dynamics of the networks. Another example from Dinnington can illustrate this. In a complex family situation involving possible non-accidental injuries to the children, the social worker was able to arrange for the children's grandmother to take them for the night and to work with Mr J's brother-in-law (himself the father of a former NAI client) in defusing a potentially hostile situation between Mr J, who had been drinking in the local club, and the police. The volatility of relationships in this and similar networks is such that an intimate knowledge of the current state of relationships is essential before work of this nature is attempted. In this case, a few months previously it would have been impossible (Seyd *et al.* 1984: 55f).

Of course there were cases where the workers operated in a more conventional way, but the beginnings of a change can be seen in the examples given above, in which the social worker is in effect sharing the discharge of his or her responsibility with lay members of the community, who may well be clients themselves. An interesting article by Parsons (1986:140) on his work in a patch team with families with multiple problems on the Moulsecoomb estate on the edge of Brighton shows a rather different pattern of working, which he describes as 'obviously still basically caseloadish'. By contrast, in the Dinnington examples the social workers show signs of acting more as one actor in a social drama. This does not mean that the social worker has abdicated his or her authority or responsibility, but the way it is being discharged is potentially markedly different from the traditional model, in that some of the responsibility is being shared. There are ethical questions about how far it is right and proper to do this but there are similar questions about how far it is right, proper, and realistic *not* to do it. A repeated question from the Maria Colwell inquiry onwards has been why more account has not been taken of what local people have heard and said. The basic question is how the relationship between the professional and the public is viewed. The ethics of this can be considered fruitfully by looking at the question of confidentiality.

Confidentiality and Gossip

It will have been obvious from the previous section that the conventional understanding of confidentiality may have to be reconsidered in developing a community oriented approach. This is a matter of deep concern to some people, who feel that basic ethical standards of social work are at risk. Leighton (1983:51), for one, is critical of patch-based social work in this respect:

Another example of values embedded in the advocacy of patch may be illustrated by just one example from *Going Local*. It is said to be a strength of the patch system that the corner shop is willing to inform the workers that a certain old lady is buying 'far too much Guinness and not "enough" food'. Here we have the fulfilment of everyone's fears about 'Big Brother' social services of 'The Welfare'. A criticism of a lifestyle is implied, a lifestyle which involves no lawbreaking or injury to any other party and no self-referral of a perceived problem. Would the 'patch' worker pick on you or me for our deviance from 'healthy' patterns of behaviour, would they carry out a friendly neighbourhood visit on the local magistrate who may also be a heavy drinker? When does 'patch' become a gross invasion of privacy?

Leighton is quite right to ask 'when does "patch" become a gross invasion of privacy?', but he shows little faith in the sensitivity and professionalism of social workers if he assumes that in the case he mentioned the social worker will stamp in and make the old lady conform. Yes, that would be an invasion of privacy. But a visit by a social worker who will respect her right to make choices about how she lives, while also being alert to ways in which she can be helped, could be an opportunity to do something valuable for a lonely old person. Locally based work may confront social workers with situations which will challenge their professional judgement, but this is a test of their training, professionalism, and proper understanding of accountability, not a sign that Big Brother is with us. The locally based approach does imply open and probably more complex relationships with people in the localities that the workers are serving. It is part of the price of treating clients and those amongst whom they live as fellow citizens with whom a partnership has to be forged. This involves awkward decisions – for example, about what to do in response to gossip, which cannot be escaped by a high-minded refusal to have anything to do with it because it is such an integral part of daily living. Confidentiality in a locally based setting cannot be a refuge to hide behind. It has to be a living principle which the worker applies with sensitivity and discrimination.

The issue of confidentiality is a central one in understanding the particular ethical issues raised by the locally based approach; we shall consider it again in the final section.

WAYS FORWARD

Underlying all the issues that have been discussed has been the belief which was quoted earlier:

that well-being, welfare and health are not technical matters for the experts but are rooted in the life, experience and competence of ordinary people and that responsibility for them is something to be shared in a partnership with professionals, not handed over to them.

(Bayley *et al.* 1989)

The key to these questions of the responsibility and rights of carers, the control function, and confidentiality, is belief that responsibility needs to be shared and that the way forward lies in finding ways of enabling that to happen. The underlying value is the belief that as members of society we do have a responsibility for one another, and that society and its individual members are the poorer the less this responsibility is exercised.

The notion of reciprocity is another way of putting this: that is, the importance of giving all people, including clients, the opportunity to give as well as to receive. This was explored by Richard Titmuss in his influential book *The Gift Relationship* (1970).

Another way of considering it is the notion of interdependence. A recent Church of England Report on the welfare state said:

What the notion of interdependence does is to reinforce the moral obligation carried by the community as a whole for the well-being and liberty of each individual member. We are our sisters' and brothers' helper!

(Church of England Board for Social Responsibility 1986: para 2.16)

The values underlying locally based work are not difficult to set out. It is the putting of these values into practice which is more difficult. But it is possible to find examples; they centre round the sharing of responsibility. Kieran O'Hagan (1980) describes how responsibility for an old man who was living by himself in a flat amongst other old people was shared by two workers and the surrounding old people who were concerned about him. Their responsibilities were not denied, nor was the reality of their fear that one day they might come into the flat and find the old man dead, 'for which they would inevitably feel some responsibility', but the workers were able to give those supporting the old man the confidence that their anxieties and responsibilities were supportable and reasonable because the workers recognized and valued the support they were giving and shared the responsibility with them. Once assured of this, the people concerned stopped agitating for the old man to be taken into residential care, and coped confidently until he died. The statutory workers did not feel the problem had been landed on them; the local people giving support did not feel exploited; the old man was able to live out his days where he wanted – in his own home. The Dinnington project cites similar examples where the responsibility for a package of care was shared by neighbours and volunteers but with the social worker having the continued and overall responsibility (Seyd *et al.* 1984: 60).

A more complex example, which also brings in elements of control and confronts the problems of confidentiality, comes from the account by Holder and Wardle (1981) of their work in a locally based Family Services Unit in Bishop Auckland in Co. Durham. They give a most illuminating case example of their work with a difficult family, in a difficult street, on a difficult estate. The stimulus for the action was that the family concerned, the Edwards family, had been served with an eviction notice and, if it was to be avoided, their house had to have a much needed clean-up. The workers decided to involve the family, the street, and other agencies in the process, and, in particular, 'Whatever changed within the family as a result of this action, we would try to direct it into an awareness of the general nature of the problem and away from scapegoating the Edwards family' (p. 88).

The process involved the workers in talking about the Edwards family by name with other people in the street and the neighbourhood, including, for example, a meeting of the estate-wide tenants' group. This approach worked. The Edwards did clean their house up and the residents in the street began thinking more about their environment rather than merely accepting it; the other families in the street joined in the clean-up. In their evaluation the authors wrote: 'A collusive tension which had been present in both our casework and community work snapped, resulting in more open and honest relationships within the street and between the residents and ourselves' (p. 93).

The authors comment: 'The preciousness of our own orientation, or method of work, was no longer important – indeed it was a hindrance because it prevented the free flow of information' (p. 131). The senior worker involved with the Edwards family wrote:

Somehow, when so many people knew about the Edwards –
probably a lot more than we did – to hide behind a barrier
[confidentiality] like that was at best humbug and at worst
added a degree of mystification to what people felt about
them. I still don't know where my barriers are in
confidentiality, but I do know they have changed. Giving up
'professional barriers', which I most certainly had to, added to
both the rewards and the difficulties. (p. 148)

The only way in which the workers could break the ineffective, individualistic, and effectively scapegoating approach of
traditional work was to 'go public' and refuse to go on allowing
the Edwards or the other people living in the same street to
pretend that they did not live in the grottiest, nastiest, dirtiest
street on the estate. Conventional notions of confidentiality were
no good: they would have strangled such an approach at birth
and left the family and the workers with their 'collusive tension'.
Furthermore, the family and the street had to be confronted
with the extent of their responsibility for the state in which they
were living. If they had not been so confronted nothing would
have happened. But that responsibility, once acknowledged, was
shared by the workers, who were able then to help the Edwards
family and the other people in the street to do something about
it. This shift was difficult and costly for the workers. It stripped
away their professional defences and made them more vulnerable, but it did enable responsibility to be shared and the
Edwards family and the street to regain a sense of their own
value and competence.
Social workers who are locally based and are seeking to work
in a genuinely community oriented way face many taxing
demands on their professional judgement; they need to be clear
about the values on which their professional judgement will
depend. The approach advocated in this chapter has sometimes
been called 'partnership practice'. The term seems appropriate:
it reflects the need to recognize that the community, and society
as a whole, need to exercise responsibility *with* the professional
worker rather than hand responsibility over *to* the professionals.
Anything less will be mere titivation. This will be a formidable
challenge to the social work profession.

©1989 Michael Bayley

Chapter Five

HOLISTIC HEALTH CARE AND PROFESSIONAL VALUES

MIKE SIMPKIN

These days we are continually being encouraged to become more self-conscious about our health by a loose coalition of political, economic, and moral interest groups which often have more than just our health in mind. Exhortations to stop smoking, eat bran, and use condoms are being proclaimed in the context of a massive reduction in public spending, loss of faith in overtly political movements as a source of social change, the reassertion of individualism, and a moral panic about AIDS. But while social workers individually may, as caricature sometimes suggests, value apparently healthy lifestyles for themselves, social work as an institution has failed to come to grips with what this might mean for practice; perhaps understandably, given resource constraints, administrative structures, and inter-professional rivalries (Simpkin 1989). Sniping by social workers at the failures of the health services and the medical model has not generally been matched by a willingness to take the responsibility for thinking through the implications of a commitment to multi-disciplinary work. In this paper I want to examine some differences in value terms between social work and medicine, and in particular to suggest that the new approach to health emphasizes old conflicts or raises new ones in ways which cannot be resolved in terms of professional values alone.

Recent years have seen many challenges mounted to the medical profession. In the ethical field, Lockwood points to 'high-tech angst', especially over developments at the frontiers of biomedical technology, and to 'populist protest' at the arrogant paternalism of much professional and administrative behaviour (Lockwood 1985). Demands for the recognition of patients' rights have forced a re-examination of long-standing professional self-justifications and assumptions about issues such as consent. Meanwhile the legitimation of lay interest and participation has added a new dimension to decisions and actions affected by the uneasy balance between the desire to avoid unnecessary suffering and legal approaches which favour minimal interference.

The assertion of patients' rights has been accompanied by a much wider scepticism about the value of curative scientific medicine and the effectiveness of doctors as guardians of the public health. Historical studies suggest that most major advances in general health care were due not to medicine but to economic and political developments (e.g. McKeown 1979). There has been increasing concern at the incidence of iatrogenic illness, whether caused by medication, simple error, or more insidious factors like institutionalization, and politicians have, from their different perspectives, drawn attention to the prohibitive cost of attempting to conduct a demand-led health service based on hospital care. More worrying still has been the publication, not without difficulty, of the failure of the NHS to diminish gross inequalities in our nation's health (e.g. Townsend and Davidson 1982).

Underlying all these developments has been the emergence of an alternative, holistic approach to health and disease. Although holism was the basis both of ancient and of eastern medicine, it was largely ousted by the scientific model of the nineteenth century (Berliner and Salmon 1980; Hastings *et al* 1981). Now that the impersonality and limitations of biomedicine are more apparent, holism's emphasis on health as a value in itself, a unity of mind, body, and spirit, which the individual has the responsibility to maintain, has proved an extremely attractive counterbalance. Holistic practitioners have still to shake off orthodox criticism of unvalidated techniques and a failure (shared with conventional medicine) fully to consider the social context and social relations of the healing process. Holism has, however, greatly increased the appreciation of different cultural approaches to health and illness, and has challenged the casual application of the assumptions of western scientific medicine both in the Third World and among immigrant and ethnic communities.

Finally, medical domination has been further challenged by the independent development of occupations and professions with which in the past medicine has been more or less loosely associated or which it has controlled. Among these are social work, nursing, psychology, and occupational therapy. Criticism of narrowly based conceptions of treatment, and a move towards more accessible and informal methods of service delivery, have led to the broadening and even dissolving of certain role boundaries as fields of concern begin to overlap. Opportunities for co-operation have also brought conflict, and the necessary reordering of professional value systems has involved a certain amount of adjustment and incorporation, buttressed by a nervously defensive reaction intended to ensure self-preservation. Accounts of professional values need to consider issues such as power, security, and status; misunderstandings or disagreements about values often wrongly present as debates about levels of competence.

Social work has, in many ways, grown up in medicine's shadow and, in searching for its own identity and status, it has often combined shrill criticism of its forebear with an aping of some of the very traits under attack. Early on, social workers offered an obeisance to doctors which developed into a role differentiation depending heavily on predominant assumptions about gender and class and often linked to their chosen social role of attending to the person as a whole in his or her social setting (Huntington 1981; Ragg 1977). But it was not until they succeeded in gaining a countervailing institutional base in social services departments that social workers could build up their own independent ethos; unfortunately both its location in local government and its bureaucratic style were guaranteed for historical reasons to wound the *amour propre* of doctors and to alienate nurses, thus causing practical difficulties for collaboration and compounding the conflict which would anyway have ensued.

Doctors have adopted a variety of strategies in response, and critics of medicine often make the mistake of treating it as a monolithic institution. Stark (1982) argues that it has often been convenient for radicals to secure their own position by shifting medicine to the right, perhaps attributing to doctors more power than they actually have. It is true that the BMA has attempted to confirm medical hegemony by, for example, reaffirming traditional ethical doctrines relating to confidentiality, autonomy, and accountability as a means towards professional solidarity (Stacey 1985); it has also been dismissive of alternative medicine. But the BMA is itself divided: many doctors recognize deficiencies in their hospital bases and in their training, and seek, either through general practice, itself now much better rewarded, or through various forms of community medicine, to render their services both more effective and more relevant. For some this is simply a recasting of the orthodox model. For others it is a return to the idealized practice of medicine, most sympathetically presented in Berger's *A Fortunate Man* (1969), a holistic but still paternalist approach, untainted by alternative techniques. Others, more radically, have sought either to integrate the new holistic medicine or to attempt forms of practice which recognize and even confront the social and economic roots of ill-health and disease.

These moves raise fundamental questions of values and boundaries which cannot be answered within medicine. In a Marxist analysis this would anyway be the case, for medicine is seen as a particular form of social relations within the capitalist system (Navarro 1986). But the problem is one for non-Marxists too. If the business and competence of doctors is in treating the sick, but factors other than sickness have to be considered for treatment to be acceptable and successful, then either doctors must recognize the limitations of their science or they must step into spheres of decision beyond their professional prerogative (Harris 1985: 56). If they are allowed to do the latter, then the consequence must be that doctors must accept the miserable as well as the sick as legitimate patients, and the rest of us must accept the corresponding extension of their power. If not, should social workers, who already have far too wide a brief, be expected to accept a legitimate interest in health care, especially when changes in the health service are associated with expenditure reductions? If social service workers are not to be involved, who is? How and by whom are the boundaries to be drawn? What is the concept of health really about?

WHAT SORT OF CONCEPT IS HEALTH?

At a time when commercial exploitation of the food and leisure markets has made healthy living chic, many regard such an earnest pursuit with some distaste, as 'a kind of elitist moralizing about what are believed to be unhealthy coping behaviours' (Crawford 1980). The inherent difficulties in defining health have traditionally led many people to regard it simply as the absence of disease. This positivism has enabled doctors not only to claim that medicine is an objective science but also to set manageable boundaries to their areas of concern. Many philosophers too, from Plato onwards, have been able to treat the purportedly undisputed analogy of physical health or illness as a benchmark for the use of the word 'good' (Hare 1986). Thus Hampshire, following Aristotle, seems to accept the existence of an ideal model of health which he contrasts with more contingent goods like friendship (Hampshire 1983:145). Writing for social workers, P. D. Shaw contrasts happiness with health, which, he says, 'is an altogether more precise concept' (Shaw 1978).

Others subsume health under more general categories. Rawls, in constructing his theory of justice, loosely accepts health as a primary good, but does not include it in his basic inventory, since income and wealth are more fundamental (Rawls 1977, 1982). Indeed contractarian approaches to society as a whole cannot deal easily with questions of illness and, more particularly, handicap since they are based on idealized constructions of social life, where nobody is sick (Daniels 1985). On the other hand Downie and Telfer, in a very thorough discussion, regard health and welfare as different aspects of one value judgement based on respect for persons (Downie and Telfer 1980).

In fact most philosophers who attend to the subject would probably agree that a major difficulty in treating health as a good is that it has both descriptive and normative content. For example, the prototypes of health we may perhaps hold, even if subconsciously, are likely to be permeated by ageist, sexist, or even racist assumptions. The distinguished anthropologist Sir Edmund Leach did not endear himself to a medical audience by suggesting that the profession bore considerable responsibility for a situation where 'an aging society which continues to search for the elixir of youth will necessarily persuade itself that it is already approaching the final stages of senility' (Leach 1975).

Furthermore, some vagueness in definition can often suit practitioners. For instance, social workers may well use a broad definition of health to justify their professional access to health-care delivery, whether through the traditional emphasis on the 'whole person' or in a more political context, but may retreat to very narrow interpretations when disagreeing with medical recommendations for compulsory admission to hospital. Similarly a psychiatrist may extend the concept of health to include employment when he considers that compulsory admission might mollify a patient's employer and thus save his or her job, but may also prefer to use restricted definitions of medical as opposed to social criteria when it comes to discharging or not accommodating patients of whom he disapproves.

Thus the definition of health can depend not just on concepts of illness or disease, but also, albeit indirectly, on the interests of those engaged in the delivery of health care; this is a significant reason for not allowing professionals any exclusive say in framing it. Additionally, while the maintenance of public health requires broad definitions to promote awareness, there is a very real risk of medicalizing not only deviance but everyday life, whether from a biomedical or a holistic framework. Crawford (1980), who has coined the word 'healthism' for this tendency, warns that by situating both problems and solutions in health and illness in the realms of the individual, we divorce them from the society in which meaning is constructed, and produce new forms of risk and disability. Indeed holism itself has been argued to be quite compatible with a totalitarian system of health care as exemplified in the American space programme (Kotarba 1983).

From this line of reasoning the search for any kind of abstract ideal of health appears not just unpromising but dangerous. Yet its importance as a political and economic issue is such that to allow it to be sidestepped for philosophical reasons would itself be a political act. Approaches are needed which view health in a more dynamic way, as a process or a capacity. For example, Whitbeck suggests that health is 'the ability to act or respond appropriately in a variety of situations', and argues that this is merely a *context* for medicine (Whitbeck 1981). This definition offers the possibility of reconciling both the broad and the narrow approaches to health; it places a value on autonomy, and can perhaps be flexible enough to be linked in different ways to different conditions. From here a link might be made with the

66

Marxist argument that the social relations of medicine must be changed through the collective promotion of health into new forms (Navarro 1986). Health, Navarro rightly insists, must be constructed and reconstructed not in theory but in practice.

VALUE CONFLICT IN COLLABORATIVE WORK

If health is part of welfare, then social workers must include the promotion of health among their goals (Downie and Telfer 1980), and the philosophy of community care demands far closer collaboration between all workers than they are used to. The nature of the network of professional relationships can often dictate not just the style of decisions, but even their content, and within this network conflicts of value have increasingly been distorted by issues of power. The problem is not peculiar to social work; nurses have often found themselves in considerable difficulty, torn between two conflicting requirements in their ethical code: their duty to obey the doctor and their duty to the patient: for example, over withholding information which the doctor does not want disclosed (Thompson 1979). Doctors, while conceding the possibility of conflict in exceptional cases, have usually failed to admit any general difficulty, given the wide-ranging obligations of their own ethic, which is claimed to bestow an overview of the patient's best interests. They are unwilling to accept that this very perspective and power can place doctors in far too remote a position accurately and conjointly to assess the information and value bases of their patients.

Social workers within medical teams may derive more protection from such conflicts through their contractual independence from medicine, but the price can be distance and mistrust. There are likely to be general differences in priorities, and a great deal of emotion can be generated over specific issues such as child abuse and mental illness, especially in those cases which involve the removal either of rights or of people. Occasional incompetence on both sides disguises how many of these disagreements are value-related misunderstandings. For example, social workers sometimes act as guardians of civil rights which exist specifically to limit what doctors may perceive as their duty to treat. Similarly the Hippocratic nostrum 'Above all, do no harm' may be subject to very different interpretations from different perspectives. Social workers are likely to be conscious not just of the limits of medicine but of those of social intervention as well.

The potential for value conflict or misunderstanding has been further highlighted in recent years as social workers have become involved in issues such as responding to medical requests to obtain legal consent for procedures which have been refused by parents for religious or other reasons. There is also some tradition of social services intervention, by request or otherwise, in the guardianship of neonates deemed to be at risk, generally because of the history or condition of the mother; this has recently, and controversially, been extended to cases of parental drug addiction and of surrogate parenthood. Discussion of the moral aspects of such situations is not well advanced in social work literature, and needs to be developed.

One further value difference which affects the respective ways in which doctors and social workers deal with conflict and anxiety lies in the value structures of their professions. Fully trained doctors are accustomed to independent and autonomous decision-making, whether they are shouldering responsibility or shrugging it off. They have little tradition of seeking support except beyond their speciality. Social workers, however, tend to value collaboration, consultation, and supervision, and are members of a bureaucratic organization, although when acting as Approved Social Workers, they do have independent responsibility. Reconciling their different rules and values is like trying to referee a ball game in which one side fields an agreed team but seems continually to vary the area of play, while the other has no power over the pitch but appears to include an indeterminate number not only of players but of substitutes.

We can take the analogy one step further. Demands for patient participation or community control can be seen as an entry into the game by the spectators and the directors. By now the ball has vanished and the whole affair resembles nothing as much as Lewis Carroll's Caucus Race. We are seeing an overall shift in the values of health care practice without adequate changes in the values of its institutions.

VALUES IN PRACTICE

To illustrate both the potential for change and some of the inherent difficulties I shall take a routine example of collaboration in a progressive primary care team.

The team, which consists of different workers employed, attached, or linked to a General Practice, is discussing a routine notification from the general hospital that Peter, a young man on the GP's list, has just been discharged after recovering from an overdose of anti-asthmatic drugs and a few tranquillizers, on top of a considerable amount of alcohol. He has been seen by a psychiatrist, who did not feel that any psychiatric admission was necessary and thought the overdose was a reaction to the loss of his girlfriend. He has returned to live at his parents' house; no follow-up has been arranged.

The GP initiates collaboration by deciding to bring this information to the team; he reports that he knows the family but not very well; mother has a long-standing and mostly subclinical depressive condition; she and her son are both rather odd in manner and speech but the family itself is stable and financially sound. Peter has considerable sexual anxiety, which he does little to disguise. All agree that Peter is likely to need further help, but how and from whom?

The GP expects that he will no doubt be requested to call on the family before long, and could make a point of asking after Peter. He could discuss what help, if any, might be useful, and then consult the appropriate member of the team. The community psychiatric nurse says that he would be willing to accept a referral if there appears to be a mental illness problem, especially if it might be amenable to some specific therapy, such as relaxation or an anti-alcohol programme. The social worker prefers not to await the vagaries of the GP's visiting rota; there are signs of underlying tensions and difficulties which could have contributed to this crisis, and help is most likely to be effective if offered immediately. He is willing to make some contact and offer Peter at least a one-off session for clarification and assessment of his problems and any appropriate resources. The practice counsellor, specializing in non-directive psychotherapy, is shocked. She will be happy to offer Peter an appointment when she has space if that is what he wants. However, the surgery is well known for its ease of approach. He will come when he wants help sufficiently to commit himself to a course of treatment. To offer something out of the blue is an intrusion and is unlikely to work. A discussion follows to which the Women's Health worker also briefly contributes. The health visitor, practice nurse, and district nurse do not speak. The outcome is an agreement that the social worker will write offering an appointment at the surgery.

After some comment on the nature of this gathering, I shall consider its operation in terms of two traditional professional values: confidentiality and autonomy.

Like most multidisciplinary teams, including some of those in hospital, this body has no formal status, nor is it a model, though its outline should be familiar. I am not concerned here with how far the term 'team' can legitimately be applied, or with team values as such (Lonsdale *et al*. 1980; Payne 1982). The grouping has an *ad hoc* existence as the result of commitments voluntarily entered into by those concerned. If the group is not able to satisfy its members, some may leave and return to independent functioning, perhaps with a direct appeal to the community. The common denominator is the perceived need to exchange information and co-ordinate action within the area. Outside workers gain regular access both to the doctor and to each other, while doctors may find unexpected sources of support. The main topic is clinically based discussion; this also renders the group exclusive, a matter I shall return to.

Informality is a key factor in disguising the power relations which still obtain, structured by all the usual elements like gender and status; the group may or may not be doctor-led, but without the doctor it loses much of its point. Each individual has a distinct accountability system. Only the doctor can assume independence; for the rest the extent of their freedom of manoeuvre is the subject of negotiation both with employing agencies and with other workers. One form of this negotiation can be witnessed in the process of bidding to help Peter from within a specific role, a discussion which involves stake-outs of prospective occupational territory and rights of access or referral. In this respect the team resembles more formal meetings like ward rounds; and teams in large health centres may resemble those in hospitals, where elaborate rituals are necessary to achieve adequate weighting and recognition for the participants. But the crucial difference from the hospital setting is that professional functions, whether conflicting or complementary, are not ordered within an institution in which they are rival factions but mediated through the community, which is actually or potentially independent of their separate interests. It seems to me that the touchstone for any real change in value terms is the extent to which this role of the community, whether direct or indirect, is recognized and acted upon by allowing users of health care services, both potential and actual, to be active partners. (See Bayley Chapter Four, Shardlow Chapter Six). If this dimension is lacking, what is going on must be either flummery or a far more effective and insidious imposition of the clinical model which had apparently been rejected.

Clearly there is no community involvement in this example. However, some progressive features can be noticed. Among them is the positive response to a piece of information, for it cannot be clearly classed as a referral, which in most surgeries and social services offices would simply be filed away. Another is the freedom, even if it is qualified, of the contributions; this is an encouraging sign for the prospects of achieving collaboration through propinquity. But how has Peter fared so far, before contact is even established? His plight is being attended to, but is there a cost? The GP could have popped round to see him instead of attending the meeting, although this might still not obviate the need for a team discussion. Peter would expect the GP to know his situation, but a stranger at the door might well be less welcome. Nevertheless an increasing number of strangers know about him.

What has happened to confidentiality?

In the ordinary business of health care it is no longer sufficient to expect that the vulnerability of the person seeking help can be protected simply by invoking a principle of confidentiality which reflects a nostalgia for a one-to-one relationship with a supreme clinician. Confidentiality has been labelled as a 'decrepit concept' by a consultant who found that the hospital records of his patients were open to legitimate inspection by between twenty-five and one hundred other staff (Siegler 1982). Peter's condition is subject to a similar information-spread in a process from which only clinics for sexually transmitted diseases are exempt. Reception staff, who may already be privy to the information, are excluded from the case discussion although other workers, who have no immediate interest or skill to offer, are present. Several criteria for this distinction may be in operation but they are far from clear. This issue cannot be examined in detail here; I raise it to illustrate the range of hidden assumptions which still need to be adequately explored before this way of dealing with Peter's problem can be justified. Life was simpler for doctors under the old system. On the other hand, many people did not get the help they needed. I suggest that the only way out of this dilemma is to build-in far more of a general dialogue about information and referral processes, and to find some way of allowing people as much choice as possible over whether to enter this system or not. This is already happening around HIV+/AIDS.

Confidentiality is a fundamental professional fetish, ostensibly based on a person's right to privacy, but with two long-standing utilitarian justifications: the likelihood that a patient will only impart intimate information necessary for adequate treatment if he is jealously protected; and, as is made clear in the Hippocratic Oath, the guarding of professional knowledge within the body of approved members. From the uneasy coexistence of an intrinsic value, however derived, and of a principle of expediency for the protection of the professions, it is often assumed and argued that it is only through the advancement of the professions that this value can be protected. This switch from a correlationship to an inference has had the further consequence that information about a person has been assumed to belong to the professional. The demand to have access to and control of information about oneself, which has been fuelled by the changing nature of information systems, is not so much one about administrative issues as about the nature and the terms of the relationship between 'client' and professional.

One other aspect of multidisciplinary teamwork can usefully be mentioned here, namely the need to distinguish between consultation and referral, particularly in matters of public importance like child abuse, where agencies are developing procedures. If it is not clear in informal discussions whether information shared constitutes a procedural notification, gross misunderstandings may result. However if information cannot be shared without also being notified, then either consultation between agencies will dwindle, or procedures will often be triggered quite inappropriately. Rules and expectations about confidentiality between agencies must therefore be redrawn.

Autonomy, self-determination and information

The issue of autonomy is highlighted in the case discussion by the counsellor, who backs up her reaction to the offer of help as an intrusion with a consequentialist argument about motivation: that help is only effective when the recipient is sufficiently engaged and committed to make a self-referral. The GP would probably go along with this view, possibly for pragmatic as well as ethical reasons; and here we return to a major value difference in the medical and social work traditions. In medical ethics debates about freedom tend to be couched in the dynamic between autonomy and paternalism. The potentially drastic and sometimes irreversible nature of medical intervention tends to lead doctors to attempt to draw some sort of boundary around situations where paternalistic intervention is justifiable, although once this line is crossed, which for some is in the act of consultation, they act persuasively about whatever treatment they consider appropriate. Medicine prefers to regard both doctor and patient as autonomous individuals, with a stress on a negative concept of liberty (Gillon 1985).

Social work, on the other hand, has always had to struggle in some confusion between an ideal of freedom based on respect for persons and the promotion of social welfare, deriving from the element of moral crusade in social work history, and reinforced in recent decades by arguments towards specific political commitment. The concept of self-determination has been developed in an attempt to reconcile these tendencies, in part by advocating a more positive ideal of liberty (McDermott 1975; Timms 1983). Thus the two professions stereotypically have been thought to balance these contradictions in different ways. The doctor limits his sphere but within it he is actively interventionist. The social worker is far more curious, often being seen as interfering, but in actual involvement may well be less inclined to definite action. To the extent that these images fit the facts, the extension of medical boundaries to fit a more positive definition of health, combined with a potential social work response of itself becoming more 'pro-active', can seem alarming.

Demands for the recognition of patients' rights (Illich 1977; Kennedy 1983) have forced some doctors to recast their defence of paternalism by suggesting, for instance, that it is not only compatible with but dependent upon the involvement and trust of the patient (Weiss 1985; contrast Matthews 1986). O'Neill, in a more sophisticated philosophical analysis, argues that autonomy is often idealized in discussion whereas in reality it is missing for many parts of all lives and throughout some. Consent is often opaque, limited, and by default; this is especially true for 'patients'. She suggests that our aim should be to make consent possible wherever we can (O'Neill 1984). This formulation obviously justifies limited paternalism, though O'Neill does go on to argue that coercion, deception, and manipulation are ruled out. But the proposal that consent should be made possible has obvious ramifications for the issue of health awareness, both at the individual and the collective levels. For instance, at what stage can or should Peter be said to know enough about the available options to make any decision about which, if any, he should try? This is an entry to the shifting territory of wants, preferences, and needs.

One (but only one) condition for choice is information on which to base a decision, and it is on this limited consumerist model that primary health care is likely to be reformed. One of the general problems with attempting to revise expectations of health care is that most people have very little knowledge either of orthodox facilities or of alternatives to them. Hence, in O'Neill's phrase, their consent is 'opaque' because they lack the information which would make consent more genuine. This professionally cultivated ignorance is one of the bases of medical paternalism. Weiss argues that the major criterion for the patient is that of outcome. But in circumstances of ignorance the common expression of gratitude and relief by patients for whom paternalist intervention has been made cannot in itself be taken as justification of such a decision. This 'thank you' test, approved by Rawls among others, is not just inadequate and illusorily simple (Culver and Gert 1982:161–2), but is also a defence of conservatism.

Now O'Neill is not necessarily wanting to defend conservatism, but her position is not developed enough to take in the question of power over definition. How and by whom is the nature of anybody's partial autonomy to be decided? She may be right to say that it is difficult to formalize consent procedures or to set any single boundary between acceptable and unacceptable behaviour. But in conditions of change we do not just need to ask what the rules are, because they are unlikely to be fixed. It is much more important to know where and by whom the rules are made. Benton, addressing a similar question in an analysis of power, calls attention to 'the paradox of emancipation': on the one hand change requires both the assent and motivation of those involved; but on the other, without outside intervention there may be no change. He adopts a dialectical approach which depends upon the argument that the social production of wants, preferences, and identities must be internally contradictory, in that the mechanisms which produce conformist patterns of wants must also produce counter-tendencies. These in turn produce the 'purchase' in real life for competing concepts of interest, and the paradox of emancipation is only resolvable, he argues, if the conditions of ideological struggle are really present in everyday life (Benton 1982). Health care is indeed increasingly the subject of ideological struggle. We ourselves are parties to these conflicts and we need a perspective which allows us to participate in maintaining the purchase necessary to create the changes of consciousness upon which progress depends without also dictating its terms.

CAN PROFESSIONAL CREDIBILITY BE SALVAGED THROUGH VIRTUE?

In recent years there has been a trend for moral reasoning to become less formal and abstract and to explore more particular relationships (Williams 1981). As pluralism becomes more acceptable (Taylor 1982), but emotivism remains insufficient (MacIntyre 1985), the Aristotelian concepts of virtue, excellence, and praxis have been redeveloped, along with constructs of identity, such as project and narrative, which derive from more recent traditions. Williams stresses the importance of 'integrity'. It is easy to see the appeal of this approach to the professional helper (Rhodes 1986; Clark and Asquith 1985), to philosophers influenced by theology, and to those who show varieties of liberal distaste for the bureaucratization of personal life (Wiggins 1978; Williams 1985; Rorty 1986). Indeed MacIntyre, whose more radical approach breaks with the distinction between fact and value which he considers to be the essence of liberalism, had previously remarked that whether someone calls themselves a Christian, a Marxist, or a liberal may be less important than what sort of Christian, Marxist, or liberal they are; the reason for this lies in the type of moral questions they ask (MacIntyre 1971:86).

One problem with this approach, despite the valuable and necessary emphasis on relationships, is the emergence of a situational ethic which must avoid not only the pitfalls of act-utilitarianism and general relativism but also more subtle justifications for an isolationist paternalism, based on existing distributions of power. Thus Sir Douglas Black, President of the BMA, has argued for a retreat from working with other professions by drawing the boundaries of medicine more closely (Black 1984). The attractions for doctors are considerable, including a reduction in legitimate demand and the avoidance of uncertainties caused by close but undefined working relationships, particularly in anomalous situations like child-guidance clinics (Bennett 1977; Appleyard and Maiden 1979; Black and Subotsky 1982). A theoretical justification may also be advanced that the formal discipline of medicine has limited norms of its own, which offer guidance towards correct medical decisions. Within these norms there can be greater autonomy, a value which would be claimed as being patient-centred. However, many would consider that the doctor is the greater beneficiary. After all, general practice, at least, is still a business. The Hippocratic Oath, with its doubtful historical antecedents, can be seen less as a public commitment to personal professional competence and moral rectitude (Carrick 1985) than as a potent but limiting myth which enables doctors 'to deduce a certain duty to their patients but no particular duty to society at large' and which, if anything, sets doctor and patient against the world (Warnock 1985).

Social workers face similar choices, both in relation to clients and to other professions; the growth of specialisms can be partially justified along the same lines. In medical settings both they and community nurses have sought independence from unco-operative medical staff. But being less powerful, they need to be more confident of being able to gain purchase by alternative means.

Nevertheless isolationism, tempting as it may be, must be seen as a contingent response to the dominant Conservative ideology which seeks to transform primary health care into a competitive market, made the more ruthless through the reduction of available resources. Individualistic constructs of health and victim-blaming health education owe little to holistic values, whose pluralism flourishes on co-operation, not competition. Consultation patterns in primary or ambulatory health care suggest that medical intervention is not appropriate in a majority of cases. Kushner concludes that a relational model of consultation, emphasizing process, is not only desirable in itself but is compatible with both deontology and utilitarianism (Kushner 1981). However, it does not follow that medicine should predominate in such a model, and if medical imperialism is not to carry the day then either medical isolationism must accept a far smaller sphere of influence than most doctors would find acceptable, or medicine must recognize that the reality which lies behind such recommendations demands a humbler approach.

The relationship with patients or clients is, of course, central for all the caring professions. It is on the sacredness of this relationship, as much as on scientific knowledge, that the edifice of medical authority is built. The same is true of psychotherapy and of psychodynamically oriented social casework; although for the more rationally centred methods which are currently fashionable in social work, the nature of the relationship is probably less central and certainly less mystical. Downie and Telfer (1980) have argued that the nature of the caring relationship, which is to cherish persons, is such as to provide much more common ethical ground than has often been recognized. From such a position it is even possible to present the professions as the conscience of society. However, while medicine's conspicuity highlights its faults, the other professions suffer similar limitations; for their concepts of morality are not neutral but are themselves 'structured along lines which favour one set of interests rather than another' (Clifford 1982).

A NEW PRACTICE NEEDS NEW INSTITUTIONS

Virtue-based professionalism, as conventionally understood, is not in itself a sufficient response to the ineffectiveness, depersonalization, and disempowering processes of much health and social care. Collier quotes Plekhanov: 'Virtue requires not to be preached but to be prepared by the reasonable arrangement of social relations' (Collier 1984). Instead, the status and possibly the very nature of the professional relationship has to be changed; moreover, the orthodox professional ideal may turn out to be as much of an anachronism as many consider classical Marxism to be. Too much is claimed for an institution whose elitism and exclusivity block many public rights and circumvent the reciprocity which holism demands. Professionalism is in danger of becoming a substitute for the real emotional, social, and economic relationships we should be recognizing and developing with and for each other. Of course, we live in a real world and there is a need for the opportunity to make intimate disclosures to another person without fear of exploitation, a need for trust in a world which often betrays it. But for this to be channelled into professionalism as the conscience of the market economy is itself a betrayal.

A possible route out of these difficulties is indicated by a conceptual distinction between institutions and practices, made in a weak way by Hampshire (1983:64), but much more radically by MacIntyre, his arch-critic. For MacIntyre, virtues exist in the context of 'certain features of social and moral life', and he defines as 'practices' certain forms of 'socially established co-operative human activity' which realize internal goods 'in the course of trying to achieve appropriate standards of excellence'. Institutions, on the other hand, are concerned with external goods (MacIntyre 1985:186–96). Health care is, I suggest, a practice in which all those who are intent on living a fulfilling life should, in principle, be engaged. By 'in principle' I mean a qualification to allow, in particular, for resistance and failure, as well as for conflicts in priorities. The definition of health need not be too specific except insofar as it must contain a recognition that health is a social construct, a social fact, and a social responsibility which gives us duties towards each other.

Health care consists both of what we informally do, in this

respect, for ourselves and for others, and also of certain institutions, including medicine and many forms of social work. These institutions have developed a variety of functions within the totality of health care and from them have also constructed values and interests of their own. There is no reason why these should be compatible; indeed some degree of conflict is to be expected and can be constructive. However, institutions are competitive, and at our particular stage of social and economic development this competition is in danger of becoming pathological and irrelevant, if not damaging, to health care. We therefore need to develop new forms of institution which permit rather than hinder the expression of values which are increasingly commonly held and expected in this new practice.

The practical values for such an institution still have to be developed, though Rhodes has produced a useful framework for analysing them (Rhodes 1986). I would expect them to include a collective commitment to health care which regarded patients or clients, both individually and collectively, as equal partners in the enterprise; a respect for difference which did not involve the universal assertion of primacy either for scientific knowledge or for some intangible form of relationship process; and an approach to individuals which would protect without disabling. This protection must also be extended to helpers and carers, whether lay or professional; it thus contains an important new element, that of reciprocity. Almost all the philosophical analysis of caring relationships concentrates on the rights of the patient or client, whose vulnerability confers power on the carer; little if anything is said about the rights of the carer, whether lay or professional. Indeed there are some forms in which it is still not considered reputable to raise them. One book which sought to establish a variant of co-counselling as the basis for a healing relationship in social work seems to have sunk without trace (Ragg 1977). I believe this disregard of reciprocity to be disabling for both parties in terms of their health. It deprives the patient, reducing the chance of compliance, and puts additional strain on the carer, whose fantasies about manipulation by the patient are allowed full rein. The consequent distance between the two cannot be directly bridged and the chance of accurate feedback for the carer is thereby reduced or eliminated.

These changes may be idealistic but so is the developing ideology of 'wholeness'. They are undoubtedly time-consuming but I believe they are capable of utilitarian as well as deontological justification. It is precisely 'close but undefined working relationships' that we need to learn to live with, not to escape from. Moral philosophy is not very helpful here because its vocabulary is too static and abstract. Nevertheless, it may be possible to develop team values either in a Habermassian framework of communicative ethics or, more pragmatically, within a contractarian approach. Contractarianism has a more obvious application to micro-societies that it perhaps has to human society as a whole; a primary care team can certainly be 'a co-operative venture for mutual advantage', and the addition of games theory not only provides a framework for negotiation but allows much more sophisticated analysis of strategy and choice (Gauthier 1986: chs 1,2).

From a practical point of view, De Wachter, a Belgian infertility specialist, gives some hints about how to proceed (De Wachter 1976). He argues, first, that teams need to develop 'communication within a coherent conceptual framework' and that this involves training the patient to be a member of the team, thus consciously abandoning any professional claims to monopoly or veto. Second, this framework should lead to openness and to a membership style which emphasizes an 'expectant' attitude to others, rather than prejudicial anticipation. This centres around recognizing both patients and colleagues as persons. Third, there should be a deployment of power which involves a genuine sharing of responsibility. De Wachter emphasizes that this sharing is not a surrender of responsibility, which, he says, has never been a sign of virtue, and he discusses some of the difficulties involved. There is a growing literature on teamwork and at least some piecemeal experimentation with this form of change. The adoption of this ideology as a whole would mean as revolutionary a transformation in health care as any biochemical or technical advance, not least because the most effective and economical use of such developments might be ensured.

But the determinants of our health ultimately lie outside the health care system. What did happen to Peter? He did not keep his appointment but two months later his mother contacted the social worker to ask if it could be arranged. Everybody in the team could feel justified! Peter embarked on a programme to reduce his drinking and was successful enough to find both a girlfriend and a job. But the courtship did not last and the job proved to be poorly paid, menial, and boring. Peter's future began to look bleaker as he abandoned both his job and his good resolutions. He returned to drinking more than he could afford and the whole process had to start again. Health is only one part of the socio-economic matrix and, whatever the composition of the health care team, it cannot any longer contemplate its work in isolation.

© Mike Simpkin

Chapter Six

RESIDENTIAL SOCIAL WORK WITHOUT RESIDENCE

STEVEN SHARDLOW

VALUES AND RESIDENTIAL CARE

We are for the most part little concerned about our values. No doubt the average residential social worker is little different from the rest of the social work profession, or indeed the general public. Certainly, there is insufficient consideration of ethical matters in the literature on residential care to suggest otherwise. Indeed, it was only very recently, in 1986, that the Social Care Association produced and adopted a code of ethics for its members (SCA 1986). It is perhaps surprising that there has not been greater interest in the ethics of residential practice, given the considerable influence and control that residential workers may exercise over the lives of those in residential care: accounts of consumers have provided ample evidence of the need for such examination (Line 1980; Page and Clarke 1977), to say nothing of events at Kincora and Nye Bevan Lodge.

This failure to undertake detailed consideration of the ethics of residential care may in part be due to disputes over the very nature of residential work and its relationship to social work. Sometimes the two have been seen as separate, discrete activities; or, by contrast, residential units are perceived as settings for the practice of social work (Davis 1981); alternatively residential work is seen as a distinct method of practice (Berry 1975; CCETSW 1973; Ward 1977); recently attempts have been made to delineate group-care practice across a range of social systems, of which residential work in the social services is one component (Ainsworth and Fulcher 1981; Philpott 1984; Wolins 1974). As Davis comments, much time has been spent on debating the precise nature of the fit between social work and residential work:

> The problem is that these distinctions tend to hold only at a very general level of discussion and any detailed examination of the activities residential workers are engaged in shows how little consideration has been given to the unique and complex problems of client-worker interaction resulting from the demands made on residential units.
>
> (Davis 1981:116)

Among the unique and complex problems are ethical issues. These are particularly ignored in such circumstances both because, as Timms suggested (Chapter Two), we avoid thinking about them unless we have to, and because when we do consider them they often seem to be inordinately difficult to contemplate satisfactorily (Lane and White 1980:3).

In so far as literature about values in residential care exists at all, two broad strands can be identified. The first takes cognizance of ethical issues which flow from the relationship between staff and residents. Primary concerns are the implications for the practitioner and resident of those ethical problems which arise from living in an environment where individuals are often powerless or under the substantial control of others. Dominant themes in this tradition are the residents' need for self-expression through participation in the structures of residential units (Line 1980), and the need for self-realization by the expression of everyday human needs (Miller and Gwynne 1972). At the heart of these concerns is the degree to which individual residents can have control within the group-living environment over money (Clough 1981:82–84), lifestyle (Dharamsi *et al.* 1979), or their own sexuality (Davis 1980) etc: in short, the degree to which those in residential care can not only retain their humanity but maximize their potential.

A second major theme concerns the function of residential care and the nature of the relationship between residential care, the family, and society. Often residential care is seen as substitute for family care, when this is no longer available (Davis 1981). Provision of a permanent substitute family is currently the preferred placement rather than residential care for the majority of children who for whatever reason are unable to live with their birth family. Similarly, for the elderly, as Norman Fowler (the then Secretary of State for Social Services) stated in his speech to the 1984 Joint Social Services Annual Conference, 'The front line of support is the family and the closest circle of support outside the family should be friends and neighbours.'

It is then hardly surprising that the individual who enters residential care may feel a failure and experience a sense of stigma bereft of the support of close family ties. The quality of care provided may be low relative to standards elsewhere in society, reflecting the worth or merit attributed to those individuals living in care. However, some radicals argue that residential care could provide a collectivist challenge to traditional family structures (Lee and Pithers 1980), and that it can provide a desirable and positive alternative for the care of some of society's dependent members. The kernel of this debate between those who argue the value of the family as the primary locus for care and those who support alternative forms of care is the nature of the relationship between the individual and the state, and the extent to which the individual as a citizen has the right to expect help from the state in adversity. Some argue that the state has only a residual function, that of supporting those who do not have families able to provide care; others would offer more by way of choice, irrespective, to some extent, of the capability of the family to provide. To further complicate this debate, new approaches to practice have emerged where residential care provides a supplement to family care (Davis 1981). Before looking at these in more detail we need to consider how values can be applied to residential units.

VALUES AND RESIDENTIAL UNITS

Individuals are often said to 'value' particular 'goods' or to hold a 'set of values'. To understand such notions we do not need to know the precise connotation of the term 'value' or 'values'. Perhaps this is as well, given the great variety of meanings that may be attached to the word 'value' (Timms 1983). Whether we believe that 'values' are ideals that have an independent existence (i.e., there are things which are worth valuing regardless of whether anybody actually does or does not value them), or alternatively that they are a form of linguistic construction with a

84

capacity to give a false impression of their independent existence (i.e., they should be more properly regarded as qualities which are attributed to particular items rather than inherent in them), is, for the purpose of the usage of 'value' or 'values', irrelevant. We are able to understand, at least in part, the values that a person holds by virtue of what he or she says, and more particularly by his or her actions. Making a free or unconstrained choice between two or more actions is an expression of the individual's values. It reveals individual preferences, from which we may deduce what is valued by that individual. We might argue that the person making a choice is providing us with an ostensive definition of his or her values, following Wittgenstein (1958). This is not foolproof: we may make mistakes, either from misunderstanding the reason for the individual's choice or by mistaking the actual quality that is valued.

So far, values have been understood only in terms of individuals rather than residential units, or groups of people. If it is difficult to understand the notion of values in relation to individuals then it is even more problematic with institutions or groups (Timms Chapter Two, Simpkin Chapter Five). We could not, for instance, say that a given residential unit holds a particular value set; to do so would be patent nonsense. This would be to commit the folly of attributing human qualities to non-human objects. It is true that when we speak of inanimate objects we frequently attribute human qualities to them: this may represent a deep psychological need to personalize the impersonal and to give meaning to the world of mechanical constructs in which we live, or it may be to do with the structure of language, which has in the past ascribed gender to nouns (as happens in some languages today) and by implication to the item signified by the word. Nevertheless, we should beware of careless ascription of values to inanimate objects or social structures such as residential units.

However, we do often want to talk about the values that underlie or are expressed, denoted, or signified by a certain institution. We can perhaps begin to understand such attributions in at least two ways. First, the unit is a nexus for an exchange of social relationships of various types: user-worker, user-user, worker-worker, family member-user-worker, etc. Although there will be substantial differences in the nature and quality of the individual relationships there will also be broad similarities for types of relationship in accord with the policy and practice of the unit. These set a framework or context in which these social interchanges occur: i.e., if a unit is committed to the involvement of parents in the care of their children who are resident one would expect to see rules and regulations that actively encourage and enable parental participation. Such structures must be perceived as helpful by the users – in this case, the parents themselves. Thus statements about the moral values adopted by residential units can be made in accordance with the way in which people are affected by their involvement in them. We might expect that users of a particular service will tend to have similar experiences at a very general level. The way in which they are treated can be used as an indicator of the values of the unit staff and the wider agency. There are many difficulties here, not least that residential units consist of teams of individuals who may have very different values. None the less, residential work is usually a team activity. In all units it will be necessary to adopt to some extent standardized work practices and policies. These may be democratically negotiated, imposed by distant bureaucracy, or benevolently applied by a charismatic autocrat. Some deviant individuals may choose not to follow the dominant values of a unit. There will always be elements of competition and conflicts between team members. Whilst our understanding of phrases such as the 'values of a unit' or the 'values of a team' will inevitably be imperfect, we can attempt to discern the effects of the structures and policies upon users as an approach to making sense of such notions.

RESOURCE CENTRES: CHANGING MODELS OF PRACTICE

Residential care is not a homogeneous entity. It caters for many different people in a variety of forms and organizational structures. Major trends have emerged in the last ten years in the provision of residential care. In regard to children, demo-graphic movements have generated pressure to close children's homes as the number of children in the population has fallen. This trend has been enhanced by an increasingly dominant ideology in social work that residential care is not a suitable long-term placement for the majority of children. Indeed at least one local authority, Warwickshire, has abolished all residential provision for children. This approach would not necessarily find favour with consumers. The National Association of Young People in Care (NAYPIC) has consistently argued that many young people prefer to live in children's homes rather than in foster care.

Despite much professional pessimism about residential care, innovatory practice abounds, whether through the work of charismatic individuals such as Bettelheim (1950) or through the application of theoretical models such as social learning theory (Gobell 1980) to the care of the mentally handicapped or disturbed adolescents, or through the work of pioneering voluntary organizations such as Dr Barnardo's at Druids Heath (Cox and McArdle 1987). In recent years we have also seen the rapid development of what have been termed 'resource centres'. It is not easy to describe the essence of a resource centre, for two reasons: first, each centre is unique, and second, although there is a growing body of literature in this field it remains scant and little can yet be asserted with any degree of certainty. A broad distinction can be made between those centres that are primarily designed for children and families, often called 'family centres', and those for elderly people, as yet without a genus name.

A key element of the resource centre was described in the Bonnington report (1984). They must be outward-looking, serving their community, not just involved in their own internal affairs, looking inwards, merely providing a home for their residents. This is not just about encouraging residents to have greater involvement in the wider community: that should be an element in good residential practice anyway. Rather, the resource centre represents a step beyond the notion that the unit should exist solely for the immediate residents. The precise form of interaction with the local community must of necessity vary from centre to centre. There is an implication that the unit will be involved in the community and similarly the community will be actively involved in the centre. As the Barclay report states, the resource-centre model is one form of community social work (Barclay 1982:209).

Family centres have proliferated in recent years, as Adamson and Warren comment:

Family centre is one of the latest all-embracing labels in social work. It is used to mean a range of different things, which have been described as 'a brave innovation', 'cheap alternative' and 'the rediscovery of community in social work'. However there is definitely a trend in social work to acknowledge the need to embrace the client, the family and the community.

(Adamson and Warren 1983:ix)

Family centres are to be found in both the local government and the voluntary sectors. A recent survey (DHSS 1988) found half of the 108 participating local authorities had one or more family centres. They offer a wide range of services (Pugh and De'Ath 1983), with little similarity between individual centres (Hasler 1984), either in physical appearance, operating principles (Birchall 1982), or particular services offered (Dennis 1981), or in their aims, activities, and staffing patterns, their degree of involvement in the community, or indeed the type of family they are designed to cater for (Goldberg and Sinclair 1984:40). Even those within the same organization are likely to be radically different from each other. In her study based on 250 centres, whilst echoing Phelan's comment that there is 'no such thing as an identikit family centre' De'Ath (1985) identified some common features of self-help family centres, including: a commitment to worc with both parents and children rather than just with children, and to relieve pressures on families whatever the cause; the intention to increase the self-confidence and self-esteem of all those who use the centre; a commitment to user participation, ranging from individual case planning to being part of management structures and working for the centre. De'Ath was writing about centres in the voluntary sector, but many of the same qualities apply to those in the local government sector. Similar developments in the care of the elderly are also apparent (McDonald *et al.* 1984; Rayfield 1985; Kelly 1987).

The origins of family centres are diverse. Some have arisen spontaneously from the efforts of local voluntary groups, others have been created by centralized bodies, be these large national voluntary organizations or local authorities. It is the latter that might be seen to be replacements for residential care, in one of two ways. Large residential units for children are being replaced in the big voluntary organizations by newer and more flexible forms of provision. Some local authorities are doing the same. The reasons for this are difficult to unravel with certainty. Can we assert then that there is a direct correlation between the development of family centres in the statutory sector and the closure of the traditional children's home or old people's home? Certainly in one case, that of the EPSU (Elderly Persons Support Unit) (McDonald *et al.*) a decision was made not to build an old people's home but to develop a community resource. Similarly, some authorities are closing children's homes and opening family centres. What are the implications of these changes for clients and workers?

CLIENTS AND WORKERS

Drawing on the writings of Paulo Friere in *Pedagogy of the Oppressed*, Hasler poses the question: why is it that those who apparently have much to gain reject the help that is offered to them (Hasler 1984:3)? For Friere this is exemplified by the illiterate in South America, who withdraw from structured opportunities to learn to read. Similarly, Hasler comments, recipients of social services often seem to be indifferent or hostile to the help being offered. He argues, in tandem with Friere, that those in receipt of welfare services need to cast off the role of passive recipient and to become 'actors' in the events surrounding them. As Marx would have argued, we all need to find self-realization to be truly human, and this can only be achieved through direct and active involvement in wage and domestic labour. To be a passive receptacle for others is to be denied the opportunity of becoming truly human; when we force others to adopt such roles we ignore their humanity, and in so doing we diminish our own.

We do not have to look far to find examples of those living in residential care being deprived of control over even the minutiae of daily living. As Willcocks, Peace, and Kelleher (1987) found in their study of one hundred homes for elderly people, little attention was paid to the social needs of the residents: the primary concern was for their physical safety. 'Residential care is rendered primarily in domestic and physical care modes, and the greatest investment of staff time is in this facet of care' (1987:62). Hence opportunities for taking risks by residents were not encouraged; this would have compromised the concern for safety. Similarly, opportunities for participation were not encouraged. The resident was for the most part perceived as a passive recipient of service rather than someone to be actively involved in the solution to their own difficulties. Similar conclusions can be drawn in respect of other groups. Berridge found in regard to children's homes that 'staff roles are limited by a predominantly tending and residential perspective, reflected in staff-resident ratios and working conditions. Yet, as we have seen, most residents are now adolescents and their needs are diverse' (1985:65). Similar evidence can be gleaned from the comments made by those living in residential care (Line 1980; Page and Clark 1977).

The challenge for the personal social services is to find ways to overcome the sense of oppression and passivity of those whom the service is designed to help. In traditional modes of social work, 'clients', those who see themselves as having a particular problem or whom a social agency has defined as needing help, seek assistance to resolve their difficulties. It may well be that the individual would rather give the responsibility for resolving the difficulty to someone else. However, to resolve the majority of difficulties it is necessary to have the active co-operation of the person seeking help. The question is then to what extent are people likely to resolve their difficulties if they are told what to do by some expert. This is both an empirical question and an ethical one. It may be the case that if we tell people what to do they will follow our instructions and resolve their difficulties. But people do not always follow instructions as given. Even if they did, we would still have to confront an ethical dilemma. Is it acceptable that individuals should be deprived of the responsibility to take action on their own account to resolve their own difficulties? Any response to this question must take account of the principle of respect for persons, which requires that individuals be treated as ends in themselves and not as means to a secondary goal (Downie and Telfer 1969). Unfortunately, this is not always part of residential care. We may be able to provide, in general, safe environments but not necessarily those which allow for the development of human potential.

Family centres may be able to challenge the traditional role of the recipient of service. Phelan notes that many have been astonished by the 'skills, energies and personal qualities that are available in what have been labelled disadvantaged communities', and by the way in which these have contributed to family centres. Ann was one such case. She was 'living in the local Women's Aid Hostel when she volunteered to help a project's welfare rights service. Shortly afterwards she was rehoused on the estate where the project was based, and subsequently co-founded a neighbourhood care scheme. She is an active member of the tenants' association and a parent-governor at the local school' (Phelan 1983:69). Similarly, Willmott and Mayne (1983) quote an example of a user whose self-confidence increased as a result of participation in a centre. This trend has been reported by the family centres located in the voluntary sector.

How are we to explain the apparent differences in the treatment of clients between traditional residential units and the more recent family centres? Role boundaries between the recipients and the providers of service are more permeable in family centres than in the traditional unit. In family centres the recipients of services are not only recipients, they may also be service providers. The implications are two-fold. First, the individual is able to feel a sense of self-esteem, which leads to increased self-confidence through making an active contribution to the life of the centre in a way that is clearly recognized. This reintroduces the notion of 'reciprocity' into client-worker and other centre-based relationships. The individual is enabled to give as well as receive through the medium of social relationships. A network of helping relationships may develop among users of the centre. Help may be deprofessionalized, and as such it may be more direct and more easily acceptable. Users are in the position of helping themselves, and of helping others through various forms of self-help. Individuals are perceived by others in a variety of different roles, including coping roles, and not merely in the dependent and passive roles of client or resident. To achieve these objectives centres must encourage active participation and must be willing to allow users to control as much as possible of what happens in the centre.

Perceptions may be equally affected when workers have practical care tasks within the centre and community social work tasks outside. This is not just the notion implied by the concept of the 'key worker', where a residential worker has specific and defined tasks in relation to one or more residents. In some centres workers may have true overlap in roles and responsibilities traditionally associated with field and residential models of practice. This generates a greater correspondence between the experience of the worker and that of the client. For example, a worker may experience difficulty in getting two or three children ready for school at the family centre before seeing other clients in the community. This breaks down the exclusivity of focus which is so often a part of traditional modes of service delivery. Workers in children's homes tend to concentrate upon the child, who is seen as the primary client. Similarly, field-workers tend to concentrate their emphasis on those living in the community, and this can exclude the child in residential care.

In these ways the barriers between the user of the service and the provider of the same service are broken down. As one worker in a resource centre has written:

> I can no longer bring myself to refer to the people I work with as clients. ... The relationship is a more equal one with more mutual respect. ... Seeing more people in the centre and around the estate I see them in various roles ... so that client is by no means the predominant role.
>
> (Simmons 1985:23)

The role of client is not then the only way in which individuals may be perceived by workers at the centre. There is a sense in which the individual's capabilities are recognized and the person is treated as if they were a whole person, with abilities as well as problems. They do not just become a 'case' or a 'resident' but remain a person. There is a close similarity here with the notion of a holistic approach to medicine (see Simpkin, Chapter Five) or the whole-person approach (see Bayley, Chapter Four). It might be argued that the approach is 'holistic social care'. This may be easier to develop in a centre catering for adults than where the centre has a role in the provision of care for children. As one manager of a local authority resource centre has written:

> One of our hopes had been that Resource Centres would have a positive role in the community, would be seen as contributing to the local community and would draw on the local community for ideas and support. I am not aware that

these aspirations have been realized. Indeed there is a conflict in the role they are being cast in. If resource centres become the places where families are assessed prior to children being removed, it will be difficult for them to retain an image of positive help to families in the community.

(Ward 1986:4)

This manager's desired solution was to increase the similarity with centres in the voluntary sector and to increase the number of preventative and day-care programmes. We do not have reliable empirical data as yet to indicate whether or not this would solve the problem, or enough evidence to suggest with certainty that new forms of practice encapsulated in the resource-centre models are more successful than more traditional forms of practice. Even so, they provide a service which can enhance the client as a person; this may in itself be a valid ethical reason to adopt this approach.

CONFLICTS BETWEEN USERS

There is always a tension between the needs of the individual and those of the wider group in residential care. This may be experienced by the individual as an adherence to rigid and impersonal routines, imposed by the organization as a response to having to deal with large numbers of people. Or the tension may result in a loss of individual freedom and a limitation on the opportunities to exercise choice, because that conflicts with the wishes of other members of the group. These problems are inherent to residential care. The means of resolution indicates much about the quality of care being provided. With the development of new forms of care, new possibilities exist for the exacerbation of such conflicts.

In resource centres, users will spend different proportions of their day at the centre. Some may attend for one hour a week for a formal group, others for much of the day on a drop-in basis, while some may live there for brief periods of time. The needs, desires, and hopes of each user may be very different. It may be more difficult to resolve conflicts between various users in resource centres than in traditional forms of residential care, because they will not necessarily share the same living experiences. An example illustrates some of the difficulties that may arise. An elderly male resident, one of ten in a small purpose-built resource centre, complains about a group that comes to the day centre once a week for two hours. The group is for mothers with their children. He objects to the noise caused by the children, saying that at his age he wants some peace and quiet and that if he had wanted to go into a children's home then he would have done so.

In this example there is a potentially irreconcilable conflict between two users of the centre. Let us assume that there is no immediately obvious practical solution to this difficulty, i.e., there is no way in which the noise of the children can be reduced, and no way in which the resident can remove himself from the centre for the time that the group is there.

In deciding between the needs of the elderly resident and the group, what kind of a decision are we being asked to make? Is it a professional judgement, based upon knowledge or skills? Are we to make a prudent decision, discreet, sagacious, and opportune? Or a policy decision, in accordance with local authority guidelines? Or is it just an arbitrary choice? There is little in the canon of social work likely to help us to make such a decision: local guidelines do not usually deal in such currency. In fact, whether we recognize it or not, what we are involved in is a moral decision, because we have to choose between the competing demands of two centre users. Were the centre a residential unit for old people then the choice might be easier, because the resident could be said to have the primary call on the facilities. Where a resource centre exists for the benefit of a community, the choice is much less clear.

There are likely in the future to be a whole new set of such competing demands. And, a second question arises: is this a question for an individual worker, the staff team, or a management committee? Here we have the space to consider only the nature of the decision – a decision which inevitably changes according to who makes it.

Which moral principles might be used to solve this problem? Much moral philosophy is concerned with the nature of moral systems and the meanings of moral words (Williams 1985). We need a mode of moral analysis that concerns itself with making judgements about the rightness or wrongness of particular actions, rather than a theory describing principles which could regulate political and social activity or a moral philosophy which all too willingly engages in abstract linguistic sophistry. There are moral theories offering guidance as to individual behaviour: deontological theories, which judge the rightness of an act by the extent to which one behaves in accordance with one's duties; motivist theories, which judge the rightness of actions by the intention of the person committing the act; consequentialist theories, which determine the rightness of an act by the effect which that act has on the person committing the act, and on others. Different people may make their moral choices in accordance with these different systems; each may lead to a different conclusion. We shall examine our present moral difficulty using a consequentialist theory.

Utilitarianism, first expounded by Bentham and subsequently elaborated and popularized through the writings of Mill, is a consequentialist theory of morality, where the virtue of a particular act or actions is measured in terms of its effects. An act is desirable to the extent that it increases the total happiness in the world, or in so far as it reduces the amount of misery in the world (Mill 1863). All individuals are assumed to be equal, and therefore to calculate the sum of human happiness it is necessary to add up the increase in happiness that would be experienced by individuals following a particular act or action.

Applying utilitarian principles, the happiness of group members and their children would at first sight greatly outweigh the unhappiness of the resident. But there is a difficulty with this rather crude application of the theory. It seems that in any such case the majority will always win. The degree of unhappiness or anguish that the resident might experience is effectively ignored for the benefit of the majority. It is possible that utilitarian principles should never be applied in this simple form to individual acts, otherwise one has something that looks suspiciously like pragmatism clothed in the garb of morality, whereby whatever the injustice to the individual the majority may do as they please. The 'rule utilitarian' would avoid this difficulty by seeking to use utilitarian principles to devise general rules for moral conduct, so that the rightness of a particular action would be tested by the extent to which it conformed to the rule. This is summed up by Smart in his definition of 'restricted' utilitarianism:

Broadly, then, actions are to be tested by rules and rules by consequences. The only cases in which we must test an individual action directly by its consequences are (a) when the action comes under two different rules, one of which enjoins it and the other of which forbids it, and (b) when there is no rule whatever that governs the given case.

(Smart 1956:345)

Restricted, or, as it is commonly known, 'rule utilitarianism' initially seems to offer a way out of our difficulty, in which an initial application of utilitarian principles to the case seemed to override the interests of the male resident. However, we cannot use restricted utilitarianism here because the example we are using clearly falls into one, if not both, of the categories of exemption. Are we then left in the uncomfortable position that the majority will always win?

There is some help to be found in the 'role reversal test' (Hare 1981). He proposes that the person making a decision should consider him or herself as bound by the judgement if the roles were reversed, and he or she were the one who was adversely affected by the decision. There are two parts to this process. First, the person making a decision must attempt to understand the world from the perspective of the individual who will be affected by the decision: this should not be an insuperable difficulty for social workers, given the emphasis on empathy in social work writings. Second, there must be an agreement to a general principle to be bound by the outcome if the worker's social role were different to that which it actually is. To return to our example, if the resident was extremely distressed as a result of the group's activity and the only way to avoid that distress was to refuse to allow the group to participate in the centre, then we have the basis within our framework for making moral decisions to take this into account.

Thus we have the bare bones of a moral theory to help us decide this particular case. It is consequentialist, and can take account of the effect decisions will have on the individual and on the majority. Even so, no two individuals need apply the same theory to the same set of facts and arrive at the same decision. Here again Hare (1963) can be of some help. He suggests that in cases of disagreement over moral judgements we should look at extreme paradigm cases to see if agreement is possible. We should gradually consider less extreme cases until we discover the point of disagreement. We may not be able to agree, because in the end the disagreement may be about a difference in belief. However, the reasons for disagreement should be much clearer.

A large number of the decisions made in resource centres may be of this kind, where individuals or groups are in direct competition with each other for scarce resources. Utilitarianism is not the only moral theory which may be able to help us resolve such conflicts. What is important is to note that without a moral theory of some description we are forced back into pragmatism.

CONCLUSION

A world without any form of residential care seems entirely fanciful, even if some authorities are moving in that direction for some groups. We may be able to replace some residential care with alternative forms of provision based on the resource-centre model. It does offer the possibility of helping to change the relationships between clients and workers, but it will also exacerbate forms of conflict between users. This is not to say that conflicts have not existed previously in residential care – clearly they have; but the conflicts in resource centres may be different in quality and, given the aims of such centres, even harder to resolve.

© Steven Shardlow

Chapter Seven

PARTICIPATION AND PATERNALISM

ERIC SAINSBURY

Among social workers – and, indeed, in the public at large – the words participation and paternalism tend to evoke knee-jerk reactions of approval and disapproval respectively. Participation is loosely associated with notions of partnership between citizens, with the sharing of power between public servants and those they serve, with ideals of greater social equality in making and implementing welfare policies, and with enhancing the freedom of individual service users to make choices in pursuing their own welfare. Paternalism, on the other hand, is taken to imply assumptions held by professionals and bureaucrats of the right to exercise controls over welfare decisions – in respect of both public and individual matters – on the basis of knowledge and expertise not generally available, and sometimes even deliberately withheld from those they profess to serve; it is thought to imply restriction of choice in the interests of achieving uniformity of disposal; and to be virtually a conspiratorial retention of power differentials in favour of elite groups. The abrupt change of attitude from the professionalization of the 1950s to the anti-professionalism of the 1960s was associated with a change in values; both owed more to political doctrine than to a greater appreciation of human needs.

In the practice of social work since the publication by BASW of *Clients Are Fellow Citizens* (1980), as Etherington (1986) has suggested, 'BASW has been concerned with making social work less like the slavish emulation of other professional groups and has attempted to create a framework in which social work can be seen as a partnership between social workers and clients, based on advocacy and ultimately as an abdication of power downwards.' Radical social work, especially Bailey and Brake (1975), or Simpkin (1983), has constituted a movement, though derived from a political philosophy characterized in practice by the centralization of power, committed to anti-professionalism, to the raising of political consciousness and political power among service-users, and to the recognition that the care and control functions, long debated as alternative concepts, are arguably both merely two facets of paternalism. Similarly, arguments from the radical right in politics have advocated the reduction of state power (in reality, the power of public servants and professionals, rather than of the state) as a means of enhancing the freedom and choices available to individual citizens, of giving people personal responsibility in free partnerships with each other in preference to dependence on the decisions taken by statutory agents. 'Britain's welfare state represents the nationalization of about £75 billion of what, for most people, should have been private spending.... The huge businesses of social security, the NHS and education are managed by public servants.... However dedicated the staffs may be, the inevitable consequences are under-investment, misallocation of resources, low morale and customer dissatisfaction' (John Hoskins, *The Times*, 22 October 1986). Thus, notions associated with paternalism are variously condemned by both left and right; and because partnership is commonly regarded as the antonym of paternalism, it is seen as a self-evident good – though, one suspects, only if compatible with the centralist intentions and controls of 'true believers' on either side.

Three reservations might be appropriate at this stage: first, to doubt whether participation and paternalism should be seen as opposed concepts, mutually exclusive of each other; second, to doubt whether paternalism is necessarily and wholly bad – for one reasonably mistrusts any blanket condemnation of an idea which is opposed by factions incapable of consensus on most other issues; third, to doubt whether participation, though self-evidently a good aim in social work practice, is any less complex a concept than paternalism when one seeks to implement it in practice.

Attitudes to participation and paternalism in social work may be seen to hinge on a fundamental assertion within the profession of the primacy due to the value of respect for persons.

Biestek's (1961) principles governing the social worker-client relationship are derived from this superordinate value; its influence may be earlier seen in the attitudes of workers in The Charity Organization Society who, despite their adherence to the essential inequalities of nineteenth-century social structure, stressed the importance of humane understanding of the motivations and aspirations of their clientele; and the principal contribution of reformers like Josephine Butler and the Police Court Mission to the philosophy of social work lay in their strengthening of respect for those previously written off as undeserving. This value is given central prominence in the BASW Code of Ethics (1975) as the source of all the operational principles of the profession.

Although, more recently, pragmatic considerations concerned with the effectiveness of intervention have been cited to justify procedures which involve clients in defining tasks and making decisions on their lives (cf. Reid and Epstein 1972, Hudson and Macdonald 1986), these would probably not have taken root so readily in the profession had it not been for a prior commitment to the essential belief in according respect to clients, and in interpreting this respect as the desirability of enhancing their self-realization and their potential for social equality, not only with more fortunate citizens but with their professional helpers. The Seebohm Committee's advocacy of actions which blur the distinction between those who give and receive help (para 492) and which involve service-users in debating the nature of the services available to them (para 491) is voiced within their report as if morally and socially self-justifying rather than utilitarian and pragmatic.

There is a tendency, therefore, as Timms (1983) has suggested, to regard this value (of respect for persons) not simply as a moral statement or ideal but as an operational principle, and to draw certain conclusions from it which have subsequently proved difficult if not impossible to sustain consistently in the day-to-day practice of social work: for example, that relationships which embody this value are self-justifying in publicly funded services (as well as in private life), irrespective of the claims of other criteria for the deployment of limited resources; and that social work practice can in all its aspects be judged by the morality of its inputs without regard to its outcomes (Timms 1983:59).

Social workers find themselves in a situation, therefore, where 'respect for persons' leads to distaste for paternalism and support for participation, while they remain concerned that the former is still present in practice (for one has no need to be concerned about something which does not exist) and that the latter is difficult to implement. Clearly, both words merit closer examination.

It is a principal theme of this chapter that, within certain limits, paternalism is an essential element in social work practice, however participatory the intentions of the social worker, and that the polarization of participation and paternalism – the assumption that they constitute mutually exclusive approaches to practice – is false.

PATERNALISM IN PRACTICE

Timms (1983) noted that paternalism is a somewhat deviant variation of the words 'paternal' and 'parental' (p. 63), and that society (through social legislation) expects social workers to adopt some parental roles – notably, of course, in the field of child care. Dworkin (1979) has defined paternalism as interference with another's freedom of action, but suggests that it may in certain situations be morally justified if reference can be legitimately made to reasons exclusively associated with the welfare, good, happiness, needs, interests, and/or values of the person dealt with. Similarly, Weale (1972), while recognizing that paternalistic activities are necessarily built on relationships in which superior and inferior status and roles are assumed, suggests that paternalism can be evaluated as appropriate or inappropriate in specific situations by reference to three criteria: the extent of the severity with which a person's choice of life style is being interfered with; the extent to which the precise focus of the activity can be linked to an aspect of the person's plans, hopes, and aspirations for his or her own life; some failure of adequate reasoning on the person's part which results in an inability, without external interference, to determine some aspects of his or her own life-goals.

In effect, therefore, elements of paternalism in social work practice may be justifiable on two grounds: first by the sanctions imposed on social workers and service-users alike by social legislation, recognizing that social workers are public servants employed to fulfil certain requirements of legislation (albeit at times appropriately critical of it); second, by the kinds of moral premises which, more generally, we associate with good parenting. Both grounds need to be present, however; paternalism may be repressive if they are seen as alternative rather than complementary grounds. The unease felt by social workers about the paternalistic elements of their work, significantly, is less expressed in respect of their child-care activities than in work with adult clients, with whom parental forms of intervention seem self-evidently inappropriate. They are right to be anxious and diffident in this matter: the exercise of power, once one gets used to it, is seductively attractive; and one is painfully aware that, for most people, the road to hell is more often paved with the good intentions of other people than with their own. Furthermore, the common vocabulary of social work – 'unmet needs', 'social inadequacy', 'under stress', etc. – tends by its nature to emphasize the impotence rather than the potential and achievements of clients, and thus it subtly encourages a paternalistic stance. On the other hand, there are situations – the complexity involved in exercising rights to adequate benefits, or the bewilderment of experiencing acutely ambiguous emotions – in which one may be glad to find a helper with certain sorts of power or one who provides a structure of certainty and comprehension within which, at times of crisis, one can *temporarily* take shelter.

Thus, despite current concerns, and an increasing lack of confidence in the exercise of professional judgements and the imposition of professional perspectives, clients of social workers (and, indeed, of all professionals) are not only made subject to professional judgements in some circumstances, but may in some instances actively seek these judgements as a means of sustaining or regaining a sense of purpose in a context of bewilderment, and occasionally even regaining a sense of their own personhood. As Clark and Asquith (1985) suggest, the interactions between individuals and their environments are the means by which personhood is created; but these interactions are also the source of limitations in the capacity to make choices. The exercise of paternalism, provided it can be purged of its undertones of exploitation, patronizing moralism, and the denial of the clients' own competence, can be justified by reference to the articulated needs of clients for help in clarifying their perceptions of situations, events, and resources, or for making sense of the criteria for judging whether the exercise of power and authority (whether by themselves or others) is legitimate and reasonable. In transactions between workers and clients, the ethic of love is not necessarily incompatible with the ethic of duty even when duty involves taking a firm (paternalistic) line. But there are pitfalls for the unwary (on both sides of this transaction) in achieving and sustaining this combination. One element in social work practice which would justify its designation as a skilled professional activity is the requirement that workers exercise authority or power with *constant* awareness of the wishes, opinions, feelings, and rights of all their clients; and that they help their clients to develop similar awareness in their dealings with others. Social workers would, however, at once recognize that this statement is an idealistic one, particularly when set in the context of a growing concern to develop participatory models of practice and greater public participation in the policies and provision of the services. In her brief history of the development of social work, Younghusband (1981) laid stress on the sincerity with which social workers in the nineteenth century emphasized the importance of treating people as individuals, the sincerity with which they referred to ideals of equality and friendship, and the sincerity of their indignant compassion for the poor and the helpless among whom they worked. But she went on to question what their striving for equality and friendship actually meant in the context of gross social inequalities. Because of these fundamental inequalities their charity *inevitably* became perceived as a combination of judgemental parsimony and sentimentality:

The organized charity, scrimped and iced,
In the name of a cautious, statistical Christ.

Is the present climate of social work practice all that different? And will the sincerity with which social workers advocate public participation and participatory practices meet a similar fate to that of nineteenth-century charity? Will participation come to be regarded as a means towards achieving greater, though covert, paternalistic powers – strengthened by technology in the way that the paternalism of the COS was strengthened by its statistical and assessment skills? Although we have moved towards the view that those who use services should have a greater say in the mode of their provisions, social work continues to be located in a social environment where attempts to develop participatory relationships within professional transactions are offset by wider, intractable social inequalities and differentials of power and where the participatory ideal of lateral accountability between workers, clients, and local communities is offset by the traditional hierarchical systems of accountability on which social services continue to be constructed.

In addition, there remains (and perhaps always will remain) the complexity associated with expertise in matters of individual welfare. In one sense, clients are undeniably expert in defining their problems and needs, and participatory models of practice are based on this assertion: social workers nowadays rarely adopt the essentially paternalistic stance of drawing a distinction between 'presenting' and 'real' problems. Yet this move calls into question the nature and validity of professional expertise; it challenges the expectation that expert methods are necessary and should be employed to formulate systematic assessments of clients' situations and to effect changes in clients' lives. Furthermore, expertise is often (though wrongly) associated in the minds of social workers with elitism, and it currently suffers the fate of this association. Thus, some workers who jib at the risk of being regarded as elitist tend also to deny or underrate their possession of expertise. Yet if they are not experts in what they do, it is hard to justify their employment; for goodwill, warmth, friendliness, and the pursuit of humane and participatory relationships cannot constitute a sufficient reason for employment in publicly financed and sanctioned services.

To a limited extent, one can get round (but not wholly resolve) this issue by distinguishing between means and ends; that is to say, by acknowledging the client's expertise as a collaborative definer of the ends to be achieved, and by limiting the worker's expertise to defining (where possible in collaboration with the client) the means by which these ends may be accomplished. Task-centred approaches to social work practice appear to adopt this position; and much community work is practised on this basis. But this is not a wholly adequate solution: the worker is, after all, encapsulated in an environment of social influences and expectations, organizational traditions, and the limitations of personal capacities and thought processes; and the means he or she adopts inevitably imply the ends which that encapsulation makes thinkable and 'desirable'. However participatory the intention, some of the characteristics of paternalism will be found in it somewhere.

The relationship between participation and paternalism cannot therefore be divorced from wider professional, political, structural, and organizational considerations. For the profession of social work, these considerations largely hinge on ideals about the desirability of achieving a greater sense of equality with clients, despite the social inequalities within which the work is undertaken. One may argue with Davies (1985) that the pursuit of social equality is a political issue rather than one with which social work should be immediately concerned. Yet most social workers would, I surmise, believe that the means they adopt (particularly in participatory modes of practice) should as far as possible demonstrate egalitarian intentions. While recognizing that people are not born equal in personal and social terms – discounting for practical purposes their equality in the sight of God – they would assert a moral view that all people have equal rights to the things which promote a sense of value and personal worth in human life. This is, I suggest, a useful principle upon which to review how services are organized, the ends they serve, and the activities of their staffs, both professional and ancillary; but, like many principles in an imperfect world, it is perhaps as well not to be carried away by it. Throughout our present society (irrespective of political allegiances) people appear to fight for differentials of income and power, and social work's capacity to mitigate for clients the effects of this environment is very limited; it does exceptionally well if, in its activities, it does not add to these differentials. Participatory practices should perhaps be concerned with this limited, somewhat negative goal rather than based on the hope of more positive achievements. Robson (1976) has suggested that equality is neither an absolute nor an overriding goal. At its worst, it can lead to debasing creativity and individuality. But it remains a good worth pursuing in the absence of stronger obligations, and it provides the basis for collective professional assertions about social justice; for equality is possible only if the social rights of citizens are in some way matched to systems of resource allocation based on principles of social justice (see Weale 1978), and we are a long way from establishing such systems.

So far, this chapter has given attention to the continuing role of paternalism in social work practice, to its inevitability in some human circumstances and within our present social structure, and to the considerations relevant to its exercise in ways which do not unduly oppress or reduce the status of clients. The chapter has also implied certain limitations in the pursuit of participation, though supporting ideals of more participatory practice. The general development of these ideals and ideas has been well rehearsed by Jones *et al.* (1978), to which reference should be made. Specifically from the standpoint of social work we shall now consider some of the complexities contained within the apparently straightforward idea of participatory practice.

PARTICIPATION AND SOCIAL WORK

For social workers, participation at its simplest is associated with asserting the rights of clients to understand the role of their social workers and the services and to contribute to decisions taken about their lives; more fundamentally, it is variously associated with freedom of individual conscience and action, with the extension of choice, with the containment of repressive controls, and with ideals of democracy (however defined). Practices based on an ideal of participation are seen as maintaining a balance between the powers of statutory agencies to determine the social conditions in which citizens live, and the empowerment of citizens to avoid encroachment on the living conditions they establish or wish to establish for themselves. They are further seen as attempts to recognize and reconcile (or mitigate the effects of) various pressures which are constantly at work within political life and which are not always mutually compatible but which have impacts, sometimes unrecognized, on the lives of citizens: pressures to maximize efficiency in the use of public resources, to meet the demands both of labour and of capital, to maintain certain ideological traditions about 'the British way of life', to maintain public-spirited but politically responsive attitudes among officials, to cope with the expediencies necessary to ensure success in elections, to prevent such hardships among the poor and disadvantaged as might lead to public scandal and electoral failure. In addressing these pressures, the ideal of public participation is to hold a balance between the tendencies to centralize and decentralize the power to make decisions; social work practice (on a smaller scale) currently follows the same intention.

Beresford and Lyons (1986) have identified the ambiguities present in both right and left in respect of centralist and decentralist tendencies. For example, the radical right's philosophy of reducing the power and resources of statutory agencies and of enhancing individual freedoms and choices has been accompanied by the increasing centralization of decisions. The left, having traditionally equated social policy with statutory regulation and provision and with the role of bureaucrats as agents of social reform, nonetheless emphasizes the rights of citizens to be heard and helped on their own terms. Both perspectives endorse the importance of mutual responsibility between all people, while at the same time looking to a bureaucratic elite to steer policies towards politically defined goals. An echo of these ambiguities has been raised earlier in respect of the nature and role of professional expertise. Further echoes are evident in current debates about community care and 'going patch': the intentions of saving public money and community power-sharing are sometimes both present in these developments – sometimes complementary and sometimes in opposition to each other. Thus there is for social work considerable scope for confusion and conflict about how participation should be implemented in respect of the activities of social services departments (and, allowing for essential differences, in probation departments also). What, in practical terms, is the nature of community social work? What is the appropriate construction of local teams? What are the implications of community involvement for the methods and skills of social work? What is the role of the professional in participatory practice? What resources are needed and how should they be allocated and deployed? What is the appropriate balance between the performance of statutory duties and the need for responsiveness to issues raised by local people which fall outside departmental priorities? If financial constraints are imposed on services, who participates in re-thinking these priorities? Is it inevitable that large-scale and monopolistic services tend to stifle initiative and create stigma and an uncomprehending dependency, all of which are essentially incompatible with the aim of developing a sense of partnership between service workers and service users?

The Barclay working party (1982:chapter 7) identified three approaches to social policy: the safety net, the welfare state (now under threat by the breakdown of the earlier political consensus), and community participation. This last approach may in part serve as an attempt to avoid the growing tension between the first two approaches; but it risks becoming a potential battlefield between those who favour giving more power to local people and those who seek to shift the 'burden' and responsibility of welfare provisions from paid to unpaid helpers. Thus, for various reasons, the current movement in social work from professionalized casework (with a limited and clearly defined remit) to community involvement has become the subject of an ideological debate (compare Appendices A and B of the Barclay report), but one with more complex sources and far-reaching implications than the subject of itself would seem to suggest. The issue is not simply one of shifting social work practice from paternalism to partnership (Bamford 1982), from predominant concern with intrapsychic difficulties to concern for material needs, and from the individualization of needs to the recognition of shared needs. These are important shifts in terms of professional intention and techniques, but they relate to more substantial political and organizational debates, of which social workers are variously aware and unaware and about which there is, appropriately, a degree of caution and uncertainty. As Bamford (1986) has suggested, while current trends in professional thinking are towards less manipulative, less directive, and more participatory involvement with clients and other local people, the issues which need resolving in support of these trends are not merely professional, but are also political (will participation become a substitute for adequate public services?), ethical (what about people's rights to seek help confidentially outside their local communities?), and managerial (how does one effectively reconcile hierarchical and non-hierarchical modes of organization and accountability?).

PARTICIPATION AND THE PRACTITIONER

This chapter has attempted to raise issues about the complexity of the concepts of paternalism and participation when applied to social work practice and to suggest that this complexity has its roots in more fundamental social structures and systems. Social workers can do little about these fundamentals; yet it is inappropriate merely to recognize their existence. Is it possible and appropriate to achieve more participatory forms of practice? Is it possible to determine how far and in what form elements of paternalism should be retained? Different social workers would address these questions differently and would, no doubt, come up with different answers. But it is possible at least to formulate some fairly simple questions about day-to-day practice which, while derived from the complexity of earlier debate, reflect the practical responsibilities of social work in achieving a balance between paternalism and participation; for example, in the practice of work with individuals:

(a) How far do the client's and worker's statements of needs, goals, and means indicate sufficient agreement, both in substance and in values, to make a sense of partnership between them possible? A sense of partnership does not require agreement on everything; it is likely that attempts to achieve full agreement may lead either to the worker coercing or patronizing the client, or to a set of compromising manoeuvres which blur issues and intentions rather than clarify them. The important question therefore is whether there is a sufficient basis of agreement to enable partnership to be developed in specific areas of activity. If so, the aim will be to enhance participation.

(b) If there is little common ground in values or intentions, differences of authority, power, and knowledge will probably lead to paternalistic reactions in the worker. These reactions can be justified only if the worker can demonstrate that his or her values or intentions are publicly sanctioned and should be implemented because the law requires it, or that the client – by reason of severe disturbance, chronic handicap, or risk to others – must be controlled and coerced. Have these conditions been satisfied? For how long and in what form will controlling methods be employed? And within what timespan will the need for them be reassessed?

(c) In sharing information and understanding between client and worker about the means of resolving a particular problem, how does the worker ensure that both sides feel they have made about equal contributions, and that respect has been accorded to the client's views, especially at points of disagreement?

(d) If the worker considers it necessary in a specific circumstance to take control or to manipulate a response, what values are breached and what values are upheld in this manoeuvre? Is it possible to strengthen the application of one value as a kind of compensation for the breaching of another?

(e) Does the worker have good grounds for believing that the client understands the worker's purposes and role in the intervention, whatever form that intervention takes? What opportunities does the client have for objecting to these purposes? What opportunity is there for the client to seek the opinion or support of another agency, worker, or independent third party?

(f) In discussion between worker and client about the needs or problems to be addressed, what allowance does the worker make for the heightened suggestibility of the client, particularly in a situation containing personal stress and differences of power, authority, or knowledge?

(g) We may assume that workers seldom lie to their clients, but they may sometimes think it necessary to be 'economical with the truth'. Is the worker aware of doing this? And how is it justified?

(h) In a specific case, is there incompatibility between the caring, expert, and employee roles of the worker? If so, how far is it possible and appropriate to share this incompatibility with the client? Is it possible to articulate the criteria for sharing and not sharing in specific situations?

(i) Are the goals of work in a specific case (i) compatible with the quality of relationships formed between worker and client and (ii) consistent with the kind of influence a worker is, consciously or unwittingly, exerting?

These questions offer a means, within work with individual clients, of assessing how far, in specific cases, greater client participation should be encouraged and certain aspects of paternalism should be retained. Reference should be made to Rhodes (1986), whose investigation of general ethical dilemmas is of particular relevance to the focus of this chapter.

In regard to the balance of paternalistic and participatory elements in professional practice in relation to community involvement, the first concern should be to determine which social work functions are properly open to formulation by local residents and potential service users, and which should be decided exclusively by the workers and the agency. It is apparent that, in periods of financial constraint, workers tend to concentrate their efforts on the performance of statutory duties (thus tending in the public view to emphasize the paternalistic aspects of their work) at the expense of preventive and promotional activities (which, because of their potential for voluntary and informal involvement, are more likely to enhance a sense of local participation). Commitment to more participatory models of social work practice implies that, both professionally and managerially, we need to seek a more even balance of concern for these two components of practice. This in turn requires – as noted earlier – a re-examination of the notion of accountability, in which some measure of compatibility is sought between the hierarchical systems of control and supervision necessarily associated with the delegation of legislative responsibilities, and the lateral pattern of shared resources and authority envisaged by the Seebohm Committee (see para. 474). In doing so, however, it will be necessary for the profession to maintain concern for those needs and problems which are usually articulated only by individuals in private rather than by local residents collectively – I have in mind intrapsychic and interpersonal difficulties, compared with the more easily expressed and collectively agreed problems of environmental and material disadvantage – and to continue to recognize that the boundaries between 'person' and 'environment' are never so clear as commonsense suggests they are. It would be disappointing if professional social work sought to reflect its concern to promote greater community involvement and participation by advocating two entirely separate groups of workers (revamped caseworkers and revamped community workers). This would be equivalent to re-inventing the broken wheel; it would have the effect of polarizing the paternalistic and participatory aspects of social intervention and would inhibit discussion and resolution of the complexities of their relationship; it would make even more problematic than at present the achievement of public understanding and recognition of the exercise and limitations of professional judgements in individual, family, and community welfare.

Finally, social workers need to be alert to the possibility that the current ideological shift from paternalism to participation may be based partly on the search for a new professional rationale. Disillusion with earlier holistic and somewhat grandiose theories of the nature, purpose, and methods of social work has left the legitimate concerns and interests of the profession at risk of absorption within those of its pay-masters; it has been left also with a collection of pragmatic, skills-based, and apparently neutralized models of practice – models which can be used to fit the demands of nearly all political and administrative schemes. The pursuit of a philosophy of participation, especially one which is so vague as to be compatible with opposed political beliefs, provides a sort of rationale for a united profession; but at worst it could leave local residents and local clients with excessive responsibilities for mutual help and self-help, and could provide workers with too easy an excuse for insensitivities and failures within the profession itself. On balance, clients would probably prefer help from paternalistic workers who hold themselves professionally responsible for the outcome of their work, rather than from workers who interpret participatory practices simply as warm, vacuous, and purposeless friendliness, or who avoid the exercise of professional responsibility (and any semblance of personal integrity) by ritualized references to self-determination and situation ethics, or who make their skills and powers available to any enterprise irrespective of its purposes and its outcomes. Professional social work cannot be reduced to a list of statements about skills, inter-personal relationships, or political ideals. It requires recognition of ways in which a variety of transactions, and the manner in which they are undertaken, reflect a range of social 'goods': a desire to promote equality of respect and to act justly; ability to articulate criteria of professional effectiveness and the efficient use of resources; respect for the opinions and choices of others, yet with the willingness to argue against them and to override them in precisely defined situations where 'goods' conflict; recognition that, as fashions

112

change in social and political policies, and as service structures come and go, there are certain principles and values which must not be lost and some which, arguably, may be adapted to changing norms and standards of service. Members of a profession united in pursuing these 'goods' could probably take in their stride where to strike a balance, in specific situations, of paternalism and participation. But we are not there yet.

© 1989 Eric Sainsbury

Chapter Eight

OPEN RECORDS AND SHARED DECISIONS WITH CLIENTS

MALCOLM PAYNE

Social work has sought, in recent years, to become a more open activity; where the social distance between social worker and client should be reduced, and the client should be more aware and understanding of the professional processes through which help is given. The move to openness can be seen particularly in a developing ideology that where decisions are made which affect clients they should influence those decisions, and that they should have access to personal information about them held in social work records. It would be wise not to exaggerate the extent to which this change has already taken place. Although much is said about 'shared decision-making' and 'access to records', they probably occur quite rarely in everyday practice. For example, a recently published study designed to promote access to records (Øvretveit 1986) reports active work with eight social work teams to this end; yet only one was routinely sharing records with clients by the completion of the two-year project.

There could be some debate about the extent of the change. Is it just, in fact, the implementation of long-standing assumptions about what is good practice? The first two sections of this chapter examine some of the ideas about shared decision-making and openness and how they have changed. The third section discusses the philosophical and moral issues which arise from this change in social work and some of their practical consequences.

THE DEVELOPMENT OF CONCEPTIONS OF SHARED DECISION-MAKING AND OPENNESS IN SOCIAL WORK

The social work ideology about shared decision-making between clients and social workers is closely bound up with the concept of 'client self-determination', which, until the 1960s, was the major expression of a set of values concerned with the human freedom of clients. The meaning of this concept and its relationship with the idea of participation has changed over the years.

In the 1920s, 'it was believed client participation created more self-reliance on the part of the client' (Garton and Otto 1964:41). In the next two decades, the idea grew that participation made the influence of the social worker more effective: 'It was not a question of *allowing* the client to participate but it was believed the client *must* do so if the experience was to be a dynamic and meaningful one to him' (Garton and Otto:92).

The therapeutic efficiency argument reflects the influence of psycho-dynamic theory on (American) casework: engagement of the client through participation in a therapeutic relationship with the social worker was considered necessary to overcome irrational psychological blocks to clients' development. This view persists. For example, in Maple's *Shared Decision-making* (1977) sharing is promoted as a way of improving therapeutic communication.

An alternative aspect of participation appeared in Hamilton's influential social work text of 1940: the development of client organizations seeking influence on service planning, management, and policy (Hamilton 1940:30). However, this disappeared from the second edition, to be replaced by comments from a therapeutic efficiency point of view (Hamilton 1951:169). Demands for client influence on policy and management appeared both in the American movements of the 1930s, epitomized by the original radical journal *Social Work Today* (Reynolds 1970:4), and in the radical political movements of the 1970s and 1980s. Radicalism on behalf of clients may well reflect the importance of economic pressures on clients during recessions rather than consistent social work values.

The classic formulation of self-determination by Biestek (1961:103) crystallized a change in approach. Self-determination was presented not as the basis of greater efficiency in social work but as a human right and professional value. Two rights are implied: one is concerned with freedom, the other with 'activating a potential', and this latter value extends the efficiency argument to propose that one of the aspects of social work is to be concerned with promoting clients' capacities in various ways. This is also a feature of Hamilton's 1951 formulation.

Another aspect of Biestek's statement is the extent of the limitations upon self-determination – only 'available and appropriate' community resources can be the object of the client's activities, and clients must be protected and controlled and not trespass beyond the agency's functions. The criticism of this analysis grew into a debate on the reality of self-determination, which is effectively summarized in McDermott's collection of articles (1975).

There came to be fundamentally three positions developing from the conception of self-determination. The *radical* position drew on Marxist analyses of social control (e.g. Bailey and Brake 1975) and argued that allegiance to self-determination was largely mythical since the structure of power in society tended to reinforce the dominance of economically and politically powerful groups to the detriment of the interests of the oppressed and disadvantaged people who are the primary objects of social work endeavour. The *intellectual* position (e.g. McDermott 1975) sought to develop a more complex understanding of the concept of freedom, which would thus inform a more sophisticated application of values in social work. The *self-realization* position, perhaps exemplified by Bartlett's influential book (1970:65–6), seeks to redefine self-determination as an aspect of achieving the best possible realization of each individual's potential, and thus the evolutionary growth of society's potential.

The radical position derives not primarily from reaction to the debate about self-determination, but to wider social and theoretical movements and their influence on social work. The individualized, therapeutic view of self-determination derives, I have already argued, from the psychological, person-oriented view of social work which predominated until the 1960s. More sociological theoretical influences began to have a stronger impact on social work and on related areas, particularly through community work, with its emphasis on collective social action rather than personal therapy.

A variety of other movements grew up in the 1960s and 1970s. In several areas of government, steps were taken to promote participation by members of the public in decisions which affected them. Planning legislation, for example, following the Skeffington report (1969), made provision for local residents to be consulted about local and structure plans for their area. In the National Health Service, community health councils were set up in every area so that consumers of the service could have influence on the local administration (Levitt 1980). Taking account of consumer opinion became an important political objective for public services, deriving from work done by pressure groups in the commercial sector such as the Consumers' Association.

Growing from these developments there was a movement in public services away from centralized, bureaucratic control to more local management, responsive to consumer needs and wishes (Hadley and Hatch 1981). This was evident in housing management, for example, as a way of dealing with the problems of managing large, poorly-planned public housing estates (Department of the Environment 1977). In social services, there was promotion of more localized, patch systems of managing 'community social work' as a means of becoming more responsive to local need and opinion (Hadley and McGrath 1984; Barclay 1982).

In the 1980s, consumerism has become one of the instruments of a social movement, initiated by the policies of one Conservative government, for the control and breaking-down of large-scale bureaucracies. Member control of trade unions, and the privatization of hitherto public services, have been designed to promote consumer choice through market systems as a means of control of apparently uncontrollable public institutions (Moran 1986).

In social work, this variety of moves both promoted and was influenced by research on consumer and public reactions to the social services (Rees and Wallace 1982). This disclosed that clients of social services often had very little understanding or acceptance of the objectives and processes to which social workers submitted them, and this in turn raised questions about the reality of the ideology of client self-determination.

Much of this came to a head when, following a speech by

Jordan (1975), the British Association of Social Workers published a report on client participation – *Clients are Fellow Citizens* (BASW 1980). Among its significant recommendations is the proposal that, as an instrument of participation, clients should be encouraged to have access to records about them which are kept by social workers. Before returning to this strand of development, however, it is useful to review the processes leading to the client-advocacy movement.

Concern about the power of large-scale bureaucracies continued. Professional discretion controlled by codes of ethics was, it was argued, harnessed to the power of such institutions, rather than being a protector against it (Illich *et al.* 1977). Organizations grew up, such as the Child Poverty Action Group, to research, promote, and advocate the rights of clients to services in a highly legalistic way, using legal action and political lobbying (McCarthy 1986). Existing organizations, such as MIND, the National Association for Mental Health, took up this trend to seek legislation or policy changes which benefitted their client group (Booth *et al.* 1985).

Changes in practice policy also began to have influences on social work. Normalization is a policy which proposes organizing institutional care in a way which is designed to promote the social and human valuation of individuals who may be devalued and stigmatized (Wolfensberger and Thomas 1981). It had a particular influence on work with mentally handicapped people (Tyne 1981), who themselves were affected by moves to promote their civil liberties. Task-centred casework proposes an explicit contract between client and social worker, each taking designated roles in their activities to the betterment of the client's situation. Various pieces of research and practice writing promoted its value (e.g. Goldberg and Stanley 1979; Goldberg *et al.* 1977; Butler *et al.* 1978).

The 1970s also saw the growth of a number of consumer organizations related specifically to the social services. The best known is the National Association of Young People in Care (NAYPIC), which grew out of the Who Cares? movement promoted by the National Children's Bureau (Page and Clarke 1977) and work done at the University of Leeds (Stein (ed.) n.d.). The National Schizophrenia Fellowship, the Association of Carers, and movements within organizations for mentally handicapped and mentally ill people picked up these trends to develop much greater consumer involvement, and the participation of the carers of people with social problems in social policy moves.

It was recognized, however, that individuals in many such groups were unable to speak for themselves. This was either because of their condition or age, or because of assumptions that people with such severe social disadvantage would not have the social status or emotional strength for participation. These factors, and perhaps resistance by professional staff anxious to avoid restrictions on their power, have prevented legislative and practice initiatives to promote participation from having much effect. Sinclair (1984), for example, carried out in one county a study of statutory reviews on children in care, where participation is encouraged by legislation. She found that 'children were only very occasionally included in reviews ... natural and foster parents were included even less often'. She suggests that inviting children to case conferences may not really involve them in decision-making because their inexperience, and the formal structure of such meetings, limits their potential influence. Jenson and Jenson (1978) have proposed smaller meetings to deal with this, Skinner (1980) a written questionnaire for children. In any case, many important decisions about children are not made in reviews, according to Vernon and Fruin's research (1986), so true shared decision-making in such cases would require much wider involvement in social work activity.

Concern that participation in decision-making would only be taken unless some way was found to facilitate it led to the movement for client and citizen advocacy. In part, this stems from the experience of using legal argument through appeal systems, particularly in social security, housing, and mental health decision-making machinery. Emphasis on the importance of advocacy on behalf of clients in formal appeals structures led to the growth in the conception that such advocacy could be used within less formal machinery, particularly for clients whose disability prevented them from full participation in decision-making. So, advocates for mentally handicapped people (Anderson, 1982:60–1), became the precursors of similar arrangements for elderly mentally infirm people, mentally ill people, deaf people, and children (Sang 1982).

119

So far, this review of changes in conception and, to some extent, practice in shared decision-making between clients and social workers has charted the development of the concept of self-determination from a view that it was concerned with making therapeutic intervention effective by stimulating activity in the client. It developed through the idea that it was concerned to stimulate psychological engagement in personal change to a view that it was a (perhaps limited) moral right deriving from the right to freedom of action, and the right to self-realization. Both of these rights were related to the idea that human beings possessed a value as individuals which should be respected. Dissatisfaction with these concepts, allied to a reappearance of ideas of the 1930s that self-determination in its therapeutic usage was related to political or democratic participation in broader social processes, has led to an increased emphasis on client participation in decision-making in the 1980s. This was, in turn, related to broader consumer movements in society. Experience of participative processes led, eventually, to the development of client advocacy, in which structures are devised to implement much more effective influence on behalf of clients in decision-making processes.

ACCESS TO RECORDS, OPEN RECORDS AND SHARED DECISION-MAKING

Where do case records fit into these developing ideas of shared decision-making? The importance given to records in the BASW client participation document, noted above, led to a re-examination by the Association of case recording in the context of the new mood of openness (BASW 1983). Other significant events were the efforts of Graham Gaskin, a former client of Liverpool City Council's social services department, to have official access to his case record in order to pursue a case for negligence against the City Council. This was refused, but at the time of writing it is still being pursued. Gaskin's case became a 'cause célèbre' (McVeigh 1982). At the same time, access by a councillor in Birmingham to records in a controversial case was permitted by the House of Lords, reaffirming the law that where there was a 'need to know' a councillor was entitled to such access. There was also concern about police access to social services files (BASW 1983). Records, and access to them, suddenly became a hot issue, and they have continued to be so.

This is unusual in the history of social work. The most significant texts on recording were those of Hamilton (1946) and Timms (1972), both concerned with the history and practice of recording. Hamilton presents the traditional picture of a record as a professional tool of the social worker, to help in diagnosing the client's problems and in organizing the social worker's thinking and work. Client access to such a record would be irrelevant; it is the private *aide-mémoire* and work organizer of the worker. In so far as recording was justified on a professional basis, it was particularly vulnerable to the criticism, noted above, that professionalism and professionalization were liable to be a form of protection for professionals rather than for clients. Records can very easily be held up as an example of professional secrecy defending the interests of the professional, and as a form of paternalism. Timms raises the issue of access. The convention was that the clients should know that a record is kept but should not be burdened with the contents. Timms asks how they may be expected to exercise a right to complain about the service received if they cannot know what 'image' is held about them in the agency's records. This concern reflects the contemporaneous move away from psychological definitions of the problems of clients, in which they are subjected to 'therapy' by knowledgeable professionals, towards sociological assumptions about the role of social workers as allies of clients, who are entitled to access to the professionals' views of them.

Timms also notes early concern about the effect of computers on clients' rights to privacy. The effect of the increasing power of computer data processing is an important strand in the growth of concern to promote access to records. In 1972 the Younger Committee produced an important report (Younger Committee 1972) expressing concern that information about members of the public kept by large commercial and government agencies was not kept sufficiently private. Also, its acquisition, retention, and use by powerful organizations without the full knowledge of the subjects of the information could invade their privacy in a number of ways. The later report of the Lindop Committee (1978) into data protection showed how the greater capacity of computers to find, link, and process personal information held in large quantities by powerful organizations created a risk of the misuse of information. For instance, it might be obtained by one agency or part of an agency for one purpose, and used much later by another agency or part of an agency for quite another purpose. Such a transfer of use invades the subject's privacy and is, therefore, often seen as unethical. It is specifically prohibited by the BASW Code of Ethics, for example.

Concern about these problems escalated with the greater power of computers until the government introduced a Data Protection Act in 1984 which restricted, and set up a system for controlling, the use of personal data in computer systems. The relevance of this concern for privacy to the growth of interest in open records in the social services may not be immediately apparent. It lies principally in the fact that a right of access by data subjects to personal information held about them in computers is a major instrument of control. Less important, but also significant, is the fact that the whole debate about data protection raised professional and public consciousness of the importance of records and their use, and drew attention to the frequency with which their contents might be inaccurate or problematic. Uncertainty about records promotes in this way insecurity about recording.

The data protection debate links to two other developments. The first is the significance of private records as a symbol of professional power and social distance between client and social worker. Thus, openness in recording tends to become allied with openness in social work generally. Second, the consumer movement has promoted access to information as a way of enforcing consumer power in a variety of fields and as a civil liberty – the right for someone to know what is being said about them. This is more than a concern about personal information. There has also been a campaign to promote access to information about policy-making processes in order to protect public interests against those of powerful bureaucracies. Campaigning about these issues (Cohen 1982) and for the access solution to them is part of the context of the use of access by the Data Protection Act as a control device.

When the BASW group produced its report *Effective and Ethical Recording* (BASW 1983), the timing was therefore propitious for it to have rapid influence. The political response in Liverpool to the Gaskin case led to a decision to permit access to records by clients. In turn, the DHSS was obliged to produce guidelines to control access arrangements (Payne 1983), which it did at the same time and in a similar format to the proposals for control of access to data held on computers. These stimulated many social services departments to introduce access (Øvretveit 1986). The DHSS Social Services Inspectorate developed a programme of seminars and inspections to investigate and promote the move towards access. BASW commissioned research in several area teams, which ran experiments to introduce a record system meeting the proposals of its working group.

The fundamental argument of the BASW group is that case recording practice should be reformed so that records are briefer, more focused, and used primarily for providing more effective service to the client. Such records would also be more ethical, because they would reduce the risk that inaccurate information would be recorded and possibly later abused. Information recorded was also said to give the social worker power over the client. The system of recording should follow the principle of the 'least restrictive alternative', so that as little power as possible should be obtained and retained through records. Access by clients is a control device to prevent inaccuracies or misuse of information, as well as a means of sharing decision-making between worker and client. When published, the later BASW research (Øvretveit 1986) demonstrated the close relationship between styles of recording, styles of work in social work practice, and basic principles of social work. The only team in the project to share records fully with their clients found that they were operating a much more open and explicit form of social work. The brief and focused form of recording promoted client involvement and shared decision-making, and more explicit planning, reminiscent of the work of Goldberg and Warburton (1979), who introduced a structured case-review form in social services teams.

It is possible to see, as the idea of access developed in the 1970s and 1980s, a substantial change in values, represented as yet unevenly in actual practice. At the beginning of the 1970s, there are the tentative signs of concern about the secrecy of recording, which grew as the shift from client self-determination, through participation, to client advocacy. The impact of the radical critique of self-determination and other aspects of traditional casework, and the reaction against psychological conceptualizations of social work, gathered pace. Changes in computer technology, and the wider civil liberty and consumerist lobbies, created a rapid change in practice ideology.

ETHICAL AND PHILOSOPHICAL QUESTIONS

Does the change in practice ideology reflect a change in dominant social work values? I argue that a considerable change in overt social work values is apparent in these developments, but that in a deeper and more general sense, fundamental value assumptions in social work are unchanged because they reflect the power of the institutionalized role of a bureaucratized profession in a complex modern state.

In making an assessment of these changes and continuities in value positions, it is necessary to clear away some factors which are not relevant. First, there is the effectiveness argument. In the case of client self-determination, participation, and advocacy, as well as in the case of shared recording, it can be argued that if they are implemented the objectives of social work intervention can be achieved more quickly, or more fully, or more permanently. This is not a moral argument, except perhaps in the sense that it can be argued that morally a more effective service is better than a less effective one. Second, there have been changes in technology, particularly as computers have been used more to process personal information. These changes do not, however, affect the ethical arguments about the rights and wrongs of shared decision-making and recording. They may affect the degree to which, or the speed at which, damage may be done by unethical practices, but they do not affect the ethical nature of those practices. Third, the advocacy of access to records as a control device is merely a practical proposal. It does not say anything about the morality of access or the right of clients to share in recording. It just suggests that problems of recording may be dealt with by giving clients a right to check on their accuracy and the uses to which they are put.

The ethical and philosophical arguments about shared recording and decision-making which remain are concerned with six areas of debate. First, there is the role of participation in official activity as part of a democratic society. Second, there is the civil-liberty argument that sharing recording and decision-making is a means of safeguarding freedom for clients from oppressive control by professionals or bureaucracies. Third, to take that point further, shared decision-making and recording can be argued to enhance the client's power in a fundamentally un-equal transaction with the social worker. Fourth, it can be argued that sharing demonstrates respect for the client as a human being. Fifth, sharing is said to have the moral value of promoting the self-realization of the client. Sixth, in moving from individual psychological definitions of the client's prob-lems towards sociological ones, sharing deals with some of the ethical problems that professionalization of social work may present. Many of these points interact, of course. For example, several are concerned with the client's freedom to act in a situation where the professional or bureaucratic power of the social worker or social work agency might limit that freedom. Nonetheless, each of these six points is in some ways a separate entity and needs to be considered as such.

1. The democratic role of openness and sharing

It is, perhaps, the essence of a democratic system that its citizens participate in decision-making. The extent to which this is so, and the means of achieving it have, however, been the subject of considerable debate.

Pateman (1970) reviews shifts in the debate. She presents the 'classical' position as presuming that active participation by citizens in decision-making characterizes a democracy. This may be criticized on the ground that effective democracies are in fact led by elites, which change slowly and are only subject to periodic election by a largely uninvolved population. Pateman, in turn, criticizes this position because, in dealing only with the national level of political life, it underestimates the extent to which active involvement in more local decision-making is rele-vant to understanding democratic systems. She argues that involvement in less significant activities is necessary to achieve enough understanding and motivation among citizens to enable them to participate in more distant (and to them less interesting and relevant) democratic activities.

Following this argument, it can be said that sharing in social work decisions and open recording present opportunities to promote the understanding of clients about how to influence decisions which affect them, and to encourage their motivation to influence such decisions by achieving some success in limited fields with social work professionals who are, perhaps, more likely to support this experience than other professional groups. The shift in emphasis from very psychological conceptions of self-determination to client advocacy suggests that within social work much greater value is being attached to such participation experience. It is a practical contribution by social workers to the democratic process in society, and aligns with the radical critique of self-determination which promotes less token and professional forms of participation. It might be significant that social workers, because they deal with many of the most disadvantaged groups in society, should have developed and implemented this ideology of shared decision-making and openness, since their clients have most to gain.

Plant *et al.* (1980), however, take a more cautious view of this position. They argue that it depends on a society in which institutions are neutral or at least responsive to influence from client involvement. In fact, political and social systems tend to distribute power according to current assumptions of right and wrong. Shared decision-making will only be permitted if its consequences are acceptable to those with power. This argument is particularly relevant to open case records. The BASW working group (1983) demonstrates that recording systems are set up by the elite in social agencies in order to enforce their policies on practitioners. The report seeks to show that case records are ineffective for this purpose, and to promote, instead, their value in service to clients. In attempting to substitute availability (and perhaps accountability) to clients, the report seems to want a redistribution of power. At the same time, the brief recording system proposed is also claimed to offer greater true accountability to management, because it is likely to produce more honest contents than lengthy but inaccessible records.

In this, the report seems to set the two aspects of its recommendations against one another. The quest for more effective recording, implying greater accountability to the governing elite, appears to run counter to the arguments for more accessible recording, which imply greater accountability to clients. Looked at more closely, however, the two may not be incompatible. Open recording would require social workers to be more accurate in recording and their records to be more relevant to clients' needs – plans, for example, would have to reflect client opinions and motivations. A manager checking on a social worker's performance would therefore have a more accurate record of what has taken place in interactions with clients than would exist with hidden records, which can and, according to the BASW report, often do, distort the reality. Thus, open recording promotes better accountability both downwards in the power structure to the client and also upwards towards management. In that managers may be more able to perceive the reality of work with clients, their power to enforce their decisions on social workers may even be enhanced. Before more accurate records were available, the social worker's activities were hidden behind a barrier of vagueness, confusion, and lengthy texts.

In general, then, only limited claims can be made for shared decision-making and open recording as a means of enhancing the client's democratic participation. They may offer more experience and capacity, which would stand the client in good stead in future life. This achievement may, however, be at the expense of enhancing the power of bureaucratic elites to enforce their policies on clients through the agency of the social worker.

2. Safeguarding the client's freedom

One of the advantages offered by open records systems is that they are said to enhance the client's freedom from oppression (Payne 1984; Doel and Lawson 1986). Information which is held about a client may be the basis on which a social worker acts towards, or on behalf of, the client. Such information is therefore powerful, in that it influences what happens to a client. The more clients are able to influence that information, the more they are able to use the power that it represents. So, as the BASW group argues (1983), the least restrictive alternative in any bureaucratic system is the one which is most likely to protect freedom.

The intellectual position on self-determination, outlined above, was concerned, in some respects, with this issue. The concept of self-determination became entwined with the philosophical debate about free will and determinism. Briefly, the issue is whether, if behaviour is 'caused' by events in a person's previous experience, it can be said that the person exercises freewill. By extension, can clients be said to be self-determining if they are entrapped in a social system, either in their ordinary lives or in their interactions with social workers, which does not offer them freedom of action? An important distinction, here, was made by Berlin (1969) between positive and negative freedom. The former is a capacity to act in some way; the latter is a lack of constraint. Thus a client may be negatively free to repair his relationship with his wife, in the sense that he is not actively prevented from doing so. Nonetheless, the history of his relationship with his wife may be such that he is unable for emotional reasons to do so.

Lack of knowledge about what powerful agencies may do, according to Plant *et al.* (1980), is an important constraint on freedom in a complex society where survival means not only staying alive but doing so 'in a condition in which one can act freely and purposively'. They argue that the most important hindrances to freedom are arbitrary power, ill-health, and ignorance. Ill-health is not relevant here, and ignorance can only be dispelled with limited gains, as I have argued in the previous section on the democratic role of openness. Arbitrary power is the situation in which one person or agency can gain control of the actions of another in such a way that the object of the control does not know the right way to act.

Open records and shared decision-making are, it is often proposed, ways of dealing with the risk of arbitrary power in social work. They clarify to the client what the social worker and agency are planning, and prevent them from making decisions according to information which is wrong, or deleterious to the client. This is because incorrect information may be put right by the client and disadvantageous material disputed. The BASW report takes up considerable space arguing that mere knowledge that the record will be available will make the social worker more careful about using dubious information or judgements.

Against this argument, it may be said that while openness may give a client negative freedom – that is, from the constraint of arbitrary power – it may do nothing to offer positive freedom – that is, the capacity to act to take advantage of knowledge. The evidence about the problems of participation in case reviews and the resistance of social workers and agencies to offering access, considered above, suggests that there are limitations on the worth of openness as a means of safeguarding the client's positive freedom.

3. Enhancing client power

To go on from the previous points, there must also be doubts, consequent on these limitations of openness, that it can enhance clients' power to achieve their wishes. The debate in relation to self-determination suggests that there are many limitations on clients' power to act as they wish, imposed by the way that principle is brought to life in social work. Biestek's restrictions have been identified above, for example.

Power, according to Lukes (1986), is not simply the achievement of, or the capacity to attain, one's wishes. There may be costs in emotional strength or in physical resources which a client, who is often poor in all sorts of resources, will find it difficult to expend. The exercise of power is a complex matter, diffused in networks of relationships so that it can be hard to identify the location of people or agencies against whom clients can use power to achieve their wishes.

Thus, although openness may offer clients knowledge and skills to use their influence, the nature of bureaucratic and professional power could often frustrate their intentions. A significant factor is that of the possession of the information resources. Cohen (1982) fundamentally argues that since the information is the clients' then the record of it should also be theirs. Legally, however, the physical entity of case records is owned by the agency, and access to it is a concession. Again, slowness in actually implementing openness suggests a recalcitrance in activating the concession, which in turn indicates that possession is indeed nine points of the law.

4. Openness demonstrates respect for the client

One of the important tenets of social work is respect for the client as a human being. It is hard to understand what this

129

means, but Brook (1973) proposes that an important feature is parity between the parties. Thus, the social worker would treat someone respectfully as another human being if there was an assumption of equality of humanity between them, if they are regarded as unique individuals, and if attitudes and activities directed towards them could not sensibly be directed towards, say, lower animals. Thus, social workers would treat clients in a personal, equal way rather than in an objective way. This is the aim behind the use of such techniques as normalization and task-centred work, considered in the discussion above of new social work techniques and openness.

It may seem curious to suppose that social workers could behave otherwise, but it is important to note that social work relationships are not supposed to be like ordinary human relationships. Social workers are, in fact, expected to treat clients relatively objectively, and their human responses to clients must be tempered by that objective stance. Otherwise, clients who expect help from an independent person may be used (consciously or unconsciously) by social workers to achieve their own personal ends. Social workers are expected to offer personal respect while retaining objectivity: this mixture of opposing factors could easily lead to an unbalanced relationship in which lack of respect took hold.

Blum (1973) suggests that deceit is an important factor in 'using' someone in a relationship. Clients would not be hurt by being used unless they were aware of the deceit in the relationship. Often, consumer research has shown, clients perceive themselves to be in a personal, equal relationship with the social worker, whereas in fact they are in an objective, unequal relationship. This is akin to the deceit which often exists in 'using' relationships. Clients run the risk of being hurt if they become aware of this difference between reality and their perception, as they would do, Blum argues, if they became aware of being used.

Openness provides some defence against these problems. The paraphernalia of access and shared decision-making draws attention to the objective, unequal nature of the relationship. So, even though it has personal features, the client is less likely to be deceived about its nature. This aspect of the arguments for openness should not, however, detract from the fact that there is inequality and objectiveness in the social-worker/client relationship. It does not, therefore, meet the sort of criteria which Brook (1973) sets up to define a relationship which respects another human being. The use of interactional techniques and objective assessments in a professional relationship still seems to negate the idea of respect for others' uniqueness which is claimed to be inherent in social work practice.

This does not contradict Watson's argument (1980), that social welfare is concerned with 'help given to the stranger'. He considers the debate concerning social welfare as an exchange. In the economic system, advantages (goods) are exchanged for economic benefits; Titmuss (1970) has sought to argue that in the social market there is no direct exchange, but benefits are received as a gift. Watson, however, suggests that altruism is a much more complex relationship, one factor in which is the knowledge that gifts are offered through the social welfare system to other human beings. In suggesting that social workers in their relationships with clients cannot treat them with respect as human beings because of the nature of their relationship, I do not dissent from Watson's argument that the fact of clients' humanity is one of the relevant reasons for offering social work help; merely that the manner in which it is offered is, as Watson proposes, organized and objective.

5. Openness promotes the self-realization of clients

One of the arguments for openness, and one of the ways of defining self-determination, has been to promote the realization of the fullest capacities of clients. The more self-directing they become, the more they can realize their capacities to control their lives. Openness is, according to this argument, vital to achieve the fullest self-control of their minds and lives by clients; secrecy and lack of involvement make them dependent upon others.

There are problems with the nature of self-realization. Plant (1970) contends that personal self-realization, and realization of community capacities to participate in decisions, both depend on social and moral assumptions about the nature of human potential, which can only be defined 'by reference to societies and the paradigms of human nature presupposed in those

131

societies' (1970:59). If this is so, Plant argues, self-realization is limited by the cultural restrictions of a society, and any broad standard of self-realization would imply a good deal of freedom to deviate from conventional norms in any particular society. The argument that openness promotes self-realization relies on the assumption that greater openness and sharing in decision-making reflects a greater preparedness to be flexible about the acceptable norms in social work interactions. I have argued already that, while such flexibility may in fact be present, it also offers the opportunity for greater social control, because, through more accurate records, elites are more aware of the reality of clients' deviations.

In considering issues of freedom and power above, it was evident that while openness may remove some constraints it is not easy to demonstrate that it has positive effects on clients' freedom and power. If the complexity of social power and restrictions on freedom are such as to deny clients' increased opportunities for freedom and power, it seems likely that self-realization will similarly not make progress. While openness offers the opportunity for greater flexibility, it remains to be achieved by other means, making use of the greater flexibility.

6. Openness, psychology, and professionalism

One of the ways in which greater self-realization might be achieved is through greater self-understanding. Schleifer (1973) argues that understanding of behaviour through psychology could be learned by laymen and thereby improve the quality of human relationships. Openness in decision-making and records could help to bring this about, by laying bare the reasons for social workers' decisions about, and reactions to, clients, and providing mechanisms for explanation and understanding.

This argument has the potential to deal with some of the objections raised previously. For example, if the professional objective relationship is understood by clients and participated in by both sides on equal terms, its nature as a contact which does not respect the humanity of the client might be lessened or negated. Another point is that openness reflects movement away from psychodynamic understandings of behaviour. Hospers (1950) considered how such explanations of behaviour, relying as they did on unconscious motivation, affected the debate on freedom. He proposed that the extent to which acts are determined by unconscious factors varies in inverse proportion to freedom. The more unconscious motivation is accepted, the less free a person may be said to be.

Openness has been presented in its alliance with a shift from seeing social workers as possessing professional power deriving from psychological understanding towards seeing them as being in an alliance with clients which might promote social understanding and social realization of clients' personal potentials. It might, therefore, be argued that it generates the opportunity for greater freedom and independence for clients from social workers and their agencies. The availability of this greater opportunity does not, however, necessarily suggest that it will be fulfilled against the many factors which can be seen to pull against greater positive freedom and power for clients.

END-WORD

In drawing this discussion of shared decision-making and open records to a close, it is important to repeat the point made at the beginning. That is, it is as yet uncertain that much real change in these practices has yet occurred, in spite of a considerable movement in social work ideology. I have argued that the evidence of slow movement identified in this chapter suggests some recalcitrance in implementing the moving ideology. Perhaps it is always true that ideas move ahead of action.

A number of factors are significant. There is no doubt that there has been a considerable movement in social work towards openness and shared decision-making. There have been recent moves to redefine and activate these ideas in ways which appear to reflect a respect for clients' freedom and power and realization of their personal potential, and, therefore, a wish for greater equality between client and social worker.

The practical difficulties for clients and agencies with open records and shared decision-making may also be an important factor. Openness may make it more difficult to defend agencies against attack, may make relationships with less open agencies more difficult, and may slow down or obstruct work with clients (Payne 1978, 1988). Openness may cause conflicts within agencies by revealing disagreements about values (Parsloe 1988). Where records are used for management control, supervision, or inspection, openness with clients may conflict with these activities, leading to dishonesty in records, defensiveness among workers, or separate record systems (Payne 1978; BASW 1983). The costs of access may be considerable, with few clients taking it up. They may prefer to be protected from unpleasant disclosures, or worried about confidentiality of information which they may not want other members of the family to know about; they may see it as a waste of time to be involved in recording when they want the worker to get on with helping them.

So it is necessary to be cautious in assessing these changes. There are many problems; progress has been slow. However, a closer analysis of the concepts of freedom, power, and self-realization suggests that openness may offer greater freedom from constraint. Whether, in a complex society, it offers positive developments against the social inertia which often restricts the powerless must be more open to doubt.

The evident slowness of real change does not detract from the fact that fewer constraints on freedom are there; the greater opportunities may, perhaps, be seized.

Chapter Nine

DISCRETION AND MANAGERIALISM

TERRY BAMFORD

The years since the reorganization of personal social services have seen a progressive accretion of power to managers and away from practitioners in the large-scale welfare bureaucracies created by the Local Authority Social Services Act 1971. Yet the individual social worker retains a degree of personal decision-making responsibility substantially greater in terms of the consequences for the clients affected by his or her decisions than is true of most occupational groups. While changes in organizational structure have been a characteristic managerial response to problems, the responsibility carried by the individual worker has been little affected. What has changed is the worker's awareness of personal vulnerability in the event of defective decision-making. The establishment of a framework for that decision-making is the subject of a tension between the organizational imperatives of the employing agency and the personal values of the social worker. The aim of this chapter is to identify the genesis of that tension, the values which govern social work practice, and the basis on which the differing perspectives are reconciled in the individual's practice.

THE IMPACT OF MANAGERIALISM

Social work is the core profession in social services departments. While only one in seven of the staff employed are social workers, the attitudes and values of social work have exercised a dominant influence on the development of departments. Initially the mode of practice was based on the values identified by Biestek – client self-determination, confidentiality, individualization, purposeful

135

expression of feelings, controlled emotional involvement, and a non-judgemental attitude (Biestek 1961). Interestingly, this set of values, while defined in the context of casework, has survived to underpin practice in social services, although it requires modification. To these values should be added what Martin Davies terms 'fundamental belief in the capacity of man to improve his own circumstances without necessarily doing so at the expense of others' – which he regards as central to the social worker's philosophy of practice (Davies 1985:4).

The early 1970s saw an explosive growth in social services. The newly established departments grew by over ten per cent each year as their workload expanded as a result of increased visibility and the open-door philosophy implicit in the Seebohm Report. The range of functions discharged by social services also increased, with major legislation affecting the chronically sick and disabled, playgroups and child-minding, adoption and child neglect. The objective of the Seebohm Report – to create a department involved in social planning – necessitated the development of a complex web of interagency relationships with housing, education, social security, and the police.

The organizational response to these developments was initially confused. Two common themes, however, emerged. First, without exception the social services department had longer chains of command than their predecessors, with at least one, and sometimes two or three, additional tiers of management interposed between the practitioner and the Chief Officer. Second, departments appointed a number of persons in an advisory role who played an important part in developing procedural guidance designed to ensure a consistency of approach. The urge towards consistency was one factor leading to an upward pull of decision-making, and this was quickened by the traumatic impact of the Maria Colwell case and its handling by the media.

Even after a succession of child abuse cases it is impossible to exaggerate the impact of the Colwell case on social workers and their managers. Parsloe and Stevenson found that

in every study of area teams social workers referred, not simply to the professional anxieties which such situations created, but to their fear of being found wanting and called to account. ... The regular flow of circulars, in turn interpreted by authorities for departmental policy, has affected the feelings of social workers at field level. More elaborate procedures, although arguably of value in child protection, have served also to increase the fear of the social workers, lest failure to follow the letter of the procedures will adversely affect their reputations, regardless of their general professional competence.

(Parsloe and Stevenson 1978:323)

Of all areas of social work practice, child abuse is the most tightly circumscribed by guidance from the DHSS, Area Review Committees, and employing agencies. The defensive practice thus generated has not proved effective in improving the quality of decision-making in child care (DHSS 1986). Even within those contraints, the individual social worker retains discretion over the style of intervention and the approach adopted with the client. The limits imposed by agencies do control practitioner discretion, but this is not peculiar to social work. 'Discretion, like a hole in a doughnut, does not exist, except as an area left open by a surrounding belt of restriction' (Dworkin 1977). Departmental guidance constitutes that belt of restriction, and the impact of managerialism has been to tighten the belt and limit the freedom of manoeuvre of the individual worker. Three illustrations of this limitation follow, showing the influence respectively of external agencies, resource constraints, and political pressures on individual discretion.

The first illustration comes from the impact of the Children and Young Persons Act 1969. The Magistrates Association mounted a vigorous campaign against the way in which the intent of juvenile courts in making care orders was being undermined by social services' decisions to return children home immediately after the court hearing. A joint agreement was reached between the Association of Directors of Social Services and the Magistrates Association that such decisions should usually be taken at Assistant Director level. Broader considerations of public policy were regarded as justifying the limitation of professional discretion. Decision-making responsibility was effectively transferred from those with detailed knowledge of the child to those with managerial authority. The quality of decision-making may not have been impaired, but the move was an explicit statement of organizational priority.

The second example is one familiar to all social workers, where a decision, correct in principle, is modified as a result of the inability of the agency to make sufficient resources available to meet the need of the client. The closure of residential facilities for children has reduced the choice of placements available for social workers. In varying forms, each agency has therefore developed filtering mechanisms to establish priorities for the allocation of places. A placement thought appropriate by a social worker and supervisor with detailed knowledge of the needs of the client may therefore be denied by an officer at a higher level in the organization. Similar examples can be found in all agencies and in work with all client groups.

The third example is one familiar in many local authorities. If a councillor becomes involved with a family and intervenes on their behalf, how should their interests be handled by the department? Requirements of fairness would dictate that the usual priorities for allocation should be followed. A utilitarian view might point out that if social workers handle the referral in the usual way, the elected member may form an impression that the department is inefficient. If the councillor is in a position of influence in the controlling group, that impression could prejudice resource-allocation decisions. While authorities may vary in their response to this dilemma, its frequency means that a policy approach, written or unwritten, to the issue will have been defined. The individual views of the social worker have to be subordinated to that approach.

The implications of these limitations for the moral basis of social work intervention will be considered below. At this stage it is important to note that, in taking a decision, a social worker may be subject to pressures from a variety of sources.

THE EXERCISE OF DISCRETION

Having focused upon some of the limitations on discretion, it is useful to balance the picture by reference to those areas of practice where the individual worker retains freedom of action. This will serve to identify some of the implicit value systems governing decision-making.

The core of social work remains the relationship between worker and client. While there is no longer the assumption that each client will receive a casework service borrowing heavily from a psychodynamic approach, the relationship established and the attitudes shown by the social worker remain critical determinants of the service offered. Warmth, openness, and respect shown by the worker can, at the lowest, provide clients with an experience of public bureaucracies different in character from that usually experienced from housing officers, social security officials, and teachers. Allied to effective intervention, those qualities can on occasion have a significant impact on the life of the client. The way in which the worker uses his or her distinctive personality is not constrained by the agency, management guidance, or the immediate supervisor.

That choice extends to decisions about the nature and focus of social work intervention. Here Dworkin's analogy of the doughnut comes into play, for the worker's freedom of choice is not absolute. First, there is an obligation to provide some response to the problem presented. Second, the response is conditioned by the resources at the disposal of the agency. A depressed single parent burdened by debt and living in damp, badly maintained accommodation can be offered psychiatric referral if appropriate, social work support, and assistance with the problems of debt and housing. What she cannot be offered is cash and decent accommodation. Third, in some areas the employing agency may have a defined policy response which shapes the worker's response. A policy of planning for permanent placement of children in care may have prescribed time limits for critical decisions about the future of children, which override the judgement of the individual worker.

These constraints are real, but most workers absorb them as part of their socialization into the job. The choice about whether to adopt a behavioural approach to the problem presented, to use family therapy, to develop groupwork, or to conceptualize the problem in a way justifying collective social action to secure changes in public policy is one for the individual worker. The ethos of supervision in social work agencies remains predominantly one of guidance, support, and advice. Only if the course of action proposed were palpably inappropriate would management supervision turn into management command. But collective social action likely to bring the agency into conflict with other public bodies is not easily accomplished, and requires a toughness and single-mindedness on the part of the worker to withstand pressures to pursue a 'softer' solution.

In addition to personal qualities and choice of method of intervention, the worker has discretion in reports to courts and other agencies and as part of the review process within the agency. Again, however, the exercise of a free choice is conditioned by agency and societal expectations. In a court report, recommendations are made against a framework of what is known of sentencing policy, judicial attitudes, and agency precedent. But within the limits imposed by a proper sensitivity to the environment and context of the report, the views expressed and the way in which they are couched will be determined by the social worker's particular perspective.

Having considered both the basis for growing managerial intervention in practitioner decisions, and the still substantial discretion exercised by individual social workers, it is time to consider the moral principles which are brought to bear on decision-making, the reconciliation of conflicting value positions which the social worker has to undertake, and the ethical framework used by social workers in determining priorities.

The preceding discussion has frequently used words like 'discretion', 'judgement', and 'choice' to describe the responsibility of the individual social worker. It has also stressed that decisions involve an interplay of factors which vary according to the particular circumstances of the client. In offering a social work service, both the worker and the agency operate from a shared assumption that the intervention will at worst be harmless, and at best will achieve a change that is in the interests of the client. At once a central dilemma can be seen – who is to determine the best interests of the client, and what are to be the criteria applied in reaching that determination?

CONSTRAINTS ON SELF-DETERMINATION

Even with the increasing interest in the involvement of consumers in the welfare system, the natural rights position of clients' self-determination about their actions is one that has to be heavily qualified. Etherington and Parker identify three areas of conflict between client interests and those interests of which the social worker is the custodian: measures of improved quality independent of the consumer's self-assessment, differential assessment of risk, and balancing the interests of the individual client with those of the supporting network of family and friends (Etherington and Parker 1986).

For many services the user will be the best determinant of quality. The satisfaction experienced by the consumer should be a key measure of success in service provision. There is an overwhelming argument for the extension of mechanisms affording consumers an opportunity to express views on service quality. But there are other measures of quality derived from principles which conflict with immediate client interests. Transport provision to adult day centres for mentally handicapped people provides an instance of a service where users, and their representatives – in this instance, families – would prefer to be picked up at their front door, but where the principle of normalization dictates use of public transport provision when available, or its analogue, collection from a central point where no public transport service exists.

Quality of service provision has to be seen not only in the context of the volume of service delivery – the input measure of most performance indicators – but also in the efficiency of the service, and the fairness of the administrative process. Securing the optimum output for a given measure of input is a legitimate managerial preoccupation. Definitional problems of output continue to trouble social work managers, but increasingly practitioners are being challenged to demonstrate the value and impact of their intervention. Inputs, however, are limited, as was discussed earlier in assessing the effect of resource constraints on practitioner discretion. The way in which limited resources are allocated is a test of quality. The client's right is not one to the provision of a service. It is a right to fair administrative procedures and defined criteria in determining how a service is distributed.

A conflict between individual and proportional justice is evident in this discussion. Social workers tend to be concerned with the unique set of needs of the client or family with whom they are working at a given time, and to promote their interests. A concern for proportional justice – ensuring that clients with equal needs receive equal treatment – is characteristically that of first-line managers. Yet even for practitioners, rationing decisions are an inescapable part of their work, for their most scarce resource, time, has to be apportioned on the basis of an inchoate sense of priority. The articulation of criteria for determining priorities can only be helpful.

The natural rights position of client self-determination acknowledges that it is limited by the qualification that it should not interfere with the rights of others. Where there is a direct risk to others from client action, the moral justification for intervention is clear. More difficult ethical issues are raised by Section 2 of the Mental Health Act 1983, which, setting out conditions for compulsory admission, states that the patient 'ought to be detained in the interests of his own health or safety or with a view to the protection of others'. On what basis do social workers form a view about the health or safety of the client, and what justification do they have for initiating compulsory admission?

The assessment of risk is an undeveloped area in social work practice. The report into the Jasmine Beckford (1985) case identified the failure to use predictive tables, the lack of knowledge of findings from earlier inquiry reports, and the lack of direct examination of the child as deficiencies in practice. A more rigorous and structured approach to the assessment of risk is a precursor of claims to superior professional competence, but that still leaves open the moral justification for imposing a personal or societal view on an individual client. Where life is threatened by deliberate self-harm, the basis for intervention derives from a Judeo-Christian view of the sanctity of human life, a view formally enshrined in the criminal law until relatively recently, and a view which remains predominant in society. Where the risk is of a lower order, or arises from protracted self-neglect – the confused elderly man living alone and rejecting assistance – the social worker has a complex ethical dilemma balancing rights and responsibilities.

That particular example overlaps with the third group of cases where client self-determination cannot be pursued as an absolute value: those situations where other family members or carers have different interests from that of the client. This can be seen when the stress of caring for a confused, incontinent elderly relative has brought the carer to physical and emotional breaking point, but where the relative is resistant to any suggestion of hospital or a residential home. As Ragg has suggested (Ragg 1980:217), what is important is not to embark on a fool's chase after the criterion of 'true' self-determination, but to consider the most rational and moral course of action in the circumstances.

Is utilitarianism enough?

So far this chapter has looked at the degree of discretion of the individual social worker and the regulatory framework for the exercise of that discretion imposed by the agency and society; it has highlighted the inadequacy of client self-determination as a basis for social work intervention. What has emerged is the importance of values, but the absence of any clearly defined framework for social work practice.

In the examples discussed, social workers seem to operate from a broadly utilitarian perspective, promoting client interests within the limitations imposed by society, the agency, and other interests. Normalization as a principle in work with mentally handicapped people can thus be viewed as promoting the welfare of the greatest number while causing anxieties and inconvenience to the carers, as can intervention to restrict the liberty and choice of a mentally disordered individual. The measurement of what is good remains a difficulty. In the example of mental handicap policy, one is according greater weight to the preferences of 'experts' than to user preferences. It is, however, consistent with utilitarian principles to examine long-term consequences of actions as well as immediate consequences.

Moral principles can be justified on utilitarian grounds. O'Hear points out that

> utilitarians should not in general recommend the weighing up of consequences of each individual action before deciding what to do. The consequences of particular actions are highly uncertain; weighing them up will take far too much time and effort; people, in assessing consequences of actions, are only too easily inclined to overlook the uncomfortable and disadvantageous ones. So, there are good utilitarian reasons for the general adoption and upholding of moral rules which will tell us what to do in particular circumstances.
>
> (O'Hear 1985:269)

Yet pursuing this argument runs into the difficulty that like is not being compared with like, and individual situations may pose problems which bring personal value systems into conflict with the collective good. Torturing suspects in order to obtain information to divert a terrorist attack is the most familiar example of utilitarian principles coming into conflict with personal values. Health care provides numerous examples of very expensive services being delivered to extend life by days, weeks, or months. Health economists point to the distortion of rational priorities when heart transplants of dubious effectiveness are funded when an extension of renal dialysis could benefit far more people for a far longer period at the same cost. Such is the value that society places on life that utilitarian principles are incomplete as a justification for action.

An alternative approach to the utilitarian is the contractual theory of welfare developed by Rawls (1977). From the premise of a veil of ignorance cloaking awareness of personality variables, Rawls argues that rational beings acting in pursuit of self-interest would create a structure of society affording the maximum political liberty compatible with liberty for all, and in which inequalities in wealth, income, and power would exist only in so far as they worked to the absolute benefit of the worst-off members of society. This conflicts with a utilitarian stance, which could justify inequalities if they operated to the good of the majority.

The idea of justice as fairness developed by Rawls is attractive to social workers, who are predominantly engaged with disadvantaged members of society whose personal problems are compounded by the manifest inequalities built into the system of distributing resources. It comes into conflict, however, with the concept of justice expressed through entitlement. Nozick argues that the role of the state is that of providing the minimal guarantees needed to allow people to exercise their rights, and sees property as a central part of individuality (Nozick 1974). It will immediately be evident that there is no neutral concept of justice. What Rawls and Nozick offer is two contrasting approaches proceeding from different ideological perspectives.

What this means for social work practice is important. If one follows Rawls' concept of fairness, personal social services can be seen in a compensatory role as the manifestation by the state of its moral obligation to provide equal respect and concern for its least advantaged citizens, and to offer assistance to them calculated to mitigate their disadvantage. Nozick's followers would favour a residual role for public welfare provision operating as a safety net and would reject any idea of a moral obligation to secure a more equal distribution of resources within society.

While much of Rawls' approach is consistent with a more egalitarian society, it is important to note the primary emphasis placed on political liberty in his formulation. The Marxist analysis of social justice presents a different picture of the role of the state. Marxists see individual freedom in broader terms of removing the barriers to emancipation and self-realization through collective action. Civil liberties under capitalism are viewed as illusory because of the degree to which they are shaped by the economic and social structure, and redefined if they threaten the established order. Political liberty can therefore be achieved only if it is hand in hand with economic liberty through a total transformation of the means of production and distribution.

Economic determinism has been somewhat qualified by later interpreters of Marxist theory to allow for the interplay of political, educational, religious, and cultural factors, albeit with economic factors predominant. The development of the welfare state is viewed by Miliband as 'part of the ransom the working class had been able to extract from their rulers in the course of a hundred years' (Miliband 1973:99). Social work has a particular function in this analysis in 'deflecting attention from structural failures by focusing on individual and community pathology' (Corrigan and Leonard 1978:xi).

In their widely read discussion of the implications for social work practice of a Marxist perspective, Corrigan and Leonard argue that public welfare services are geared to individuals through the process of assessment and delivery. Group work and community work have been used as ways of locating problems in groups or particular communities. A vivid description of the worker-client contact comes from a novel, *The Caseworker*:

His system is depressingly lacking in complexity, his income wretched, his physical surroundings dreary, his vision

145

blurred, his burden heavy. His freedom of action is below average, his drives, which are without direction, conflict and sometimes collide head-on. When this happens, the traffic jams up and official intervention is needed to start it moving again. Since my job is to protect children and safeguard the interests of the state, the most I can do is to reconcile him with his circumstances and oppose his propensity for suffering. I do what the law and my fumbling judgement permit; then I look on, mesmerized, as the system crushes him.

(Konrad 1975:16)

While that description comes from Eastern Europe, it is a compelling account of the impotence of both client and worker in the face of structural pressures.

Marxist social workers have to reconcile their structural analysis with their knowledge of individual needs. Their sensitivity to the anguish and pain of clients prevents them from following a hard-line approach that relieving suffering is applying a poultice to the festering sore of society, and thus delays the structural change required. Corrigan and Leonard suggest that social work has 'to understand individual experience and the features of individual personality ... not only in relation to the family as a reflection, at least in part, of the dominant economic structure, but also the other wider structures with which individuals interact' (Corrigan and Leonard 1978:22). In this way links can be drawn for the client to facilitate a realization that his experience is part of a collective experience to be addressed through collective action.

This brief discussion of a Marxist approach to practice has identified a distinctively different view of values to that expressed by Rawls, Nozick, or Biestek. For these writers, values stand as a discrete personal statement without being viewed in the context of the socio-economic system. For Marxists, values, attitudes, and beliefs come together in an ideological perspective.

Technical Solutions to Value Conflicts

Some of the different perspectives affecting social work decision-making have been presented. It is evident that there is no congruence within social work about the values which should govern practice. The traditional statement, articulated most clearly by Biestek, has been absorbed into the dominant culture of social work, but is not wholly adequate because of its over-emphasis on client self-determination and individualization. Rawls' theory of social justice has been adopted as the basis for a construct of social welfare services by a wider constituency than egalitarian socialists, and has been interpreted in different ways (Weale 1980; Etherington and Parker 1986). Corrigan and Leonard acknowledge that much more work needs to be done to offer a fully developed analysis of social work from a Marxist viewpoint, but offer signposts to practice.

Confronted with this range of approaches, social workers showed a lack of intellectual rigour vividly described by Parsloe and Stevenson:

> Social workers showed little interest or capacity to analyse their rationale for determining the frequency of contact, nor whether it took place at the client's home or in the office. Social workers seemed to make such decisions without conscious thought and, when pressed, implied that they acted 'by intuition' or that their behaviour was determined not by the individual client's need but by what they thought was the tradition of the local authority or by some practical feature such as a lack of interview accommodation.
>
> (Parsloe and Stevenson 1978:339)

The explosive growth of social services functions and staffing in the early nineteen-seventies brought into social work staff who rejected the imposition on clients both of a middle-class value system and of a psychodynamic model of social casework inappropriate for the volume and the urgency of the problems being confronted. Values other than empowerment of clients were suspect. Without a clear ethical framework for decision-making at individual level, the response of employing agencies was to fill that vacuum by rationing procedures, by statements of priorities, and by attempting to structure client contact.

Initial attempts to set priorities were somewhat crude. They emphasized the legal basis of intervention and, as subsidiary factors, the element of risk involved and the likely effectiveness of intervention. A more sophisticated approach, using a client-problems dictionary, was developed by Algie and colleagues at the National Institute for Social Work (Algie and Miller 1976), and further refined in a matrix matching service options and problem severity (Whitmore and Fuller 1980). Similar concepts were incorporated in a workload management system which focused on the classification of cases according to goals (Vickery 1977). The prescription of contact based on client goals was:

(a) Behavioural change. Contact: weekly or more

(b) Support or maintenance of a social situation. Contact: 2 – 4 weeks

(c) Personal maturation. Contact: several times weekly

(d) Responding to a crisis. Contact: substantial over a short period.

(e) Environmental change and provision of practical/material help. Contact: estimate calculated on basis of local knowledge.

(f) Reassessing client situations. Contact: as required

(g) Assessment. Contact: as much as may be required to formulate goals and plans for intervention.

The implications for practitioner discretion of this managerial approach are self-evident.

The significance of these developments is that they substitute bureaucratic definitions and prescriptions for individual moral judgements. Rhodes identifies four ways in which bureaucracies operate to undermine ordinary concepts of morality (Rhodes 1986). First, social relations are defined impersonally. Clients are categorized or pigeonholed, and then an appropriate response is delivered in terms of frequency of contact or pattern of service. This is objectionable from both an individualist and a Marxist perspective. It fails to recognize the set of particular problems and the individual's contribution to their solution. Equally it fails to locate the clients in their social situation, and to offer any possibility of collective action. By depersonalizing the worker-client contact, it distances workers from clients and binds them more tightly to the employing organization.

Second, large-scale bureaucracies deal with problems presented to them by developing a specialized response. Again, the ascription of special knowledge and expertise has a distancing effect from ordinary moral responses. It gives extra weight to the culture of specialization, to the rite of passage, whether through training or experience, that leads to the designation of specialist, and to the language and concepts deemed to require special skills. Thus specialist workers in child abuse are trained and equipped to spot warning signals, but their existence has a deskilling effect on other workers, and their role conditions their response.

Third, the hierarchical structure of bureaucracies, with some decisions expressly removed from the front-line worker, and with formal rules and procedures over which the individual worker has little influence, reinforces the sense of distance between worker and client. True, they share an impotence in the face of the bureaucracy; but impotence is a poor basis for joint work on the problems presented.

Fourth, the personal obligations of the worker to his client and to his sense of morality have to be subordinated to organizational requirements. Most social workers have had to take coercive action, whether in child care, mental health, or probation work, while knowing that the likely consequences of the action taken would be prejudicial to the interests of the client. Legal requirements, neighbourhood pressures, the expectations of other agencies can all bring powerful influences to bear on organizations. A vagrant might normally expect one pound towards a sandwich and a cup of tea from a compassionate, socially concerned individual, but when that individual is a social work duty officer in a busy inner city office the response received by the vagrant will be dictated by organizational norms, not by an individual's moral views about the distribution of power and wealth.

These comments are valid in the organizational structures hitherto favoured by local authority social services departments. The debates about genericism and specialization, about functional and geographic structures, about devolution and centralism, patch-based work and communities of interest, and, most recently, the proposal for a 'fourth-generation social services department' produced by The University of Bath (1987), all fail to address the central issue of the social worker's distancing from ordinary judgements. The weight of the organization, however structured, has that effect.

TWO CURRENT ISSUES

Social Work Education

There has been a long-standing debate within social work about the relevance of social work education to the issues facing the beginning social worker. Some Directors of Social Services have been active critics of much of the content of current training courses, contending that they do not constitute an adequate preparation for the realities of working within a hierarchical bureaucracy. While the development of Certificate in Social Service schemes has been constrained by resources, such schemes are seen by many managers as affording more relevant training for the tasks that actually have to be undertaken by social services.

Current proposals for training are much closer in concept to the Certificate in Social Service than to the current Certificate of Qualification in Social Work. While presented as a partnership between employing agencies and academic institutions, they represent a victory for managerialism by giving management for the first time a wide measure of control over the content and organization of social work training. It is premature to sound the deathknell of professional values independent of the employing agency, but the management structures to be established for social work education will become the fulcrum of the tension between those two value systems.

Political Intervention

With the exception of the ethical dilemma posed by the priority to be accorded to referrals from individual councillors, elected members have rarely been directly involved in the decision-making process. Their role in policy has been focused on the issue of resource allocation, staffing structures, and new service developments.

The inadequacies of social work practice in addressing key issues of social policy have led a handful of local authorities to adopt a more interventive approach, establishing policies at member level which govern social work practice. An example of the moral issues which such a policy can produce can be seen in the context of transracial fostering, where some authorities have moved to an insistence that black children should be placed only with black families. An ideological view that ethnic identity should be accorded primacy over other interests is the basis for the policy.

Individual discretion about the appropriateness of a placement with foster-parents is limited by the primacy given to ethnicity. The scarcity of black foster-parents can produce pressures to alter standards for assessment, a pressure to which predominantly white social workers are vulnerable when they are told by political leaders and by representatives of the black community that their colour makes it impossible for them to form objective judgements. The limited options for placements may mean that black children remain in residential care for a longer period because the pool of potential foster-parents has been reduced by a politically imposed restriction.

The example can be argued as a utilitarian view: the councillors believe that children placed with proper recognition of their ethnic identity will grow up as better-adjusted members of society, and that the agency will respond by targeting campaigns at black foster-parents. It demonstrates the subordination of the self-determination of the individual client, whose views are assumed rather than sought. And it illustrates another of the many complex factors which impact upon the decision-making of practitioners.

Towards a Synthesis

The earlier quotation from Parsloe and Stevenson suggested an eclecticism in selection of methods of social work intervention. A similar eclecticism exists in the value system used by practitioners, sufficient to undermine most generalizations about the basis adopted for decisions. It is important, however, to draw together some of the themes considered, and see how social work values are shifting in response to the challenges from managerialism and Marxism.

Clark and Asquith (1985:7) refer to Laycock's neat summary of the present state of the art: 'Social work is in the peculiar position of having many worthwhile skills without either a coherent unifying philosophy or a sufficiently strong scientific foundation to subject skills to rational enquiry.' From this Clark and Asquith suggest that the result of this vacuum is that

> social workers are content, rightly or wrongly, to adopt conventional norms and wisdoms. Where clear standards are not readily available, they are built up over time as a sediment of practice within social work agencies. This process established the relationship between the self-determination which social workers aspire to promote and the social control which, however reluctantly, they admit as a consequence or end of social work. Social workers act as agents of social control by defining the area within which self-determination is to be allowed: that is, in precisely what respects the right is particular and qualified.
>
> (Clark with Asquith 1985:32)

That view is consistent with the argument advanced above, which lays great emphasis upon the socialization process within the employing agency as the means, often unarticulated, whereby values are transmitted.

The question regularly asked of social workers is 'why did you take up social work?' If that question had to be answered in detail, one might begin to move towards an agreed social philosophy. Certain base statements would find common agreement – democracy, for one – although as has been shown, these concepts would mean different things to different people dependent on their political philosophy.

Liberalism places a high premium on the individual, and takes as its reference point the effect of measures on the individual. It is thus readily compatible with the concepts of respect for persons and individualism which are accorded a prominent place in Biestek's classical statement of values.

Social work is utilitarian in the sense that the overall benefits to society of social work intervention are seen to outweigh the disbenefits in terms of interference with individual rights. Nevertheless, that utilitarian perspective has not led to the development of a collectivist perspective and commitment to social reform in the way argued by Corrigan and Leonard, and practitioners who wish to develop that perspective frequently find themselves challenging the norms of their employing agency (Simpkin 1983).

The dichotomy between individual action and social action is reflected in the Codes of Ethics adopted by the British Association of Social Workers (BASW) and the National Association of Social Workers in the USA (NASW). Both are individualist in their orientation, but BASW states that social workers have a duty 'to bring to the attention of those in power, and of the general public, ways in which the activities of government, society or agencies, create or contribute to hardship or suffering or militate against their relief' – a definition significantly worded in terms of an obligation to publicize rather than to engage in direct social action. NASW's code asserts as a 'primary obligation the welfare of the individual or group served', which includes action for improving social conditions. Both Codes are at a level of abstraction which render them of limited utility for practitioners.

Professionalism in the sense of the official ethical statement of the professional association has little to offer the social worker, but there is an important way in which a strongly developed professional view can act as a countervailing force against organizational, bureaucratic, and managerial values. If, as has been suggested, practice values are usually dictated by the employing organization, professionalism may be the best protection for social workers when their personal sense of morality brings them into conflict with organizational goals.

Giller and Morris' study of decision-making in work with juvenile offenders found evidence of social workers' knowledge of theory, but less of their use of that knowledge. They suggested that social workers generated 'practice-orientated ideologies ... sets of ideas about categories of cases and means of dealing with them' (Giller and Morris 1981:102). These ideologies were used to assimilate issues, events, people, and behaviour. Rees developed the concept further with a threefold typology of casework ideology, based on the use of inter-personal relationships; service ideology, geared to the delivery of immediate benefits and services; and relief ideology, geared to the provision of compensatory services, whether in cash or kind, to the disadvantaged. That description helpfully draws together the key elements in the approach used by social workers (Rees 1978).

Does it matter if social work has no agreed value system? I believe it does, for two reasons. First, the professional aspirations of social work have little substance if the value base for practice is so diverse. It matters little that social work knowledge is drawn from a range of different disciplines, but the absence of agreed values is more damaging. While Biestek's statement still has much utility, it has to be heavily qualified: authoritative restatement is urgently needed. Second, the growth in managerial power consequent on the size of social services departments and their bureaucratic structure threatens to subjugate ordinary morality to organizational morality. Social work's contribution as a humanizing influence within the welfare system will itself be threatened if this trend continues. Thinking about values is hard work. Without that thinking, the survival of social work as anything other than a local government function is in peril.

© 1989 Terry Bamford

Chapter Ten

TAKEN FROM HOME

OLIVE STEVENSON

In this chapter, the circumstances of, and moral justification for, the compulsory removal from home of children and some adults are explored. It focuses attention on three situations in which social workers may be involved. These are the admission of children to care, of mentally disordered adults (including old people) to mental hospitals, and of old people to institutional care, under specific provisions of the National Assistance Act 1948.

This analysis is undertaken at a time when British social workers' actions and decisions are subject to scrutiny as never before. Public attention is focused most sharply on cases of child abuse, especially, currently, sexual abuse, in which the dilemmas as to when to remove children from home are often agonizing. However, in the past decade, despite an absolute decline in the numbers of children in care, there has been a growing interest in the way in which social control functions in respect of children generally are exercised. Social workers' powers in relation to the removal of mentally ill people from home have also been widely discussed, particularly in the debates preceding the passing of the Mental Health Act 1983. For reasons which are later addressed, the issue of intervention in the lives of elderly people has been less discussed, despite the substantial increase in the numbers of very old, frail people, whose care may involve intervention. It raises ethical issues every bit as important and complex as those which are raised in relation to the other two groups, and it is therefore here accorded the same weight.

The discussion assumes that such action is taken without the consent of the persons involved. This is itself problematic. Some of those concerned are clearly incapable of giving consent – for example, a baby. Some are deemed to be incapable – for example, a person with advanced dementia. Some refuse consent but their wishes are overriden. However, these decisions often give rise to difficulties. We have to assess another's competence, by virtue of maturity or mental capacity, to make decisions about his or her own life. Furthermore, as we shall later show, such assessments necessitate an evaluation of the risk involved to the person or others of leaving him or her at home. Considerations both of competence and of risk always involve the value systems of workers, whether in such matters as child-rearing standards, the way mental illness is viewed, or domestic hygiene.

To remove any person from their home against their will is considered to be one of the most extreme forms of coercion. In the cases which we shall be considering, it also always involves placing them somewhere else, not of their choosing. The primary, explicit motive is protection, whether of the individual concerned, of those who may directly engage or be involved with him or her, or the wider society which, it may be considered, is placed at risk because of the behaviour of the individual. This is not to ignore secondary or hidden agendas, nor to pass over the complexity of the decisions which have to be taken about such protection. Indeed discussion of such matters forms the core of the chapter. It does, however, focus attention on a double coercion: to be taken from home and to be required to live somewhere else, often quite unlike the home which has been left.

Although this chapter is concerned with certain specific acts of compulsion, it raises much more general issues about social control and, in particular, about social workers as agents of the state. These matters are vitally important, but they are not considered in depth here, lest they detract from a more immediate and practical purpose, to examine the ethical and professional dilemmas which arise, or should arise, for social workers in their day-to-day work with individuals who may have to be 'taken from home'. It is only too easy to take refuge in generalities and avoid the challenge of improving the quality of what has to be done now.

At the level of individual practice, the exercise of compulsion raises questions about the nature of the relationship between worker and client, about power, influence, persuasion, and coercion. Heraud (1970:192) argued that 'the difference between persuasive and coercive control is in most casework situations one of degree only'. Whilst that may be so, the question of degree is not trivial. The invocation of legal powers in the situations which we shall be discussing is a kind of 'brake', in the sense of a check. It is also a kind of 'break' in the continuum between persuasion at the one end and crude compulsion at the other. It is perceived by the social workers as a distinctive kind of action – one which arouses considerable anxiety and misgivings. Furthermore, some clients may believe that they have only 'Hobson's choice': that if they do not agree to a certain course of action, compulsion may ensue.

In short, to embark on a consideration of this specific issue is like casting a stone in a pond: the ripples spread wider and wider into the social and legal context in which social work is practised and into the social work relationship. This phrase, so often trivialized, is crucial to an informed understanding of ethical matters.

MORAL DEVELOPMENT – A FEMINIST PERSPECTIVE

The philosophical debate which underpins discussion of these matters runs deep and wide. It revolves around two questions, fundamental to the organization of society. First, to what extent am I my brother's or sister's keeper? Second, how do we balance the freedom of the individual with the freedom of those with whom he or she interacts? Much that is written about these issues seems disappointing and of little help to the student or practitioner. Recent feminist writings have illuminated possible explanations for such disappointment, particularly the work of Gilligan (1977;1982), Rhodes (1985;1986), and Noddings (1984), whose arguments underpin this chapter.

Briefly, Gilligan asserts that theories of moral development have failed adequately to explore the difference between the sexes. She points out that the influential work of Freud and Piaget has been used by men, notably Kohlberg (1981), to elaborate further hierarchies of moral development and, in so doing, they have found women morally deficient according to the standards set by men! This may be explored by reference to the domestic context in which women have traditionally operated (the italics are mine):

> The repeated finding of these studies is that the qualities deemed necessary for adulthood – the capacity for autonomous thinking, clear decision-making and reasonable action – are those associated with masculinity but considered undesirable attributes of the feminine self. The stereotypes suggest a splitting of love and work that relegates the expressive capacities requisite for the former to women while the instrumental abilities necessary for the latter reside in the masculine domain. Yet ... *these stereotypes reflect a conception of adulthood that is itself out of balance, favouring the separateness of the individual self over its connection to others and leaning more toward an autonomous life of work than toward the interdependence of love and care. The relational bias in women's thinking ... now begins to emerge in a new developmental light. Instead of being seen as a developmental deficiency this bias appears to reflect a different social and moral understanding.*
>
> (Gilligan 1977:482)

Thus, research by Kohlberg and Gilligan shows fundamental differences in the value systems of men and women.

> The moral imperative that emerges repeatedly in the women's interviews is an injunction to care, a responsibility to discern and alleviate the 'real and recognizable trouble' of this world. For the men Kohlberg studied, the moral imperative appeared rather as an injunction to respect the right of others and thus to protect from interference the right to life and self-fulfillment. Development for both sexes then would seem to entail an integration of rights and responsibilities through the discovery of the complementarity of these disparate views.
>
> (Gilligan 1977:511)

We are not here crudely allocating these views to men and women, as if there were no overlap between the sexes. However, the dominance of men in the public domain has resulted in the masculine formulation being put forward more powerfully, and this is mirrored in the preoccupation of moral philosophers, with many of whose books I have struggled in vain.

As Noddings (1984:3) puts it:

The very wellspring of ethical behaviour [is] in human affective response ... It is necessary to give appropriate attention and credit to the affective foundation of existence. Indeed, one who attempts to ignore or to climb above the human affect at the heart of ethicality may well be guilty of romantic rationalism. What is recommended in such a framework simply cannot be applied to the actual world.

Some applications of these ideas to social work have been explored by Rhodes (1985). In particular, she seeks to relate Gilligan's analysis to social work ethics (Rhodes 1985:101). There are

two general modes of reasoning about ethical choices and about the world. One, 'responsibility', focuses on caring, responsibility ... in accordance with people's needs. The other mode, 'rights', stresses reasoning based on moral principle, particularly principles of justice, equality and individual rights.

What has all this to do with our theme? It is relevant at three levels. First, it allows us to assume as given that decisions about compulsory removal from home should be rooted in caring.

The focus of our attention will be upon how to meet the other morally. Ethical caring ... will be described as arising out of natural caring – that relation in which we respond as one [who cares] out of love or natural inclination. The relation of natural caring will be identified as the human condition that we, consciously or unconsciously, perceive as 'good'. It is that condition toward which we long and strive, and it is our longing for caring that provides the motivation to us to be moral.

(Noddings 1984:5)

That view is similar to those of other moral philosophers, such as Downie and Telfer (1969), and Plant (1970), who suggests that respect for persons is not in itself a moral principle but rather underpins notions of morality. However, the phrase 'respect for persons' describes a more distant, less direct response than Noddings' formulation. By linking an ethic of caring to

159

informal interactions, arising from the domestic setting, the ideal is softened and enhanced. It is suggesting that, in our professional relationships, we should strive to replicate (within certain constraints and limitations) some of the best, most worthy impulses which arise spontaneously in personal relationships. High on that agenda, as Gilligan found in her interviews with women about moral responsibility, is a deep desire 'not to hurt others, and the hope that in morality lies a way of solving conflicts so that no one gets hurt' (Gilligan 1977:486).

The second level of analysis concerns the tension between responsibilities and rights as modes of thought. This is closely related to ideas concerning justice, especially the distinction between what Tillich (1960) described as creative and proportional justice. These ideas are explored elsewhere, using different terms, such as distributive justice (Rawls 1977). However, Tillich's terminology is attractive in this context because it seems to highlight the link with gender. Creative justice approaches individuals as unique human beings; in this kind of justice, we are all special cases, needing different things. Proportional justice strives towards equity, towards treating people in the same way. It seeks to find common elements in different situations or cases which will enable consistency of treatment. This tension is to be found in all our social institutions, in more or less degree, whether it be the family, how parents behave towards their children, the courts (as between 'the tariff' and recognition of individual circumstances), or the social security system (as in discretion or entitlement in single payments). The emphasis which individuals give to each, however, seems to be gender-related, although notions of creative justice become increasingly harder to sustain and implement as we move outside the private and into the public domain and from smaller to larger systems of interaction. The application of these ideas to compulsory removal from home is extensive and complex. It is bound up with the balance between the use of courts and other similar regulatory mechanisms and the exercise of professional discretion.

The third level of analysis, developed by Rhodes (1985), helps us to place some of the dilemmas of social work in historical context, again related to gender. The history of social work, casework in particular, has always been characterized by its direct concern for the well-being of the individual. Its most eminent theorists have all stressed the centrality of relationships to casework. Two problems arise from this:

> First, a caseworker's care, responsibility and doing for others may be at the expense of the client's autonomy and self-determination. Nurturance may be distorted into coercive control ... Second, decisions made in a case-by-case basis may lead to arbitrary and unfair treatment.
>
> (Rhodes 1985:102)

However, the 'rights' approach is crude and approximate and by definition cannot tailor decisions to fit individuals. As Rhodes suggests, it may

> lead to indifference to particular circumstances and to bureaucratization of the social work process. Following rules may take precedence over meeting people's needs.
>
> (1985:103)

Gilligan makes the link with gender:

> Thus it becomes clear why a morality of rights and non-interference may appear frightening to women in its potential justification of indifference and unconcern. At the same time, it becomes clear why, from a male perspective, a morality of responsibilities appears inconclusive and diffuse, given its insistence on contextual relationism.
>
> (Gilligan 1982:22)

Rhodes considers the history of social work, traditionally seen as women's work, and concludes:

> The struggle by nineteenth-century women to care for others in the face of the individualistic and competitive public world parallels the struggle by social workers today to balance caring with maintaining right in a bureaucratized and atomistic society.
>
> (Rhodes 1985:104)

This helps us to understand better the internal tensions which social workers experience in making such decisions about their clients; it opens up the likelihood that the nature of this experience is related to gender.

Against this background, we turn to examine the key ethical issues which arise in 'taking from home': firstly, the notion of 'risk'.

RISK

The justification for compulsory removal from home is that the person concerned is at risk by reason of his or her actions or the actions of others, or that the person concerned is placing others at risk. We need, therefore, to consider in some detail the nature of those risks, which fall, broadly, into five categories. All raise problems of definition and of degree.

First there is the question of physical injury or systematic neglect caused by another person. The victim is usually a child. Although the decision concerning the extent of injury or neglect which justifies removal may be contentious, the underlying principle that, in certain circumstances, children must be protected from physical harm caused by their caretakers is not. (This, of course, was not always the case; it marks a significant social and legal change from the notion of 'child ownership' by parents to one of children's rights.) Recent concern about child sexual abuse raises the issue in a new form. What kinds of physical abuse caused by sexual activity will be considered grounds for removal?

Although the main focus in this matter has been upon children, the case for protecting vulnerable adults from injury by their caretakers needs to be addressed. Concern about physical abuse of very old people is increasingly expressed (Cloke 1983). Although this does not cause public outcry as do cases of children, it is highly probable that it will attract growing attention as the numbers of the very frail elderly increase. Nor is it difficult to envisage situations in which mentally ill or mentally handicapped people are similarly at risk.

A second, very problematic, group comprises those who are considered to be at risk emotionally or socially, rather than physically, from their caretakers' behaviour towards them. This is, of course, a conceptual and legal minefield because of the difficulties of defining terms adequately and of producing evidence sufficiently 'hard' to allay the suspicion of values being unreasonably imposed by outside agencies. Thus, although child-care law enables care proceedings to be taken on the grounds that a child's proper development is being avoidably impaired, the courts have been reluctant to remove children from home on such grounds, unless the nature of the caretaker's 'misbehaviour' is flagrant. So far as adults are concerned, such action is almost unknown, although, as with physical injury or neglect, it is not hard to imagine situations in which the suffering of a vulnerable adult might be intense. Social and emotional neglect and ill-treatment are now given as grounds for concern about, and even for closure of, residential homes. However, the idea of intervening in family life in a similar way is not yet acceptable, nor, in the case of adults, are legal powers yet available so to do.

The third category concerns the physical risk to others in the immediate environment which the behaviour of the individual may occasion. This is most frequently seen in the case of mentally ill adults. Whilst this on occasions leads to diagnostic disputes, there are some situations (such as severe post-puerperal depression) when such decisions are relatively clear-cut. More complex are the decisions which arise when children and young people are alleged to be uncontrollable by their parents. Other difficult situations not uncommonly concern elderly people. An elderly spouse, for example, may continue the abusive behaviour of a lifetime but inflict it on a partner who is now too frail to 'take it'.

All these situations involve direct interaction between the individual and his or her caretakers or family members. Discussion of compulsory removal from home tends to encourage a view of events which defines victims and perpetrators in a way which many would challenge. Theoretical frameworks for the understanding of family and group dynamics have encouraged professionals to think of the ways in which so-called 'victims' – children and adults – may provoke hostile behaviour in others. Such provocation may be conscious or unconscious, or may be a consequence of behaviour not intended to be aggressive (such as a crying baby). Such a way of looking at things undoubtedly offers those who seek to intervene a useful model. It enables them to work on the assumption that a changed style of interaction between victim and perpetrator may reduce provocation and hence aggressive behaviour. Yet this approach can slide into 'blaming the victim', a view of the situation which fails to acknowledge the power of the perpetrator over the victim and which, in shifting the responsibility, also shifts the locus for action. Feminists concerned with domestic violence are understandably negative about such a formulation. For our purposes here, the problem is, of course, when to draw the line, when to say, 'No matter what goes on here we cannot any longer risk the harm which may ensue if we do not take action to remove one of the parties.' That judgement is not easy to make, especially if a worker has become involved with, and eager to help, the perpetrator(s), as has been demonstrated in some child abuse inquiries (Beckford 1985: Spencer 1976).

Fourth, there is what we may describe as social risk – a much more elusive concept and certainly more open to exploitation by those in power. This is most clearly seen in the case of children and young people who are taken from home on care orders because of the offences which they have committed or because they have not attended school. Whilst, on occasion, their behaviour constitutes a physical danger to others, such as in cases of violent robbery or arson, large numbers of young people have been compulsorily removed because they have placed property rather than people at risk. Hooligans, it is argued, have to be kept in order or anarchy will ensue. This, then, is a more generalized notion of risk to the community and to the rule of law and order.

Lastly, some adults, usually old, are considered to be an environmental risk. That is to say, their mode of life is thought to constitute an unacceptable hazard to others. The extent of the offence which certain behaviours give is partly related to the proximity of neighbours. Acceptance of an individual's right to live life as he or she wants, like all aspects of liberty, has limits. In a block of flats, for example, squalor that leads to infestation, incontinence which leads to smells, and erratic behaviour (such as leaving on taps or wandering at night) can intrude excessively into the liberty of others. Situations like this, which are not rare, pose serious dilemmas for professionals.

It may be argued that in both the last two categories an element of concern for the 'offenders' is also present, and the decision to take from home is partly 'in their own interest'. However, as we shall see later, the value to the individual of removal to another environment is dubious; however disguised, it is the protection of others which is here the primary goal.

Weighing these different kinds of risk lies at the heart of decisions about the use of compulsory powers and raises profound questions about the nature of liberty, the role of the state, and the extent to which we (as agents of the state) are our brothers' and sisters' keepers. Moreover, a 'good' decision must take into account highly specific situations in which the nature and balance of the factors involved are immensely variable.

THE LEGAL CONTEXT

Coercion is not necessarily achieved through legal process; indeed the latter is intended in part to protect individuals from the excesses of 'a police state'. The law interposes a regulatory structure between the state and the person who may have to be 'taken from home'. However, between the client groups here considered there is a sharp contrast in the way the law is used and the courts are involved in the process. In decisions about children and young people, the role of the courts is central. Care proceedings and, increasingly, wardships are at the centre of the legal process by which children are removed. Even (temporary) Place of Safety Orders must be signed by a magistrate.

By contrast, under the powers of the Mental Health Act, 1983, a mentally disordered person may be removed from home and detained in hospital without recourse to the courts at all. The provisions of the National Assistance Act (Section 47), which will be discussed later, require the order of a magistrate for a person (usually old) to be compulsorily removed. But there is no right of appeal for six weeks after the order has been made; because of the characteristics and situation of the people so removed, the legal process in itself offers little protection to their rights.

There is a continuing debate about the effectiveness of the courts in protecting the liberty of vulnerable individuals. The law, it is suggested, is a blunt instrument in matters of this kind: the courts have to lean on professional expertise in forming a view. Furthermore, the adversarial tradition of the courts affects the way evidence and information are presented and may create an artificially formal environment for the making of 'welfare'-type decisions. Greater involvement of the judiciary, therefore, has not been seen as unequivocally good. Indeed, as Bean (1980) points out, pressure for reform before the 1959 Mental Health Act came in part from a clash between those who advocated 'legalism' and those who sought to 'medicalize' the care and control of the mentally ill. Is it significant that we have moved towards a more court-centred process in respect of children and young people, and, on the whole, away from it in respect of adults? Can it be that, as the concept of parents owning children as property was abandoned, checks and balances were none-theless built in to safeguard parents' rights as well as those of children? Such an element of arbitration is missing when adults are the focus of attention. Furthermore, in matters concerning mental illness, the growth and establishment of psychiatry as a medical specialism has been influential.

Bean (1980:47) uses the term 'therapeutic law' to describe processes in which 'strong emphasis is placed on *parens patriae*', the role of the state in caring for therapeutic people. Therapeutic law permits extensive use of discretion by the administrators.

The case of the mentally ill nicely illustrates the recurring dilemma between the use of administrative law, in this case described as 'therapeutic', and the use of judicial process. As we have pointed out, the latter is not necessarily an appropriate context for the management of situations in which people are emotionally disturbed and in which individual circumstances vary so greatly. Yet the exercise of discretion, by definition, limits the formulation of case law, a mechanism by which proportional justice ('fairness') is established. Public awareness of what is going on is damped down and the professionals are not effectively challenged.

We have not yet found a proper balance between the use of administrative law and the courts in relation to those 'taken from home'. Children and young people are more effectively pro-tected than adults against arbitrary exercise of compulsory powers. However, it would be simplistic to infer from this that an extension of court process in the case of adults would be wholly beneficial. One way forward is to introduce or strengthen clear-cut procedures for the involvement of courts, or similarly constituted bodies, in appeals or reviews of decisions taken. This has been attempted, as in the Mental Health Review Tribunals, so sharply criticized by Gostin (1976), and, subsequently, the

Mental Health Commission, set up in 1983, whose functioning has not yet been adequately reviewed. In the end, however effective such bodies may be, the elusive question of 'quality control' of the professionals who exercise such power is critical. For no system of legal or quasi-legal process can eliminate the exercise of individualized discretion.

CLIENT GROUPS CONSIDERED

We turn now to consider the client groups in turn, drawing on a framework which Rhodes (1986:108) has suggested for analysing coercive action. Rhodes asks (*inter alia*):

i) what values are violated by the coercive act?

ii) what is the good of the coercive act?

iii) is the person competent to make the decision?

The dilemmas which these questions raise underly the discussion which follows. Two assumptions are made.

First, social workers, like anyone else, are children of their time and of the social milieu in which they happen to have been born. The judgements which they make and the decisions which they take are never value-free, although it is important that they become more aware of their assumptions. Nor does respect for others' beliefs, attitudes, and value systems necessarily lead to a cultural relativism which refuses to prefer one behaviour to another. Greater understanding of the temporal and social context of our own and other belief-systems should, however, make us much slower to assert our 'rightness' and much more cautious about condemning the life-style of others. A sensitive and sophisticated social worker has a much harder time in reaching decisions; the development of self-and-other-awareness in these matters is in itself an ethical duty as we seek to avoid causing grave, sometimes irreparable, hurt in coercive action.

Second, there is no escaping from the 'messiness' of most ethical problems, which, as Rhodes puts it, '[defy] any neat moral analysis' (1986:108). Such 'messiness' usually arises, first, from the need to form a judgement about the degree of risk to the person concerned or those around him or her and, second, from the need to decide about 'lesser evils'; whether more harm will be done by such action than by 'leaving ill alone'. These points are at the heart of most decisions about people who may be 'taken from home'.

Old People

The rights and needs of old people who may be taken from home have been seriously neglected. Although compulsory powers have been relatively rarely used, the growing numbers of very frail old people, including a substantial number suffering from forms of mental infirmity, especially dementia, make it inevitable that difficulties in deciding 'what is for the best' will arise more frequently. Increasing emphasis on community care in recent years places a heavy burden of responsibility on all those who support and care for such elderly people. Small wonder, then, if the cry 'she would be better off in a home' is heard more often. Furthermore, the issue of old-age abuse by carers, formal and informal, is bound to arise more often; that in turn focuses attention upon the inadequacy of the present legal powers adequately to protect old people.

There are two routes by which old people may be 'taken from home'. The first uses the general powers of the Mental Health Act for compulsory short-term admission and subsequently for guardianship. (The guardian may decide where a person lives.) There are complex problems of definition. As Greengross (1986:87) points out, 'Even if [old] people are not diagnosed by a psychiatrist as suffering from mental disorder or impairment, they may be behaving in a manner which suggests that they cannot cope without intervention.'

The right to intervene, therefore, arises in cases where the mental state of the old person is not such as to make obvious their incompetence to decide their own destiny. In practice, the use made of compulsory powers under the Act, especially guardianship, is highly variable between authorities, reflecting the uncertainty which exists about its applicability and justification.

Old people may also be removed from home under the provision of the National Assistance Act 1948 (Section 47). These powers are not in fact limited to old people, but it is significant that they are never, or very rarely, invoked in respect of younger people. The provision allows for adults to be removed from home if they:

i) are suffering from grave chronic disease of being aged, infirm or physically incapacitated, are living in insanitary conditions and
ii) are unable to devote to themselves and are not receiving from other persons proper care and attention.

Again, there is very wide geographical variation in the use of Section 47 and some local authorities never use it at all.

Although community physicians, not social workers, are responsible for implementing these procedures, it is highly likely that social workers will be involved in such cases. It has been estimated that these powers are used in respect of about 200 elderly people a year (Greengross 1986:39).

Section 47 has been widely criticized, mainly on the grounds of 'the difficulty in defining insanitary conditions and of the need to protect the liberty of the individual' (Greengross 1986:42). Norman (1980:31) points out that the power 'appears to derive not so much from a wish to protect the elderly person at risk, as from the need to facilitate slum clearance or prevent infection'. This historical perspective illustrates the different elements in the concept of risk, discussed earlier. It would be naive to ignore the difficulties which the behaviour of a small number of old people poses even in today's society. Insanitary conditions may at best give grave offence to neighbours and at worst are a health hazard. Old people are no more exempt from the normal constraints on liberty than anyone else, although the risks of the provision being abused are obvious. The present legal framework, however, is unsatisfactory and needs radical reform, perhaps along the lines suggested by Greengross (1986).

Returning then to the questions posed by Rhodes; the decision to use compulsory powers may on occasion be taken to protect others, but this severe infringement on the liberty of the old person necessitates the most careful consideration of the degree and extent of the nuisance or danger posed. However, the arguments of Gilligan and Noddings, previously rehearsed, places the responsibility to care, rather than 'non-interference', as a prime ethical duty. Such a view will lead us to ask, 'What is best for this person?' The coercive act violates that value, the duty to care, if the actions taken are based on an inadequate understanding of what may be 'best' or if the views, feelings, and needs of others (neighbours, relatives, other professionals etc.) are given undue weight.

The situation in which compulsory powers are, or might be, used must assume 'incompetence' in the old person. At its tragic extreme, usually because of dementia, it will not usually be necessary to invoke compulsory powers, the person being manifestly unable to cope. Indeed, the fact that legal powers are so rarely used shows that even in less clear-cut cases persuasion is usually successful. That, of course, places a heavy moral responsibility on the workers involved to analyse the motives for such persuasion. In whose interests is the action being taken? Whose good is served by the action? These questions must be asked whether the intervention involves legal compulsion or not. There is some evidence that old people's reaction to 'relocation', whether to residential care or life with relatives, is affected, maybe even determined, by their willingness to move, and is reflected in how long they live. If that is so, it follows that there will be very few instances in which coercive powers to remove old people from home permanently should be used unless their needs have to be overridden.

Children and Young People

We turn now to children and young people. As earlier discussed, coercive powers are broadly of two kinds, those designed to protect children and young people from being harmed by their caretakers and those designed to protect society from them. Of course, the line is a fuzzy one – hence the debates about the treatment of 'the deprived' and 'the depraved' in the juvenile court system and the continuing tension between 'justice' and 'welfare' models of intervention.

The notion of 'competence' in relation to children and young people is related to age and to the maturity and capacity of the children or young people concerned. For our purposes, discussion of competence will centre upon the ability of the children or young persons to express a view on whether they wish to leave home and what weight to give to it, and whether voluntary care is an option. Such views have less relevance, of course, when the protection of society against the offender is the focus, but may be highly significant in cases of older children or young people 'at risk'. Even here, however, other factors intervene, as in the reluctance to leave a child at home who has been sexually abused whilst the abuser is still there.

We are unclear about the weight to be given, at different ages and stages, to the wishes of children and young people, and, some would say, to their rights as human beings to exercise choice over their own lives. Specifically, more work needs to be done in linking what is known about children's intellectual and moral development to their capacity to make informed choices. Without this, pronouncements on children's rights become rhetorical and unhelpful to practitioners.

However, parental competence is also an issue. This plunges us at once into the steamy waters of cultural relativism. It is obvious that assumptions about acceptable standards of child rearing are profoundly affected and, to an extent, determined by cultural and racial norms and those of social class.

Few would argue that respect for other people's child-rearing norms and practices should be absolute if they offend the wider (sometimes the host) society. For example, the practice of female circumcision would be generally condemned in Britain, and there is now a law which prohibits it. Whether a Social Services Department will now initiate action if warned of such a ritual remains to be seen. By the same token, feminist social workers working with some Muslim families will find some values and practices unacceptable. We have to recognize that there is, for us all, 'a bottom line', a set of assumptions about acceptable and unacceptable child-rearing practices on which the right, indeed duty, of the state to intervene is based. However, it is essential to analyse those assumptions and to become aware of the profound subjectivity, social and personal, involved in the assessments of other people's family lives. It is also important to seek to understand other people's value systems and so to avoid simplistic stereotyping of the 'Afro-Caribbean parents over-chastise their children' type. Only in this way can one walk the tightrope between cultural relativism and cultural arrogance. There is an ethical duty, therefore, to use available knowledge to enhance professional awareness in order to make the best judgement possible at the time.

Second, the question 'what good will the coercive act do?' reminds us of the depressing findings of so much research over the past thirty years, that life for children in care can be bleak and damaging. Thus, the decision compulsorily to remove a child must be 'a last resort'. When we break a family, we cannot predict the consequences; we have no certainty that what we shall provide is better, as the recent tragic death of a child, sexually abused at home, allegedly at the hands of his foster-father, so graphically illustrates. Decisions to intervene when children are seriously at risk at home will continue to be taken in the hope that what is provided will be better. It can only be a hope, however. In the context of our frequent failure to provide adequate alternatives to the child's parents, recent emphasis on partnerships with parents and in shared care, with a reduced emphasis on coercion, is welcome.

These issues take a rather different form in relation to delinquent children and young people. We now have ample evidence that removal from home to the type of institutional care usually provided for delinquents does not effect improvements in behaviour. Given the fact that a large number of young offenders 'grow out of it', without intervention, and that the environment in which they have been placed is expensively counter-productive, it seems self-evident that compulsory powers to remove from home should usually only be taken for the protection of society. Occasionally, the delinquency is a product of emotional disturbance rather than social rebellion and in such circumstances – as, for example, when there are very destructive family relationships – the decision to remove a delinquent child or young person from home may be genuinely believed to be in his or her best interests. This, however, is rare. More commonly, the balance between the rights of the child or young person and the rights of those against whom he or she has offended is the source of ethical tension. In such matters, there may be a difference between the social workers and the courts in the weight attributed to each. The ethical dilemma may be institutionalized and split between the parties. However, research (Vernon and Fruin 1986) indicates, surprisingly, that, despite our knowledge of the ineffectiveness of custodial care, social workers frequently recommend it. Whether this reflects a kind of fatalistic acceptance of the status quo or more deep-seated attitudes towards offenders is not clear. The proven ineffectiveness, and indeed dangers, of custodial measures suggest that

172

'taking from home' is only justified when the danger to the public is clear and substantial. Yet as offences grow more serious, the rough justice of the present system, which legitimates anger and outrage through the tariff, brings removal from home inexorably nearer. As with the adult penal system, we seem locked in a situation in which the interests of the public and those of the offender cannot be reconciled.

Since these matters are not within the jurisdiction of individual workers, ethical dilemmas over particular cases may not be experienced as acute. The ethical problem for social workers is rather more general. Can they continue to work within a system in which pressure seems continually to mount for 'tougher' measures, usually custodial, whose justification and outcome are so doubtful?

Recent research (Fisher *et al.* 1986) throws new light on the way parents see problems with their children and the role of the local authority. One finding of this study stands out. There was 'an extensive lack of concern on the part of the majority of parents over whether care had affected their rights as parents' (p. 56). 'Rather than infringement of their rights, therefore, many of these parents instead experienced a sense of relief that their request for help had been heeded. The intervention of others in their family life was positively sanctioned by some parents rather than regarded as unwarranted interference' (p. 57).

Criticism of social workers centred much more upon their failure to understand the difficulties under which the parents were labouring or their relief when children were removed. Fisher *et al.* discuss this important and interesting finding. They suggest that 'essentially, parents seem to be offering the view that rights flow from responsibility ... to care for, guide, enlighten their children .... The issue for parents became, not so much whether entry to care infringed their rights, but whether it was consonant with their conception of their responsibility to their children, whether it was "the best thing" and whether they were "in good hands"' (p. 60).

Thus, many who felt that they had failed 'on the job' did not challenge the entry of their children to care. Whilst we may wish to understand more about the fatalism and apparent rejection which the researchers encountered in these disadvantaged families, these consumer views again point us in the direction of the 'duty to care' rather than 'not to interfere'. They do not, of course, necessarily point to the use of coercive powers, since children and young people may come into care voluntarily. Fisher *et al.* fear that social workers may increasingly want to protect themselves through the laws and that 'the public care of children will be further identified with compulsory removal, and this is antipathetic to family care' (p. 122).

In Packman's (1986) view, this would be regrettable. From her research she concludes that 'being *compelled* into care carries a high risk that the admission will be hasty, ill-prepared and even traumatic'. Parents, children, and social workers will 'experience loss of control over decisions' which affect children's lives. She suggests that 'the compulsory mode of entry, and the sense of outrage which it so often presents, creates considerable difficulties for both the helpers and the helped. By comparison, voluntary reception into care is generally better managed and much more acceptable to parents' (pp. 187–8).

With children at risk, compulsory admission has conventionally been justified on the grounds of the protection of the child from its parents, the assumptions being that parents might claim their children back or children and young people might discharge themselves from care. Whilst situations do arise when the security of a legal order is needed, there is little doubt that skilful social work can often achieve a voluntary agreement. However, there are those who will see dangers of covert influence, persuasion, or even manipulation of parents who will not have the protection of the courts, especially if the possibility of care proceedings hangs over them.

Whatever route to care is taken, in the light of the combined research findings summarized by Rowe (1987) the professional ethical responsibility must be expressed through improved child-welfare practice, in the assessment, planning, and intervention, for and with children and parents, which precedes entry to care. There is no aspect of social work which more urgently requires individualized or creative justice.

Mentally Ill People

Finally, we turn to consider the exercise of compulsion to remove mentally ill people from home and admit them to

174

hospital. An extensive literature now exists on the concept of mental illness. Its relevance to, and impact on, our theme are excellently summarized by Sedgwick:

> Whatever exaggerations the more radical anti-psychiatrists and labelling-theory sociologists have engaged in, they have shown convincingly that both diagnoses and treatment measures in psychiatry are founded on ethical judgements and social demands whose content is sometimes reactionary, often controversial, and nearly always left unstated. Mental illness is a social construction; psychiatry is a social institution, incorporating the values and demands of its surrounding society.
>   ... To say that somebody is mentally ill, or to announce oneself as mentally ill, is to attach complex social meanings to acts and behaviours that in other societies, or in different contingencies within our society, would be interpreted in the light of quite different concepts.
>
> (Sedgwick 1982:25)

The sense of unease which many social workers experience in the role of 'Approved Social Workers' dealing with compulsory admissions arises in part from the influence of those to whom Sedgwick refers. The combination of the 'literature of dysfunction' concerning institutional regimes, of theories of deviance and labelling which demonstrate some of the processes by which people come to be defined as mentally ill, and of growing awareness of variations in time and between societies in the way mental illness is regarded, creates powerful negative feelings in some social workers about their role.

Another powerful influence on social workers has been the civil libertarians, to whom Sedgwick also trenchantly refers.

> The civil-libertarian ethic, in mental health as in other fields where power over the politically weak has manifest capabilities of abuse, has an honourable and indeed essential role. Nevertheless, it has the crucial defect of being unable to focus therapeutic policy on any question other than the misuse of medical power. Consequently, civil-libertarians find themselves cast in the role of a permanent reforming opposition to the main structures of authority and decision in

psychiatry. Because their voice is essentially reactive, they depend on medical practitioners to initiate and conduct treatment before they themselves can appear in the next phase of the cycle as protestors and resisters. A further move beyond this partially negative stance is, of course, open to civil-libertarians in mental health: that of a complete negation of the legitimacy of any psychiatric intervention whatever. Rather than taking confinement and ill-treatent as the misuse of therapies which are basically sound, we are bidden to see them as the normal use of an authoritarian power which is basically evil. Defensive libertarianism in the mental-health field can be pushed, in the absence of a positive programme for valid therapy, into an all-round condemnation of the psychiatric enterprise itself.

(p. 217–8)

Sedgwick suggests that we have a choice 'between the language of abuse and that of use' (p. 218). Those who write of abuse, he suggests, generally presuppose that 'there is a legitimate use of similar procedures'. Yet for others, as Szasz put it, the problem is 'not how to improve commitment but how to abolish it' (in Sedgwick, p. 218). Social workers in the statutory sector who fall into the latter category will have great difficulty in fulfilling their assigned role and are probably best out of it. However, most social workers are, at least in theory, concerned to limit abuse, in the sense of preventing unwarrantable interference with another's liberty, but also with the 'duty of care' when they encounter individuals whose distress and disturbance, whatever its origins, is intense.

As we have seen earlier, the issue of 'competence' in such cases cannot be divorced from the question of risk. Those considered likely to harm others physically present few ethical dilemmas (though the professional judgements may not be easy). No-one has 'a right' to injure another; if he or she seems likely to do so they forfeit their right, if only temporarily, to run their own lives and to stay in their own homes. In that sense, they are deemed incompetent. However, as we saw earlier, such judgements are complicated when family interaction is seen to produce disturbed behaviour in a particular member. Whilst such understanding should affect the mode of intervention adopted over a period of time, social workers involved in compulsory admission are usually involved at a point of crisis. Judgements about present risk to others must be made whatever the assessment of the underlying causes of the problem may be.

More difficult ethically are those cases in which the danger is to the person concerned, notably in cases where suicide is attempted or threatened. (However, it is often less clear-cut: anger may be directed outwards, inwards or both ways.) The right to intervene in such cases is, in general, highly problematic, in particular, of course, where a person is terminally ill or in great pain. The broader implications cannot be explored here. In relation to those defined as depressed whom the social worker is likely to encounter in the situation we are considering, it is commonly assumed that the intense despair which some experience will pass and is, to an extent, remediable. Therefore, it is agreed, it is ethically proper that we should seek to prevent a final act of self-destruction. The duty to 'save people from themselves' is commonly placed above the rights of self-determination. However, ethically, the mere act of preventing suicide is surely not enough. The social and emotional troubles which may have precipitated the attempt should also be the concern of the professionals. Sadly, these are often neglected, as Fisher *et al.* (1984:167) noted.

Fisher *et al.* (1984), in the only recent comprehensive analysis of mental health social work, raise many points which are pertinent to this discussion, although the findings have been overtaken to some extent by the introduction of Approved Social Worker training and consequent raised awareness of good mental health practice. Above all they show, especially through case examples, how complex and how 'messy' is the reality of practice in this field. Social workers are required to make judgements about cases in which they have not usually been involved beforehand (p. 163). The proportion of schizophrenic clients (about 50%) is much higher than in other forms of admission (p. 164), which may produce situations of great tension.

Social workers' views differed substantially from those of the doctors (less so when psychiatrists rather than G.P.s were involved), in more than a third of the cases studied (p. 167). For various reasons, social workers in these cases believed that compulsory admission was not necessary. This might suggest that the civil-libertarian aspect of their role, and the ethical considerations arising from that, loomed large. However, the authors' findings on the quality of individual practice are depressing:

> A request to assess for compulsory admission was regarded by workers as a distinct category of social work practice, in which they tended to set aside their wider professional concerns in favour of the more limited role of legal applicant. (p. 170)

> There was little attempt to assess whether the presence of risky behaviour was wholly the consequence of mental disorder, or evaluate risk against the normal level of risk-taking in the community at large, or the risks intrinsic to hospital admission. *This stood in marked contrast to social workers' attitudes towards the assessment of children at risk.* (p. 161: my italics)

These findings, combined with a lack of follow-up work, suggest that a kind of 'bureaucratization' of the process, in which people are categorized and thus depersonalized, has set in. The ethical implications are alarming, not least because of the factors associated with culture, race, and gender which affect judgements about mental illness as they do everything else in this field.

Of particular concern is the treatment of black people under the Mental Health Act. Some evidence on this point focuses on the police use of powers (Section 136) (Rogers and Faulkner 1987). However, the need for social workers to examine their assumptions about mental illness in those of different ethnic origins is clear. As Rack (1982) discusses, it is highly desirable that those working in this field should seek to understand more sensitively the effects of cultural and ethnic background on manifestations of mental illness. However, this understanding has to be required and used in the context of a raised awareness of racism and the ways this affects interaction between the helper and the helped.

If social workers today demonstrate a capacity for thought independent from the medical profession, and concern to protect clients from inappropriate coercion, one is reassured about the ethical development of the profession in relation to human rights. If they fail to relate general ethical principles, and their social work knowledge and skill, to the unique circumstances of individuals, social workers fail adequately to exercise their responsibility. The client is betrayed.

CONCLUSION

The argument of this chapter may be summarized as follows. A discussion of the ethical issues which arise in the use of compulsory powers focuses upon the tension between the principle that one should interfere as little as possible with another's independence and the principle (or presupposition) of 'caring', the responsibility to look after each other. This tension is related to gender, to the different priorities which men and women accord to these principles. However, given the evidence which exists of the adverse effects which result from compulsory intervention of this kind, those who accord priority to 'caring' will exercise extreme caution in using such powers. It is further argued that the tension between notions of 'creative' and 'proportional' justice is gender-related. Whilst both have a significant part to play in society, the dominance of the masculine model of proportional justice in the public domain needs to be corrected. In considering the need for compulsory intervention, there is an ethical obligation on practitioners to assess and to plan meticulously for the person concerned. We are not acting morally when the process is bureaucratized or becomes insensitive to the feelings of the individual. Attention to detail, which is the hallmark of creative justice, is at the centre of good social work practice. This is not to belittle the part played by those who pursue ideals of proportional justice, for example, through emphasis on civil liberties. It is a plea for balance, and for constructive interaction between the two.

© 1989 Olive Stevenson

Chapter Eleven

THE MORALITY OF PRIVATE SOCIAL CARE: PRIVATIZATION IN SOCIAL WORK

STUART ETHERINGTON

Social policies of the post-war consensus were based upon the notion of social citizenship. Marshall's (1964) seminal work, arguing for a level of social spending to assist participation in social citizenship which would mirror that which had been attained in political citizenship, gained acceptance in the detailed policies which followed the Beveridge Report. Whilst the development of social citizenship had been criticized, these criticisms had come from the left, who claimed that insufficient resources had been invested to ensure the full participation of all citizens. The late 1970s saw the culmination of a new set of theories from the right of British politics which questioned the very basis of social citizenship.

These trends have been well documented, but in summary they flow from the thinking of the Institute of Economic Affairs, and, to a much lesser extent, from its sister-ship the Institute of Social Affairs. In essence these ideas represented neo-Liberal thinking based on the teachings of Hayek (1944 and 1960) and Friedman (1962). They place particular emphasis on individual freedom, on competition, and on efficiency; they argue for a need to reduce the role of the state's provision of services and for a growth in private decision-making and the dominance of market philosophies. Running alongside these neo-Liberal theories, which can be said to have directly contributed to a growth in the private sector, New Right thinkers also represented another strand within Conservative thinking, in particular the emphasis placed on the responsibilities of the family and the notion of the moral responsibility of individuals to care for themselves and each other in a voluntary way. These two sets of ideas are by no means separate. Both Hayek (1960) and Nozick (1974) make reference to voluntary giving as being the main expression of welfare. They argue that the state *per se* had no power to expropriate individuals' money or wealth as far as welfare was concerned, because those individuals whose money or wealth was being taken could not be held to be responsible for the misfortunes of others for whom their money was being used. However, individuals could freely contract to give their money by charitable giving or by purchasing services for themselves.

The Social Affairs Unit (Anderson *et al.* 1981) was in many ways more constrained. Its criticism was primarily mounted at the efficiency and effectiveness of public welfare services. They argued that these services were not responsive to consumers and were populated by free-roving professionals who were subject to very little public scrutiny and whose quality was questionable.

The writings of both the Institute of Economic Affairs and the Institute of Social Affairs attack the very heart of social citizenship as embodied in public welfare solutions.

This chapter is not concerned to analyse these trends in detail. This has been done elsewhere (e.g. Wicks 1987). Rather, the chapter looks specifically at that trend of thinking which leads to neo-Liberal solutions in welfare and in particular at whether or not it is possible to develop a framework which can assess the extent to which services should be provided within either the private or the public domain. In doing this, it will draw on a body of literature which has looked at the notion of social and natural rights. It is important to do so because it is only by examining this body of theory that it will be possible to establish the extent to which theories from the New Right can legitimately hold sway in welfare and where they should be legitimately rejected.

Arguments such as these are no longer restricted to the realm of rarefied philosophical debate. They are the everyday stuff of politics and social policy. The current Conservative administration clearly displays a mistrust of statutory solutions. The growth of the private sector has continued apace under their policies. In some areas this has not been quantified, but in private residential care (which has) the growth has been astronomic. In 1982 £39 million was spent on private residential care; in 1983 this figure had increased to £104 million; in 1984 it was £200 million.

By 1986 £459 million was spent to assist residents in private residential care. There are no figures showing the amount of private social work or domiciliary care; however, the increase in private residential care alone represents a phenomenal growth in public expenditure. This growth has been demand-led, and has been assisted directly by the provision of benefits by central government.

A BASIS FOR MORALITY

Establishing moral rules or moral rights is no easy task. A starting point is to examine the different ways in which morality can be conceived to see if there are any suggestions as to how we might develop a framework by which to assess those areas of welfare which could justifiably be in the private domain.

There are essentially three ways of conceptualizing moral rights. The first is to conclude that morality does not exist because it is impossible to establish any generalizable moral rules upon which to base behaviour. Although this is difficult to refute in some circumstances, it nevertheless conflicts with our ordinary ways of thinking. If there were no morality then it would be impossible to chastise, on moral grounds, people for any form of action: this runs against our commonsense view of the world and is of limited value in examining aspects of social policy. Following a nihilistic position in relation to private care would simply mean that it wouldn't matter whether or not people were exploited in private care more than in public care, as there would be no moral way of judging one against the other. Such a position is therefore of limited value in relation to this set of arguments.

The second, and more powerful, case for the establishment of moral laws, particularly in relation to rights, is the naturalistic position.

Whether or not social rights, which underpin much of social care, are rights at all is a contentious argument. However, it has been asserted that certain forms of natural rights, which form the basis of a moral code, can be established. This argument is developed by Hart (1967) and is perhaps best summed up in his seminal essay:

Rights are possessed by individuals and these expressions reflect the conception of moral rules as not only prescribing conduct, but as forming a kind of moral code for individuals to which they are, as individuals, entitled. (1967:112)

They provide a moral justification for limiting the freedom of others. These types of moral rights, which might be termed natural, arise in two circumstances. The first is where they relate to particular types of transaction, and the second arises when the right is invoked to resist interference from somebody else. The first of these Hart terms special rights: in the main they flow from promises or contracts. That is, we have a right to claim what people promise they will do for us. This is not based on any particular moral authority but because people have conducted some form of voluntary transaction. Rights may also be accorded by a part cular individual allowing or authorizing another person to interfere in matters which, without this consent, the individual would be free to determine for himself or herself. Interestingly, this could well provide the basis of citizen advocacy.

The third source of rights identified by Hart he terms mutuality of restriction. By this he means that people who conduct some form of joint enterprise, according to rules that restrict their liberty, have a right to require similar submission from people who benefited from their own submissions. This is the basis of the structure of legal rights and duties.

In addition to these special rights – contract, the voluntary giving of rights to somebody else and mutuality of restriction – there are a number of general rights which are defensive or negative rights: resisting somebody else's sphere of activity over you, the ability to reject any coercion. These do not arise out of any particular relationship and they are not therefore specific to particular individuals. To assert this form of general right is, of course, to claim freedom of action where special rights do not afford a restriction of that action, that is, in Hart's words, 'The assertion of general rights directly invokes the principle that all men equally have the right to be free' (1967:150).

Here we have a clear group of moral rights, which are essentially a right to certain forms of freedom. These freedoms are absolute and can only be constrained by the opposing rights which it is possible to assert in particular cases. The free tests of these general moral rights which Cranston (1973) has developed are universality and paramount importance. This is important for later arguments in this chapter because it makes a clear distinction between these moral rights and social or economic rights, which may indeed not be rights at all.

Many of the traditional civil and political liberties – freedom of speech, religion, association and travel – are conceivable in a natural state. These rights require non-interference in the right holder's action. The absence of government does not mean that facilities are lacking for the right holders to undertake the appropriate actions. In other words, the traditional civil and political rights do pass the test of being imaginable in a state of nature.

There are certain moral positions which flow from a set of natural rights. These natural rights justify much of our civil and political activity. They assume that people have a certain range of freedoms which they would expect to find in nature. Having identified these 'core' natural rights, and before examining the development of private social care in relation to them, I wish now to look at the slightly less well defined area of social rights.

It is clear that social or economic rights vary over time, and it therefore becomes much more difficult to justify them as absolute moral rights. Indeed, the task is impossible if by a natural moral right we mean a moral right that could be established within a state of nature. However, Hare (1952) and Shue (1980) have, in different ways, provided some way forward in this area. Hare has argued that morality is essentially a set of principles accepted by a group of people, so that if I accept that it is wrong to do a certain thing, and enough people also agree that it is wrong thus to do, it then constitutes a moral law applicable to that society at that time. In this way it is possible to establish at least temporary claim rights, which advance or recede depending upon the prevailing view at the time. Thus, it would be possible to argue that because people are legally entitled to claim social security at this particular juncture they have a social right to income support, but that it is not a natural right because such a right could not be said to exist in nature, nor could a right to any major form of sustenance. So, on the one hand, we have a set of natural rights which are essentially rights to negative freedoms; on the other we have certain positive rights, and some might argue that these constitute moral rights which vary over time. Between these two extreme positions we have a group of theories which have been developed in order to construct a set of rights which is not dependent on the state of nature nor upon the ebb and flow of what is acceptable to the majority. This group of ideas has taken many forms. Historically it has been associated with a utilitarian viewpoint, which in crude terms asserts that there is a moral reason for doing what is most likely to promote the general welfare. Most who have advocated this position have never pretended it to be a theory of natural rights, but rather a moral framework for decision-making.

Presented with various options, it is possible to suggest that the correct course of action is that which would maximize the general welfare; indeed it could be argued that this could be used directly to contradict a position taken in relation to natural law. An example provided by Harman (1977) ably illustrates this. I am given money by a man on a desert island who asks me to give it, if he dies, to a long-lost nephew. The man subsequently dies and I am rescued. Nobody knows that I have the money. When I arrive at the mainland I discover that the nephew is rich and selfish. I could act under a contractual right of the deceased person and give the money to the nephew. Alternatively, I could apply utilitarian principles and give the money to a charity because I believe that this action would benefit the greatest number of people. This illustrates a direct conflict between the natural contractual right and the utilitarian claim of the greatest happiness of the greatest number.

Utilitarianism, however, is but one of a number of codes which have attempted to develop some idea about rights, independent of their being natural rights. Lately, considerable attention has been given to contractual theories, in particular those of John Rawls (1977). In essence, his theory is based on the notion of the likely agreed system of distribution by self-interested parties. This is the idea of the 'original position', which imagines a group of men and women who come together to form a social contract. These are men and women with ordinary tastes, talents, and ambitions, but each is temporarily ignorant of the features of his or her own personality; they must agree upon a contract before the self-awareness returns. Rawls argues that if these men and women are rational beings and act only in their own self-interest, they will choose two major principles of justice and distribution. These principles are:

1) That every person must have the largest political liberty compatible with like liberty for all.
2) That inequalities in power, wealth, income, and other forms of welfare distribution must not exist except in so far as they work to the absolute benefit of the worst-off members of society.

This position implies that people are conscious of risk. If they are risk-neutral, then social welfare will consist of the aggregation of the sum of individual welfares, which would in effect be a utilitarian position. However, assuming that people are averse to risk, then people would be prepared to forgo the prospect of some gain in order to secure for themselves a higher minimum standard. Social welfare provision would therefore give greater weight to the gains and losses of poorer members and lower weight to those of richer members. It is an important component of Rawls' second principle to ensure that any distribution works to the distinct advantage of poor sections of the community. What is forbidden, in this theory, is the imposition of losses on the rich with no gain for the poor. It is essentially an equalization formula based on a contractual theory of welfare into which self-interested partners would enter.

This position does not imply an absolute system of welfare. Many shades of welfare provision would fulfil the two sets of principles. These principles fall short of many people's egalitarian ideals. As Dworkin (1977) points out, they subordinate equality and material resources, when this is necessary, to liberty by making the demand of the first principle prior to that of the second. Nor does the theory take account of relative deprivation, because it justifies any inequality when those worse off are better off than they would be in absolute terms without the inequality. Dworkin, in his analysis of Rawls, asserts that the theory implies that individuals have the right to equal concern and respect in the design and administration of the political and social institutions that govern them. The right to equal concern and respect implied by social contract theories is by no means unproblematic, but it tends to imply a style of care rather than of welfare provided at any particular level. Clearly, no social welfare at all would imply inequalities which diminish the exercise of even the natural rights outlined previously but, at the other extreme, absolute equality in outcome of the provision of social welfare might imply a substantial erosion of individual liberty. The notion of autonomy, which is at least implied in the natural rights thesis and is certainly explicit in Rawls' theory, together with equal concern and respect in the design of social institutions, becomes of paramount importance. In a more recent essay Dworkin (1985) has argued that Rawls' thesis about the existence of rights based upon contract does not contradict utilitarian principles, but provides trump cards that can be played in order to supersede utilitarian arguments.

Weale (1983:140) argues that equal concern and respect for persons in the design of institutions can be codified into a system of procedures of fairness. He outlines five conditions:

1) The decision-maker should be authorized to make the decision.
2) The decision taken should be within the decision-maker's sphere of competence.
3) The decision should be made on relevant considerations.
4) The decision should be equitable between beneficiaries of a similar status.
5) The beneficiary's standing in the matter should be respected.

In this section of this chapter, I have suggested a three-tier framework for understanding rights. The first tier is the solid rock of natural rights, essentially rights to certain freedoms which are only restricted when there are three possible sets of counter-claims: first, that of contract, second, where rights are afforded to others without coercion, and third, mutuality of restriction.

The second tier of rights is that which flows not from natural positions but from contractual ones, of which Rawls and Dworkin represent the chief modern exponents. From their position it is possible to build a notion of procedural fairness to govern the operation of social institutions – although because these rights are 'non-natural' they may ultimately prove to be less well grounded. Even if this is not the case, one important aspect to note here is that the advancement of personal liberty and freedoms is still the primary consideration of contractual theories: in this sense they are consistent with the notion of natural freedoms.

The third aspect of the framework which I have proposed is inevitably the most challenging. It suggests that whatever is agreed by a group of people to be a moral position constitutes such a moral position, so if I believe it to be a principle and convince enough people that it is a principle, then that is sufficient. Laws thus arrived at can hardly be called unchangeable moral laws, but they may nevertheless govern behaviour and, therefore, a distributive system of welfare.

The problem in using this latter framework to examine welfare in the context of this chapter is simply that it is very difficult to assert what is right or wrong, other than to state the prevailing view of the private sector. All that could be said with reference to this latter position is that large numbers of people disagree about whether or not private care is a good or bad thing. Indeed, one of the features about the development of private care is that the number of people who ultimately claim that it is a bad thing has receded with a rapidity which must have surprised many.

THE PRIVATE SECTOR

I do not intend to restrict this argument to private residential care; although this may provide a useful illustrative example it is too restrictive a framework. By the private sector I mean any form of welfare which is provided for profit. To a certain extent this distinction starts to blur the borders between the private and the voluntary sector. Although the voluntary sector is meant to be non-profit-making one could envisage a situation where surpluses from service development in the voluntary sector are being accrued to assist in development elsewhere. Such developments can only serve to blur the distinction in the terms which are being used within this chapter. The purpose of this section of the chapter is not to document the growth of the private sector but rather to examine the private sector in the context of the moral framework that has been developed earlier.

An exposition by Gilbert (1983) has considered the developing private sector by reference to two criteria: that of moral opposition to private care, and that of opposition on the grounds of efficiency. He considers moral opposition to the private sector only briefly. In the paragraph which refers to it, he quotes

188

Utting and Mendelsohn as his two primary sources. Each of these sources has one thing in common, i.e., the moral objection to the private sector is grounded in the notion that the public conscience is disturbed more by the intrusion of pecuniary interests into spheres of service traditionally associated with family duty than by the fact of profit being made from vital services – which in any case occurs regularly in the market economy. Altruism and love, therefore, are the moral grounds for opposition to the private sector. This may be true, but this chapter argues that we perhaps need to look at the private sector in relation to a more developed framework of moral principles. However, Gilbert's book is useful in another sense, for the greater part of it considers the efficiency arguments in relation to private care and concludes, from an examination of empirical data, that 'It is important not to determine the universally superior form of organization but to understand the particular conditions under which profit- or non-profit-oriented service may be the most suitable provider of social services' (1983:2).

He goes on to suggest four conditions that might bear on the choice between profit-making and non-profit-making providers for certain social services. These conditions are the nature of the service, the client's degree of competence, whether or not the service is invested with coercive powers, and whether or not there is scope for potent regulatory environments for social service agencies. Most of these arguments are concerned directly with the efficiency of providing services from a particular basis, although some of them are more rooted in the notion of morality, particularly those conditions which relate to coercion and client competence.

To my mind, the efficiency argument is less important that the moral one. It should be possible to argue from the moral framework set out above that some areas of care could be provided either by the public or private sector by reference to certain key principles. If this were possible, then it would make the debate about whether or not services should be provided via profit- or non-profit-making service a little more sophisticated than is currently the case.

Let us then return to the framework that we set out earlier, and, first, to the framework of natural rights. These are essentially to do with freedoms, but it will be recalled that there were certain circumstances in which freedoms might be curtailed. Let us look at each one of these in turn.

As far as contract is concerned, freedom of action is curtailed by the implied or explicit contract between two or more parties who are free to engage in contractual arrangements. This is relevant to private care. There are a number of issues which we must consider when assessing this. The first is in relation to vulnerability; linked with this is the notion of competency. Are vulnerable people, whether they be mentally ill, mentally handicapped, elderly, or physically handicapped, in a position freely to enter into contracts with private proprietors? The evidence is clearly that they are not perfectly competent: often decisions about entry into residential care or the receipt of other private services are negotiated between the relatives of the client and the proprietors without reference to the consumers themselves. So in many ways the notion of a contract freely entered into is somewhat suspect. But does this differ in any way from the statutory services? In some ways it may. One of the developments which has been of the most significance in relation to private care is the by-passing of any assessment of alternatives by other professionals. It is difficult to be sure exactly what professionals were doing at the point of entry into various public resources, but in theory at least they were meant to be assessing the extent of social need. But they were also attempting to ensure, in the best practice, that the consumer was readily entering into some contractual agreement with the public sector. This, however, in practice was far from satisfactory. One is forced to say that a notion of contract should be an important part of welfare, particularly if one considers a natural rights position to be at the core of welfare provision. This is often not respected, in either the private or the public sector, and remedies to ensure the effective implementation of contract arrangements between consumer and provider are as necessary in the public as they are in the private sector. In short, there is little to demonstrate that the private sector is any worse at this than the public sector was. This, of course, is not an argument for abandoning the notion of contract, but it is an argument against discriminating between the public and private sector on this count alone.

The notion of contract, particularly with reference to contractual arrangements where the person is vulnerable, or not competent to make decisions, brings us to the second area of natural rights, that of voluntarily giving rights to another. In welfare terms, this might be conceptualized as citizen advocacy, or delegating authority to act to a professional. Is the private sector any less willing to engage in the provision of an advocate or agent than the public sector? Again, we are forced to conclude that there is very little evidence that the public sector is engaged in advocacy to any great degree, except in isolated examples like the Mental Health Act Commission, although a more residual strategic role concerned with monitoring care might alter this. The existence of a code of practice and a legislative environment may provide a better foundation for the development of advocacy services than that which currently exists in relation to statutory services.

However, there are balancing factors in relation to this. At the very least statutory care is subject to some review, however removed, by local authority members who are publicly accountable. They will, on occasion, visit establishments and could, in certain circumstances, act as advocates for individual consumers, although it must be admitted that this happens rarely. There is little evidence that the public sector is particularly good at advancing the notion of advocacy, although this may change as the Disabled Persons Act is slowly brought into force. So, in summary, there appears again to be no real distinction between public and private sector here, other than the implicit contract that there might be in allowing an elected member of a local authority or a member of a health authority to act on your behalf. This is admittedly a rather tenuous application of rights in relation to either private or public care.

Finally, we have mutuality of restriction – that is, the assertion that people's rights can be restricted when they can be held to have benefitted by the submission of others. A good example, of course, is the area of political obligation. But is this similarly true in relation to private care? Clearly not. For example, the restrictions that I undergo in choosing state care cannot be held to be obligations on others to give up private care, because my choice of state care has not benefitted them and I cannot therefore require their submission. There may be some exceptions to this rule. For example, it could be argued that in using state care in a large way, groups of people ensure that workers are trained to provide that care. Thus it follows that people may be receiving a service within the private sector from those who have received their training to service the public sector. In these circumstances I could legitimately place an obligation on them to use state care and give up private care. This, of course, assumes that large numbers of people working within the private sector are indeed trained in the state sector, and this may be increasingly true in both health and social services. It is not true, however, in the provision of some services, such as psychotherapy. Indeed, in the United States this argument is used as a justification for social workers continuing to participate in the private sector, the reason being that they have not been trained by the public sector and therefore service recipients are under no obligation to use the public sector. However, because in this country significant numbers of private-sector workers are trained by the statutory sector then the public-sector workers should be compensated by a levy on the private sector based on the number of publicly trained staff employed.

So, in relation to the restrictions on the natural rights position, there appears to be no reason by reference to the normal conditions for the waiving of natural rights to assume that the private sector should have a diminished role in relation to the welfare of citizens. The fact that others may not have such rights does not in itself create a moral condition where we are obliged to extend the public sector at the cost of the private sector. But, of course, in reality it is not even as simple as this, for much private care is publicly funded: all that has happened is that the supplier has changed whilst the pay-master has remained the same. Although at the time of writing this is restricted mainly to the residential care sector, there is no reason why similar arguments could not be advanced in relation to domiciliary and day care; indeed, the next ten years may see quite large-scale growth in these areas.

So far we have looked at the principles of natural rights and concluded that, with some exceptions, there is no intrinsic reason why those who are attempting to take a moral stance based on these principles should necessarily oppose private care. But what of the principles based on contractarian views? Does

the operation of private care run counter to notions of procedural fairness which might be embedded in a (less well
established) view based on an acceptance of social rights? To
look at the first question first, we are guided by the principles
which follow from Rawls' (1977) original contract. These, as
readers may recall, suggest that there are two guiding principles
which follow from the original position: first, each person
participating in a practice, or affected by it, has an equal right to
the most extensive liberty compatible with a like liberty for all;
second, inequalities are arbitrary unless it is reasonable to expect
that they will work out for everyone's advantage, and that the
positions and offices to which they are attached, or from which
they may be gained, are open to all. Rawls suggests that these
principles express justice as a complex of three ideas: liberty,
equality, and reward for services contributing to the common
good. The burden of proof lies on those who would depart from
the principle of equal liberty.

Clearly, the existence of private care does not offend this
principle: the availability of private care does not in itself restrict
liberty. Publicly financed private care, it could be argued,
extends the liberties of individuals and can in fact create a like
liberty for a large number of people. The fact that at the
moment large numbers of the population can only choose
residential care is not in itself a damning indictment of the
private sector, but of the way in which the public subsidy system
operates.

The second principle, which is subsidiary to the first, is
a consideration of equality of access and, as Dworkin has
demonstrated, of equal concern and respect. Will inequalities
engendered by private care work out to everyone's advantage?
There is nothing to suggest that they will not. In policy terms
they could lead the public sector into a position to develop
innovative schemes or, perhaps more effectively, to monitor and
influence the development of social care untrammelled by the
need to confront their own internal problems. Private care is, in
a very real way, open to all because of the existence of a public
financing system. It is open to all in a much more real way now
than it was when residential care only existed in the public
sector. For when this was true, various gate-keepers stood in the
way of individuals who may have actually wanted good-quality
residential care.

But what of the equality of concern and respect? It has been argued that this is at the basis of social citizenship, and that it implies an active consumer of welfare services who is able to exercise choice, to take risks, to participate, and to be afforded certain rights and responsibilities. Is there anything implicit in the private sector which runs counter to this? It may be argued that economic concerns lead to the provision of a scale of resources which are not conducive to choice, risk-taking, and participation. Large-scale residential facilities may not present positive images of disabled people which would be in accordance with equality of concern and respect. But on the other hand, experience of private residential care has tended to suggest that it scores particularly highly on positive images of homeliness and ordinariness. So it is by no means clear that even on the rarefied considerations of equality of concern and respect the private sector scores particularly badly.

Finally, it is important to judge the private sector by reference to rules of procedural fairness. As I have suggested earlier in this chapter, Weale (1983) characterizes procedural fairness by reference to five principles, which I shall restate here. The first is that the administrator responsible for making a decision on benefits should be duly authorized to make the decision. Clearly, the administrator, in this case, is the proprietor: they are authorized to make the decision by reference to the fact that they run homes which have been registered by the local authority. Even in the less well established provision of domiciliary or day care, where no registration is required, the authorization is implied by the contract between the consumer and the provider. It may well be that as the private sector grows into these latter areas, some form of publicly accountable authorization will have to be necessary, particularly in the area of provision of food-stuffs through private meals on wheels. So, in the first condition there is clearly an authorization to the administrator.

The second condition relates to competence, that is the decision taken must be within the administrator's competence. By this Weale means a possibility of referring to an institutional set of rules which entitle the administrator to make certain decisions. The example cited by Weale is that of social workers using receptionists to deter clients instead of themselves explaining the situation. Is there anything here in the private sector that offends this procedural fairness test? In so far as administrators have already agreed to be authorized to make the decisions, they may be more directly concerned with the ability to pay as a major criterion. It may also mean that the spheres of service are more closely defined. For example, there are many circumstances in private care where a tariff of charges is given to the resident, which may include additional charges for other services such as chiropody and hairdressing. By defining the area of competence in this way, an appeal to some contract-based procedural fairness is deliberately being set out, and in many ways this may be a more productive relationship – one indeed which could be extended to private social work.

The third condition set out by Weale does perhaps cause more problems. It is that decision-makers must act only on relevant considerations. In the private sector, where there is no public scrutiny of entry into particular services, it is easy to conceive of situations where proprietors make decisions about entry into care on a number of criteria which are not directly relevant to the decision. Thus, particular homes may take a particular type of less dependent client, or a client of a particular religious persuasion, in circumstances which could be held to reflect a certain bias in the desire for a type of consumer which included irrelevant considerations.

Weale's fourth condition relates to treating cases equitably, that is treating like cases in a like way. These are often special cases of the third consideration, and again with the increased power of proprietors, who lack public scrutiny, it may well be that they do not treat like cases in like ways. This introduces an inevitable sense of preference or arbitrariness in the negotiations between consumer and supplier which is characteristic of commercial relationships based on spending power rather than on the assessment of need. Private institutions are not required to eradicate sources of bias.

The fifth consideration outlined by Weale is that administrators should recognize the beneficiary's standing. That is, potential recipients should be able to acquire relevant information about the benefit being allocated and should be aware of their rights and obligations under the relevant procedures. There is some evidence that the private sector has in fact pioneered work in this area, with the best homes being much better at providing information, detailing contracts and providing statements of rights and obligations far in advance of what many consumers would expect to find in the public sector. Not all of the private sector would score highly in this respect, but there may be more of a tendency for this to happen in a sector which is more explicitly regulated.

Whilst the examples drawn here are from residential services there is no reason why the arguments cannot be extended both to domiciliary care and to social work.

Table 1 summarizes the comparisons we have been making between the private and the public sector.

Table 1

	Private	*Statutory*
Natural Rights		
Contract	Vulnerability with little accountability Limited help from advocates	Greater accountability through public scrutiny Limited help from advocates
Mutuality of Restriction	Problems with use of workers where the state has paid for training	
Social Rights		
Freedom of Action	Encouragement of choice if subsidy to consumer exists	Leads to competitive stance of regulating
Equality of Concern and Respect	Tendency to large units. Possible reduction in positive image	Ghettoization of public facilities
Procedural Fairness		
Responsibility for Decision	Contract based and clear	Often unclear
Competence	Perhaps greater clarity of responsibility defined by tariffs	Greater levels of professional training
Relevance of Criteria	Supplier can choose 'easier' groups	No choice from supplier. A ghettoed service
Equity	Major bias based on cost criteria	More moves to eradicate bias
The Active Recipient	Contracts may be clearer. More active consumer	Residual consumer

So what conclusions can we arrive at about the relationship between morality, rights, and the private sector? I have argued that the notion of morality and rights is by no means unproblematic. I have put forward a framework which suggests various orders of rights, starting with the strongest, or natural rights position, and moving to the weakest, or 'accepted' view of rights. I have argued that the hardest view of first-order natural rights does not run counter to the existence of the private sector. It is compatible with the notion of liberty and, particularly if advocates were appointed, would indeed be consistent with the application of natural rights by the able adult. As far as the weaker definitions of rights are concerned, private care does not offend all the conditions of procedural fairness and indeed scores higher than the public sector on some. This implies not only that it is desirable to accept a pragmatic response to the private sector on efficiency grounds, as Gilbert (1983) has argued, but also that it may be possible to argue pragmatically for the acceptance of aspects of private care on moral grounds. In short, the private sector may have something to learn from the public sector, but the converse may also be true.

This chapter has considered the extent to which notions of natural and social rights can be used to assess the appropriate balance between public and private welfare. In the recent past the dominance of public welfare solutions has given way to a battle of ideological slogans – 'public good' and 'private bad', or vice versa. This chapter has suggested that there are ways, in terms both of efficiency and of morality, in which it is possible to assess those areas of welfare which should be exclusively public, those which should be exclusively private, and those areas where there is an option. Making assessments either on efficiency or moral grounds as to the appropriate suppliers of welfare is likely to be crucial in the post-Thatcherite era. It is important for social workers and policy makers alike that they have a framework to refer to, in terms of both efficiency and morality. This chapter has attempted to provide such a framework.

REFERENCES

Adamson, J. and Warren, C. (1983) *Welcome to St. Gabriel's Family Centre*, London: Children's Society.

Ainsworth, F. and Fulcher, L. C. (eds) (1981) *Group Care for Children*, London: Tavistock.

Aldgate, J. (1980) 'Identification of factors influencing children's length of stay in care', in Triseliotis, J. (ed.) *New Developments in Foster Care and Adoption*, London: Routledge and Kegan Paul.

Algie, J. and Miller, C. (1976) 'Deciding Social Services Priorities', *Social Work Today* 6(22):678–82; and 6(23): 717–20.

Allan, G. (1983) 'Informal Networks of Care: Issues raised by Barclay', *British Journal of Social Work* 13:417–33.

Anderson, D. (1982) *Social Work and Mental Handicap*, London: Macmillan.

Anderson, D., Late, J., and Marsland, D. (1981) *Breaking the Spell of the Welfare State*, London: Social Affairs Unit.

Appleyard, J. and Maiden, J. (1979) 'Multidisciplinary Teams', *British Medical Journal* 4:1305–7.

Austin, J. (1975) *How to do things with Words*, Oxford: Clarendon Press.

Baier, A. (1985) *Posture of the Mind*, London: Methuen.

Baier, K. and Rescher, N. (eds) (1969) *Values and the Future*, New York: The Free Press.

Bailey, R. and Brake, M. (1975) *Radical Social Work*, London: Edward Arnold.

Bamford, T. (1982) 'From Paternalism to Partnership', *Community Care* 415:1.

Bamford, T. (1986) 'Unresolved issues: A United Kingdom Perspective', *British Journal of Social Work* 16 Supplement: 169–72.

Barclay Committee (1982) *Social Workers: Their Role and Tasks*, London: National Institute for Social Workers/Bedford Square Press.

Bartlett, H. M. (1970) *The Common Base of Social Work Practice*, New York: National Association of Social Workers.

BASW – *See* British Association of Social Workers.

Bayley, M., Seyd, R., and Tennant, A. (1989) *Local Health and Welfare: is partnership possible*, Aldershot, Gower.

Bean, P. (1980) *Compulsory Admissions to Mental Hospitals*, London: Wiley and Sons.

The Beckford Report (1985) (Report of the committee of inquiry into the death of Jasmine Beckford) *A Child in Trust*, London: London Borough of Brent.

Beehler, R. (1978) *Moral Life*, Oxford: Basil Blackwell.

Beiner, R. (1983) *Political Judgement*, London: Methuen.

Bennett, B. (1983) 'A view from the field', in Sinclair, I. and Thomas, D. (eds) *Perspectives on Patch*, London: National Institute for Social Work.

Bennett, J. (1977) 'Multidisciplinary Teams', *British Medical Journal* 4:1584–5.

Benton, T. (1982) 'Realism, Power and Objective Interests', in Graham, K. (ed.) *Contemporary Political Philosophy*, Cambridge: Cambridge University Press.

Beresford, P. (1984) *Patch in Perspective, Decentralizing and Democratizing Social Services*, London: Battersea Community Action.

Beresford, P. and Croft, S. (1986) *Whose Welfare: Private Care or Public Service?*, Brighton: Lewis Cohen Urban Studies Centre.

Beresford, P. and Lyons, K. (1986) 'Training Focus', *Social Services Insight* 1(9):18–19.

Berger, J. (1969) *A Fortunate Man*, Harmondsworth: Penguin.

Berlin, I. (1969) 'Two concepts of liberty', in McDermott, F. E. (ed.) (1975) *Self-Determination in Social Work*, London: Routledge and Kegan Paul.

Berliner, H. and Salmon, J. W. (1980) 'The Holistic Alternative to Scientific Medicine: History and Analysis', *International Journal of Health Services* 10 (1):133–47.

Berridge, D. (1985) *Children's Homes*, Oxford: Basil Blackwell.

Berry, J. (1975) *Daily Experience in Residential Life*, London: Routledge and Kegan Paul.

Bettelheim, B. (1950) *Love is not enough*, New York: Free Press.

Biestek, F. P. (1961) *The Casework Relationship*, London: Allen and Unwin.

Birchall, D. (1982) 'Family Centres', *Concern* 43:16–20.

Black, Sir D. (1984) 'Iconoclastic Ethics', *Journal of Medical Ethics* 10(4):179–82.

Black, D. and Subotsky, F. (1982) 'Medical Ethics and Child Psychiatry', *Journal of Medical Ethics* 8 (1):5–8.

Black, J., Bowl, R., Burns, D., Critcher, C., Grant, G., and Stockford, D. (1983) *Social Work in Context: A Comparative Study of Three Social Services Teams*, London: Tavistock.

Blum, L. (1973) 'Deceiving, hurting and using', in Montefiore, H. (ed.) *Philosophy and Personal Relations*, London: Routledge and Kegan Paul.

Bonnington Report (1984) Surrey: Social Care Association.

Booth, T. (1985) *Home Truths*, Aldershot: Gower.

Booth, T., Melotte, C., Phillips, D., Pritlove, A., Barritt, A., and Lightup, R. (1985) 'Psychiatric crises in the community: collaboration and the 1983 Mental Health Act', in Horobin, G. (ed.) (1985) *Responding to Mental Illness*, London: Kogan Page.

Bowlby, E. J. M. (1953) *Child Care and the Growth of Love*, London: Pelican.

Brearly, P., Hall, F., Gutridge, P., Jones, G., and Roberts, G. (1980) *Admission to Residential Care*, London: Tavistock.

British Association of Social Workers (1975) *A Code of Ethics for Social Workers*, Birmingham: BASW Publications.

British Association of Social Workers (1980) *Clients are Fellow Citizens*, Birmingham: BASW Publications.

British Association of Social Workers (1983) *Effective and Ethical Recording*, Birmingham: BASW Publications.

Brook, J. A. (1973) 'How to treat persons as persons', in Montefiore, H. (ed.) *Philosophy and Personal Relations*, London: Routledge and Kegan Paul.

Browning, R. C. 'Bishop Blougram's Apology', in Pettigrew, J. (ed.) (1981) *Robert Browning 1812–1889: The Poems vol. 1*, Harmondsworth: Penguin.

Bruce, M. (1968) *The Coming of the Welfare State*, London: Batsford.

Butler, J., Bow, I. and Gibbons, J. S. (1978), 'Task-centred casework in marital problems', *British Journal of Social Work* 8(4)393–410.

Carrick, P. (1985) *Medical Ethics in Antiquity*, Dordrecht: Reidel.

CCETSW (1987) *Paper 20.6*, London: Central Council for Education and Training in Social Work.

CCETSW (1973) *Residential Work is Part of Social Work* (Discussion paper 3), London: Central Council for Education and Training in Social Work.

CCETSW (1988) *Statement of Minimum Requirements of the Social Worker at the Point of Qualification* (Paper 20.9), London: Central Council for Education and Training in Social Work.

CCETSW (1976) *Values in Social Work* (Paper 13), London: Central Council for Education and Training in Social Work.

Cheetham, J. (1976) 'Pregnancy in the Unmarried: The Continuing Dilemmas for Social Policy and Social Work', in Halsey, A. H. (ed.) *Traditions of Social Policy*, Oxford: Basil Blackwell.

Child Care Act (1980) London: HMSO.

Children Act (1980) London: HMSO.

Children and Young Persons Act (1969) London: HMSO.

Church of England Board for Social Responsibility (1986) *Not Just for the Poor: Christian Perspectives on the Welfare State*, London: Church House Publishing.

Clark, C. L. with Asquith, S. (1985) *Social Work and Social Philosophy*, London: Routledge and Kegan Paul.

Clifford, D. (1982) 'Philosophy and Social Work', *Radical Philosophy* 31 Summer:23–6.

Cloke, C. (1983) *Old Age Abuse in the Domestic Setting*, London: Age Concern England.

Clough, R. (1981) *Old Age Homes*, London: George Allen and Unwin.

Cohen, R. (1982) *Whose File is it Anyway?*, London: National Council for Civil Liberty.

Collier, A. (1984) 'Milton Fisk. Marxism and Ethics', *Radical Philosophy* 36 Spring:20–6.

Corrigan, P. and Leonard, P. (1978) *Social Work Practice under Capitalism*, London: Macmillan.

Cox, D. and McArdle, I. (1987) *The Druids Heath Experience*, Birmingham: Birmingham Polytechnic.

Cranston, M. (1973) *What Are Human Rights?*, London: Bodley Head.

Crawford, R. (1980) 'Healthism and the Medicalization of Everyday Life', *International Journal of Health Services* 10 (3):365–87.

Crellin, E., Kellmer Pringle, M. L. and West P. (1971) *Born Illegitimate*, Slough: NFER.

Culver, C. and Gert, B. (1982) *Philosophy in Medicine*, Oxford: Oxford University Press.

Daniels, J. (1985) *Just Health Care*, Cambridge: Cambridge University Press.

Davies, M. (1985) *The Essential Social Worker (second edition)*, Aldershot: Gower, Community Care.

Davis, A. (1981) *The Residential Solution*, London: Tavistock.

Davis, L. (1980) 'Sex and the Residential Setting', in Walton, R. G. and Elliot, D. (eds) *Residential Care*, Oxford: Pergamon.

De'Ath, E. (1985) *Self-help and family centres: a current initiative in helping the community*, London: National Children's Bureau.

Dennis, S. (1981) *What are family centres?*, London: London Borough of Lambeth.

Department of the Environment (1977) *Housing Policy: A Consultation Document*, London: HMSO.

Determination of Needs Act (1941) London: HMSO.

De Wachter, M. (1976) 'Interdisciplinary Teamwork', *Journal of Medical Ethics* 2 (2):52–7.

Dharamsi, F., Edmonds, G., Filkin, E., Headley, C., Jones, P., Kyprianou, P., Naish, M., Scott, I., Smith, E., Smith, H. and Williams, J. (1979) *Caring for Children*, Ilkley: Owen Wells.

DHSS (1988) *A National Survey of Family Centres Run by Local Authorities*, London: Social Services Inspectorate.

DHSS (1986) *Decision-making in Child Care*, London: HMSO.

Doel, M. and Lawson, B. (1986) 'Open records: the client's right to partnership', *British Journal of Social Work* 16 (4):407–30.

Downie, R. S. and Loudfoot, E. M. (1978) 'Aim, skill and role in social work', in Timms, N. and Watson, D. (eds) *Philosophy in Social Work*, London: Routledge and Kegan Paul.

Downie, R. S. and Telfer, E. (1980) *Caring and Curing*, London: Methuen.

Downie, R. S. and Telfer, E. (1969) *Respect for Persons*, London: George Allen and Unwin.

Dworkin, R. (1979) 'Paternalism', in Laslett, P. and Fishkin, J. (eds) *Philosophy, Politics and Society*, Oxford: Basil Blackwell.

Dworkin, R. (1985) 'Rights as Trumps' in Waldron, J. (ed.) *Theories of Rights*, Oxford: Oxford University Press.

Dworkin, R. (1977) *Taking Rights Seriously*, London: Duckworth.

Emmet, D. (1979) *The Moral Prism*, London: Macmillan.

Etherington, S. (1986) 'Essays discussing social work and citizenship', *Social Work Today* 18 (14):6.

Etherington, S. and Parker, C. (1986) *Unpublished paper to Social Services Inspectorate Conference.*

Finch, J. (1985) 'A Response to Robert Harris "End Points and Starting Points"', *Critical Social Policy* 4 (3):123–6.

Finch, J. (1984) 'Community Care: developing non-sexist alternatives', *Critical Social Policy* 3 (3) Spring:6–18.

Fisher, M., Marsh, P., Phillips, D., Sainsbury, E. (1986) *In and Out of Care. The Experiences of Children, Parents and Social Workers*, London: Batsford.

Fisher, M., Newton, C., Sainsbury, E. (1984) *Mental Health Social Work Observed*, London: George Allen & Unwin.

Flathman, R. (1976) *The Practice of Rights*, Cambridge: Cambridge University Press.

Friedman, M. (1962) *Capitalism and Freedom*, Chicago: University of Chicago Press.

Fuller, R. and Stevenson, O. (1983) *Policies, Programmes and Disadvantage*, London: Heinemann.

Garton, N. R. and Otto, H. A. (1964) *The Development of Theory and Practice in Social Casework*, Springfield, Illinois: Charles C. Thomas.

Gauthier, D. (1986) *Morals by Agreement*, Oxford: Oxford University Press.

Gilbert, N. (1983) *Capitalism and the Welfare State*, Yale: Yale University Press.

Giller, H. and Morris, A. (1981) *Care and Discretion*, London: Burnett Books.

Giller, H. and Rutter, M. (1983) *Juvenile Delinquency: Trends and Perspectives*, Harmondsworth: Penguin.

Gilligan, C. (1982) *In a Different Voice: Psychological theory and women's development*, Cambridge, Massachusetts: Harvard University Press.

Gilligan, C. (1977) 'In a Different Voice: Women's Conception of Self and Morality', *Harvard Educational Review* 47 (4):481–516.

Gillon, R. (1985) 'Autonomy and Consent', in Lockwood, M. ed., *Moral Dilemmas in Medicine*, Oxford: Oxford Univers ty Press.

Gobell, A. (1980) 'Social Learning Theory in Residential Care', in Walton, R. G. and Elliot, D., *Residential Care*, Oxford: Pergamon.

Goldberg, E. M. and Sinclair, I. (1984) *Family Support Exercise: Research Report*, London: National Institute for Social Work.

Goldberg, E. M. and Stanley, J. S. (1979) 'A task-centred approach to probation', in King, J. (ed.) *Pressures and Changes in the Probation Service*, Cambridge: Institute of Criminology.

Goldberg, E. M., Walker, D., and Robinson, J. (1977) 'Exploring the task-centred casework method', *Social Work Today* 9 (2):9–14.

Goldberg, E. M. and Warburton, R. W. (1979) *Ends and Means in Social Work*, London: Allen and Unwin.

Gostin, L. (1976) *A Human Condition*, London: Mind.

Greengross, S. (1986) *The Law and Vulnerable Elderly People*, London: Age Concern England.

Griffin, J. (1986) *Well Being*, Oxford: Clarendon Press.

Guay, J. (1986) *The Local Community Service Centres: The Quebec Experience in Decentralization*, Decentralization of Public Services Seminar, Brighton: 27–30 May 1986.

Hadley, R., Dale, P., and Sills, P. (1984) *Decentralizing Social Services: A Model for Change*, London: Bedford Square Press.

Hadley, R. and Hatch, S. (1981) *Social Welfare and the Failure of the State*, London: Allen and Unwin.

Hadley, R. and McGrath, M. (1984) *When Social Services are Local*, London: Allen and Unwin.

Halmos, P. (1949) 'The Training of Social Workers and the Teaching of Psychology', *Social Work* 6 (1):251–8.

Hamilton, G. (1946) *Principles of Social Case Recording*, New York: Columbia University Press.

Hamilton, G. (1940) *Theory and Practice of Social Casework*, New York: Columbia University Press.

Hamilton, G. (1951) *Theory and Practice of Social Casework* (second edition), New York: Columbia University Press.

Hampshire, S. (1983) *Morality and Conflict*, Oxford: Blackwell.

Hare, R. M. (1963) *Freedom and Reason*, Oxford: Oxford University Press.

Hare, R. M. (1986) 'Health', *Journal of Medical Ethics* 12 (4):174–81.

Hare, R. M. (1981) *Moral Thinking*, Oxford: Oxford University Press.

Hare, R. M. (1952) *The Language of Morals*, Oxford: Oxford University Press.

Harman, G. (1977) *The Nature of Morality*, Oxford: Oxford University Press.

Harris, J. (1985) *The Value of Life*, London: Routledge and Kegan Paul.

Hart, H. L. A. (1967) 'Are There Any Natural Rights?', in Quinton, A. (ed.) *Political Philosophy*, Oxford: Oxford University Press.

Hasler, J. (1984) *Family Centres: different expressions same principles*, London: Children's Society.

Hastings, A., Fadiman, J., and Gordon, J. (eds) (1981) *Health for the Whole Person*, New York: Bantam.

Hayek, F. A. (1960) *The Constitution of Liberty*, London: Routledge and Kegan Paul.

Hayek, F. A. (1944) *The Road to Serfdom*, London: Routledge and Kegan Paul.

Heraud, B. J. (1970) *Sociology and Social Work*, Oxford: Pergamon Press.

Holder, D. and Wardle, M. (1981) *Teamwork and the Development of the Unitary Approach*, London: Routledge and Kegan Paul.

Holman, R. (1975) 'Unmarried Mothers. Social Deprivation and Child Separation', *Policy and Politics* 3 (4):25–41.

Hoskins, J. (1986) 'Still Wanted: A Strategy for Prosperity', *The Times* October 22:16

Hospers, J., (1950) 'Free-Will and Psycho-analysis', in Sellars, W. and Hospers, J., *Readings in Ethical Theory*, Englewood Cliffs, New Jersey: Prentice-Hall.

Hudson, B. L. and Macdonald, G. M. (1986) *Behavioural Social Work*, London: Macmillan.

Huntington, J. (1981) *Social Work and General Medical Practice*, London: Allen and Unwin.

Illich, I. (1977) *Limits to Medicine*, London: Boyars.

Illich, I., Zola, I. K., McKnight, J., Caplan, J., and Shaiken, H. (1977) *Disabling Professions*, London: Marion Boyars.

Jenson, G. and L. (1978) 'Reassuring reviews', *Community Care* 234:31.

Jones, K., Brown, J., and Bradshaw, J. (1978) *Issues in Social Policy*, London: Routledge and Kegan Paul.

Jordan, B. (1975) 'Is the client a fellow citizen?' *Social Work Today* 6 (15):471–5.

The Karen Spencer Inquiry (1976) Derbyshire County Council. Derbyshire Area Health Authority.

Kelly, D. (1987) 'Resource centres as centres of excellence', *Social Work Today* 18 (33):20.

Kennedy, I. (1983) *The Unmasking of Medicine*, London: Granada.

Kohlberg, L. (1981) *The Philosophy of Moral Development*, London: Harper & Row.

Konrad, G. (1976) *The Caseworker*, London: Heinemann.

Kotarba, J. (1983) 'The Social Control Function of Holistic Healthcare in Bureaucratic Settings', *Journal of Health and Social Behaviour* 24 (3):275–88.

Kushlick, A. and Blunden, R. (1974) *Proposals for the Setting up and Evaluation of an Experimental Service for the Elderly*, Winchester: Health Care Evaluation Research Team, Wessex Regional Health Authority.

Kushner, T. (1981) 'Doctor–Patient Relationships in General Practice', *Journal of Medical Ethics* 7 (3):128–31.

Lane, D. and White, K. (1980) *Why Care?*, London: Residential Care Association.

Leach, E. (1975) 'Society's Expectations of Health', *Journal of Medical Ethics* 1 (2):85–9.

Lee, P. and Pithers, D. (1980) 'Radical residential care: Trojan horse or non-runner?', in Brake, M. and Bailey, M. (eds) *Radical Social Work Practice*, London: Edward Arnold.

Leighton, N. (1983) 'Patch in Perspective', in Sinclair, I. and Thomas, D. (eds) *Perspectives on Patch*, London: National Institute for Social Work.

Leighton, N., Stalley, R., and Watson, D. (1982) *Rights and Responsibilities*, London: Community Care, Heinemann.

Levitt, R. (1980) *The People's Voices in the NHS*, London: King Edward's Hospital Fund.

Lindop Committee (1978) *Report of the Committee on Data Protection (Cmnd 7341)*, London: HMSO.

Line, B. F. (1980) 'Resident Participation – a Consumer View', in Walton, R. G. and Elliot, D. (eds) *Residential Care*, Oxford: Pergamon.

Lockwood, M. (1985) *Moral Dilemmas in Medicine*, Oxford: Oxford University Press.

Lonsdale, S., Webb, A., Briggs, T. (eds) (1980) *Teamwork in the Personal Social Services and Health Care*, London: Croom Helm.

Lukes, S. (ed.) (1986) *Power*, Oxford: Basil Blackwell.

McCarthy, M. (1986) *Campaigning for the Poor*, London: Croom Helm.

McDermott, F. E. (ed.) (1975) *Self-Determination in Social Work*, London: Routledge and Kegan Paul.

McDonald, R., Qureshi, H., and Walker, A. (1984) 'Sheffield Shows the Way', *Community Care* 534:28–30.

MacIntyre, A. (1967) *A Short History of Ethics*, London: Routledge and Kegan Paul.

MacIntyre, A. (1985) *After Virtue* (second edition), London: Duckworth.

MacIntyre, A. (1971) *Against the Self Images of the Age*, London: Duckworth.

McKeown, T. (1979) *The Role of Medicine*, Oxford: Basil Blackwell.

McVeigh, J. (1982) *Gaskin*, London: Jonathan Cape.

Mandell, B. (1973) *Where are the Children?*, New York: Lexington Books.

Maple, F. (1977) *Shared Decision-making*, Beverly Hills: Sage Publications.

Marsden, D. (1969) *Mothers Alone*, London: Allen Lane.

Marshall, T. H. (1963) 'Citizenship and social class', in *Sociology at the Cross Roads and Other Essays*, London: Heinemann.

Marshall, T. H. (1964) *Class, Citizenship and Social Developments*, New York: Doubleday and Company.

Matthews, E. (1986) 'Can Paternalism be Modernized?', *Journal of Medical Ethics* 12 (3):133–6.

Mental Health Act (1983) London: HMSO.

Miliband, R. (1973) *The State and Capitalist Society*, London: Quartet Books.

Mill, J. S. (1863) 'Utilitarianism', in Lindsay, A. D. (ed) (1968) *Utilitarianism, Liberty and Representative Government*, London: J. M. Dent.

Miller, E. J. and Gwynne, G. V. (1972) *A Life Apart*, London: Tavistock.

Millham, S., Bullock, R. and Cherret, P. (1975) *After Grace – Teeth*, London: Human Context Books.

Milo, R. D. (1986) 'Moral Deadlock', *Philosophy* 61:453–71.

Moran, M. (1986) 'Industrial relations', in Drucker, H., Dunleavy, P., Gamble, A., and Peele, G. (eds) *Developments in British Politics 2*, London: Macmillan.

Morris, A. (1981) *Care and Discretion: social workers' decisions with children*, London: Denton.

Morris, A. and Giller, H. (eds) (1983) *Providing Criminal Justice for Children*, London: Edward Arnold.

Morris, T. P. (1963) *Pentonville*, London: Routledge and Kegan Paul.

NASW (1980) *Code of Ethics of the National Association of Social Workers*, Washington, D.C.: National Association of Social Workers.

National Assistance Act (1948) London: HMSO.
Navarro, V. (1986) *Crisis, Health and Medicine*, London: Tavistock.
Nissel, M., Maynard, A., Young, K. and Ibsen, M. (1980) *The Welfare State – Diversity and Decentralization*, London: Policy Studies Institute.
Noddings, N. (1984) *Caring. A feminine approach to Ethics and Moral Education*, Berkeley: University of California Press.
Norman, A. (1980) *Rights and Risk*, London: National Corporation for Care of Old People.
Nozick, R. (1974) *Anarchy, State and Utopia*, Oxford: Blackwell.
O'Hagan, K. (1980) 'What if something terrible happened?', *Community Care* 338:16–18.
O'Hear, A. (1985) *What Philosophy Is*, London: Pelican.
O'Neill, O. (1984) 'Paternalism and Partial Autonomy', *Journal of Medical Ethics* 10 (4):173–8.
Øvretveit, J. (1986) *Improving Social Work Records and Practice*, Birmingham: BASW Publications.
Packman, J. (1986) *Who needs care? Social Work Decisions about Children*, Oxford: Basil Blackwell.
Page, R. and Clarke, G. A. (eds) (1977) *Who cares?*, London: National Children's Bureau.
Parsloe, P. (1988) 'Social services: confidentiality, privacy and data protection', in Pearce, P., Parsloe, P., Francis, H., Macara, A. and Watson, D. *Personal Data Protection in Health and Social Services*, London: Croom Helm.
Parsloe, P. and Stevenson, O. (1978) *Social Service Teams: The Practitioner's View*, London: HMSO.
Parsons, R. (1986) 'Practice and Patch: Passivity Versus Participation', *British Journal of Social Work* 16 Supplement:125–49.
Pateman, C. (1970) *Participation and Democratic Theory*, Cambridge: Cambridge University Press.
Payne, M. (1988) 'Access to social services records', *Journal of the Royal Society of Health* 108 (2):41–4.
Payne, M. (1983) 'Clients and a secret society', *Social Work Today* 14 (44):1.
Payne, M. (1984) 'Involving families in recording', in Froggatt, A. and Shuttleworth, J. (eds) *Family Involvement: Access and Participation*, Bradford: FSU and BASW.
Payne, M. (1978) 'Problems with social work records', *Social Work Today* 9 (32):11–13.
Payne, M. (1982) *Working in Teams*, London: Macmillan.
Phelan, J. (1983) *Family centres: a study*, London: National Children's Bureau.
Philpott, T. (ed) (1984) *Group Care Practice*, Surrey: Business Press International.
Plant, R. (1970) *Social and Moral Theory in Casework*, London: Routledge and Kegan Paul.
Plant, R., Lesser, H., and Taylor-Gooby, P. (1980) *Political Philosophy and Social Welfare*, London: Routledge and Kegan Paul.

Polsky, H. W. (1966) *Cottage Six: The social system of delinquent boys in residential treatment*, New York: Science.

Pugh, G. and De'Ath, E. (1983) *The Needs of Parents: Practice and Policy in Parent Education*, London: Macmillan.

Rack, P. (1982) *Race, Culture and Mental Disorder*, London: Tavistock.

Ragg, N. (1977) *People not Cases*, London: Routledge and Kegan Paul.

Ragg, N. (1980) 'Respect for Persons and Social Work: Social Work as doing philosophy', in Timms, N. (ed.) *Social Welfare: why and how*, London: Routledge and Kegan Paul.

Randall Close Team (1986) *Social Work and Social Care at Randall Close Family Resource Centre*, London: London Borough of Wandsworth.

Rawls, J. (1977) *A Theory of Justice*, Oxford: Oxford Clarendon Press.

Rawls, J. (1982) 'Social Unity and Primary Goods', in Sen, A. and Williams, B. (eds) *Utilitarianism and Beyond*, Cambridge: Cambridge University Press.

Rayfield, M. (1985) *The Gouldings Resource Centre for Elderly People*, Isle of Wight: Isle of Wight Social Services Department.

Rea-Price, J. (1987) 'And though it in the centre sit ...', *Social Services Insight* 2 (20):12–18.

Rees, S. (1978) *Social Work Face to Face*, London: Edward Arnold.

Rees, S. and Wallace, A. (1982) *Verdicts on Social Work*, London: Edward Arnold.

Reeve, A. and Ware, A. (1983) 'Interests in Political Theory', *British Journal of Political Science* 13:379–400.

Reid, W. and Epstein, L. (1972) *Task-Centred Casework*, New York: Columbia University Press.

Rescher, N. (1969) Preface in Baier, K. and Rescher, N. (eds) *Values and the Future*, New York: Free Press.

Reynolds, B. (1970) 'An American namesake and what it stood for', *Social Work Today* 1 (1):4.

Rhodes, M. (1985) 'Gilligan's Theory of Moral Development', *Social Work* March/April:101–10.

Rhodes, M. L. (1986) *Ethical Dilemmas in Social Work Practice*, London: Routledge and Kegan Paul.

Richmond, M. E. (1917) *Social Diagnosis*, New York: Free Press (1965 edition).

Robson, W. A. (1976) *Welfare State and Welfare Society*, London: George Allen and Unwin.

Rogers, A. and Faulkner, A. (1987) *A Place of Safety*, London: Mind Publications.

Rorty, R. (1986) 'The Contingency of Community', *London Review of Books* 8 (13).

Rowe, J. (1987) 'Social work decisions in child care – implications for social workers', in McHugh, J. (ed.) *Creative Social Work with Families*, Birmingham: BASW Publications.

Rowe, J. and Lambert, L. (1973) *Children Who Wait*, London: Association of British Adoption Agencies.

Sang, B. (1982) 'A question of power', *Open Mind* 17.

Schleifer, M. (1973) 'Psychological explanations and interpersonal relations', in Montefiore, H. (ed.) *Philosophy and Personal Relations*, London: Routledge and Kegan Paul.

Sedgwick, P. (1982) *Psycho Politics*, London: Pluto Press.

Seebohm, F. (1968) *Report of the Committee on Local Authority and Allied Personal Social Services*, London: HMSO (Cmnd 3703).

Sen, A. and Williams, B. (eds) (1982) *Utilitarianism and Beyond*, Cambridge: Cambridge University Press.

Seyd, R., Tennant, A., Bayley, M., and Parker, P. (1984) *Community Social Work. Neighbourhood Services Project, Dinnington, Paper No. 8*, Sheffield: Department of Sociological Studies, University of Sheffield.

Shaw, P. D. (1978) 'Medicine and the Market Place', in Timms, N. and Watson, D. (eds) *Philosophy in Social Work*, London: Routledge and Kegan Paul.

Shue, H. (1980) *Basic Rights*, Princeton: Princeton University Press.

Siegler, M. (1982) 'Confidentiality', *New England Journal of Medicine* 307 (24):1518–21.

Simmons, S. (1985) 'Becoming Part of the Network', *Community Care* 574:23–24.

Simpkin, M. (1983) *Trapped within Welfare* (second edition), London: Macmillan.

Simpkin, M. (1989) 'Health Issues. Social Services and Democracy', in Langan, M. and Lee, P. (eds) *Social Work in Recession*, London: Hutchinson.

Sinclair, R. (1984) *Decision-Making in Statutory Reviews on Children in Care*, Aldershot: Gower.

Skeffington Report (1969) *People and Planning: Report of the Committee on Public Participation in Planning*, London: HMSO.

Skinner, P. (1980) 'Our experiment in involving children in reviews', *Social Work Service* 22:43–6.

Smart, J. J. C. (1956) 'Extreme and Restricted Utilitarianism', *Philosophical Quarterly* 6:344–54.

Social Care Association (1986) *A Code of Practice for Social Care*, Surrey: Social Care Association.

Social Services Committee (House of Commons) (1984) *Children in Care Vol. 1*, London: HMSO.

Spencer Report (The Karen Spencer Inquiry) (1976) Matlock: Derbyshire County Council and Derbyshire Health Authority.

Stacey, M. (1985) 'Medical Ethics and Medical Practice', *Journal of Medical Ethics* 11 (1):14–18.

Stark, E. (1982) 'Doctors in spite of themselves: The limits of radical health criticism', *International Journal of Health Services* 12 (3):419–57.

Stein, M. (ed.) (no date) *Ad Lib In Care Group Story*, Leeds: University of Leeds Centre for Social Work and Applied Community Studies.

Taylor, C. (1982) 'The Diversity of Goods', in Sen, A. and Williams, B. (eds) *Utilitarianism and Beyond*, Cambridge: Cambridge University Press.

Thompson, I. (1979) 'The Nature of Confidentiality', *Journal of Medical Ethics* 5 (2):57–64.

Thorpe, D. and Paley, J. (1974) *Children, Handle with Love*, Leicester: National Youth Bureau.

Tillich, P. (1960) *Love, Power and Justice*, Oxford: Oxford University Press.

Timms, N. (1972) *Recording in Social Work*, London: Routledge and Kegan Paul.

Timms, N. (1983) *Social Work Values: an enquiry*, London: Routledge and Kegan Paul.

Timms, N. (1986) 'Value-Talk in Social Work: Present Character and Future Improvement', *Issues in Social Work Education* 6 (1):3–14.

Titmuss, R. (1970) *The Gift Relationship: From human blood to social policy*, London: Allen & Unwin.

Tizard, B. (1977) *Adoption: a Second Chance*, London: Open Books.

Townsend, P. and Davidson, N. (eds) (1982) *Inequalities in Health*, Harmondsworth: Penguin.

Tutt, N. (1974) *Care or Custody: community homes and the treatment of delinquency*, London: Darton, Longman and Todd.

Tyne, A. (1981) 'The impact of the normalization principle on services for the mentally handicapped in the United Kingdom', in Reinach, E. (ed.) *Normalization*, Aberdeen: Department of Social Work, University of Aberdeen.

University of Bath (1987) *Review and recommendations on Brent Social Services*, Bath: Social Policy Studies, University of Bath.

Vernon, J. and Fruin, D. (1986) *In Care: A Study of Social Work Decision-making*, London: National Children's Bureau.

Vickery, A. (1977) *Caseload Management*, London: National Institute for Social Work.

Ward, L. (1977) 'Clarifying the residential social work task', *Social Work Today* 9 (2).

Ward, M. (1986) *Area Family Resource Centres*, London: London Borough of Wandsworth.

Warnock, M. (1985) 'The Artificial Family', in Lockwood, M., *Moral Dilemmas in Medicine*, Oxford: Oxford University Press.

Watson, D. (1980) *Caring for Strangers*, London: Routledge and Kegan Paul.

Weale, A. (1978) *Equality and Social Policy*, London: Routledge and Kegan Paul.

Weale, A. (1972) 'Paternalism and Social Policy', *Journal of Social Policy* 7:157–72.

Weale, A. (1983) *Political Theory and Social Policy*, London: Macmillan.

Weale, A. (1980) 'Procedural Fairness and Rationing the Social Services', in Timms, N. (ed.) *Social Welfare: Why and How*, London: Routledge and Kegan Paul.

Weiss, G. (1985) 'Medical Paternalism Modernized', *Journal of Medical Ethics* 11 (4):184–7.

Whitbeck, C. (1981) 'A Theory of Health', in Caplan, A., Engelhardt, H. T., and McCartney, J. (eds) *Concepts of Health and Disease*, Reading, Massachusetts: Addison-Wesley.

Whitmore, R. and Fuller, R. (1980) 'Priority Planning in an Area Social Services Team', *British Journal of Social Work* 10 (3):277–92.

Wicks, M. (1987) *A Future for All*, Harmondsworth: Penguin.

Wiggins, D. (1978) 'Deliberation and Practical Reason', in Raz, J. (ed.) *Practical Reasoning*, Oxford: Oxford University Press.

Wilkes, R. (1981) *Social Work with Undervalued Groups*, London: Tavistock.

Willcocks, D., Peace, S., and Kelleher, L. (1987) *Private Lives in Public Places*, London: Tavistock.

Williams, B. (1985) *Ethics and the Limits of Philosophy*, London: Fontana.

Williams, B. (1981) *Moral Luck*, Cambridge: Cambridge University Press.

Willmott, P. and Mayne, S. (1983) *Families at the Centre: a study of seven action projects*, London: Bedford Square Press/NCVO.

Wimperis, V. (1960) *The Unmarried Mother and Her Child*, London: Allen and Unwin.

Wittgenstein, L. (1958) *Philosophical Investigations*, Oxford: Basil Blackwell.

Wolfensberger, W. and Thomas, S. (1981) 'The principle of normalization in human services: a brief overview', in Reinach, E. (ed.) *Normalization*, Aberdeen: Department of Social Work, University of Aberdeen.

Wolins, M. (1974) *Successful Group Care*, London: Aldine.

Wollheim, R. (1984) *The Thread of Life*, Cambridge: Cambridge University Press.

Wynn, B. M. (1964) *Fatherless Families*, London: Michael Joseph.

Young, K. (1982) 'Changing Social Services in East Sussex', *Local Government Studies*, March/April 1982:18–22.

Young, L. (1954) *Out of Wedlock*, New York: McGraw-Hill.

Younger Committee (1972) *Report of the Committee on Privacy*, London: HMSO (Cmnd 5012).

Younghusband, E. (1981) *The Newest Profession*, London: Community Care Press.

NAME INDEX

Adamson, J. 87, 88
Ainsworth, F. 82
Adlgate, J. 28
Algie, J. 147–8
Allan, G. 53
Anderson, D. 119, 181
Appleyard, J. 76
Aristotle 65
Asquith, S. 76, 102, 151
Austin, J. 17

Baier, A. 16
Bailey, R. 99, 116
Bamford, T. 108
Bartlett, H. M. 116
Bayley, M. 50, 58, 92
Bean, P. 166
Beehler, R. 13
Beiner, R. 22, 40
Bennett, B. 48
Bennett, J. 76
Bentham, J. 95
Benton, T. 75
Beresford, P. 50, 52, 107
Berger, J. 64
Berlin, I. 128
Berliner, H. 62
Berridge, D. 90
Berry, J. 82
Bettelheim, B. 87
Biestek, F. P. 5, 100, 115, 116, 129,
    135–6, 146, 147, 152, 154
Birchall, D. 88
Black, Sir D. 76
Black, J. 47
Blum, L. 13, 40, 130
Blunden, R. 47

Booth, T. 25, 118
Bowlby, E. J. M. 25, 30
Brake, M. 99, 116
Brook, J. A. 130, 131
Browning, R. C. 41
Bruce, M. 52
Butler, J. 100
Butler, J. 118

Carrick, P. 76
Cheetham, J. 26
Clark, C. L. 14, 76, 102, 151
Clarke, G. A. 82, 90, 118
Clifford, D. 77
Cloke, C. 162
Clough, R. 83
Cohen, R. 122, 129
Collier, A. 78
Corrigan, P. 145, 146, 147, 152
Cox, D. 87
Cranston, M. 184
Crawford, R. 65, 66
Crellin, E. 31, 32, 33
Croft, S. 50, 52
Culver, C. 74

Daniels, J. 65
Davidson, N. 62
Davies, M. 105, 136
Davis, A. 82, 83, 84
Davis, L. 83
De'Ath, E. 88
Dennis, S. 88
De Wachter, M. 80
Dharamsi, F. 83
Doel, M. 127
Downie, R. S. 3, 27, 65, 67, 77, 159

Dworkin, R. 101, 139, 186, 187, 193

Emmet, D. 20, 21
Epstein, L. 100
Etherington, S. 98, 140–1, 147

Faulkner, A. 178
Finch, J. 52, 53, 54
Fisher, M. 28, 173, 174, 177
Flathman, R. 16, 17
Fowler, N. 84
Friedman, M. 180
Freud, S. 157
Friere, P. 89
Fruin, D. 119, 172
Fulcher, L. C. 82
Fuller, R. 148

Garton, N. R. 115
Gauthier, D. 80
Gert, B. 74
Gilbert, N. 188, 189, 197
Giller, H. 25, 153
Gilligan, C. 157, 158, 159, 160, 161, 169
Gillon, R. 73
Gobell, A. 87
Goldberg, E. M. 88, 118, 123
Gostin, L. 166
Greengross, S. 168, 169
Griffin, J. 16, 19
Guay, J. 50, 51
Gwynne, G. V. 83

Hadley, R. 48, 50, 117
Halmos, P. 13
Hamilton, G. 115, 116, 121
Hampshire, S. 65, 78
Hare, R. M. 3, 46, 65, 184
Harman, G. 185
Harris, J. 64
Hart, H. L. A. 182, 183
Hasler, J. 88, 89
Hastings, A. 62
Hatch, S. 117
Hayek, F. A. 180, 181
Heraud, B. J. 157
Hohfeld, W. N. 19
Holder, D. 59
Holman, R. 31
Hoskins, J. 99
Hospers, J. 132–3
Hudson, B. L. 100

Huntingdon, J. 63
Huws Jones, R. 1

Illich, I. 74, 118

Jenson, G. 119
Jenson, L. 119
Jones, K. 106
Jordan, B. 118

Kelleher, L. 89
Kelly, D. 88
Kennedy, I. 74
Kohlberg, L. 157, 158
Konrad, G. 146
Kotarba, J. 66
Kushlick, A. 47
Kushner, T. 77

Lambert, L. 28
Lane, D. 83
Lawson, B. 127
Laycock, J. 151
Leach, E. 65
Lee, P. 84
Leighton, N. 2, 4, 56, 57
Leonard, P. 145, 146, 147, 152
Levitt, R. 117
Line, B. F. 82, 83, 90
Lockwood, M. 61
Lonsdale, S. 70
Loudfoot, E. M. 3
Lukes, S. 129
Lyons, K. 107

McArdle, I. 87
McCarthy, M. 118
McDermott, F. E. 14, 73, 116
Macdonald, G. M. 100
McDonald, R. 88, 89
McGrath, M. 48, 50, 117
MacIntyre, A. 21, 75, 76, 78
McKeown, T. 62
McVeigh, J. 120
Maiden, J. 76
Mandell, B. 32
Maple, F. 115
Marsden, D. 31
Marshall, T. H. 180
Marx, K. 89
Matthews, E. 74
Mayne, S. 91
Mendelsohn 189

Miliband, R. 147
Mill, J. S. 95
Miller, C. 148
Miller, E. J. 83
Millham, S. 25
Milo, R. D. 20, 21
Moran, M. 117
Morris, A. 35, 153
Morris, T. P. 25

Navarro, V. 64, 67
Noddings, N. 157, 159, 169
Norman, A. 169
Norzik, R. 144–5, 146, 181

O'Hagan, K. 58
O'Hear, A. 143
O'Neill, O. 74, 75
Otto, H. A. 115
Øvretveit, J. 114, 123

Packman, J. 174
Page, R. 82, 90, 118
Paley, J. 36
Parker, C. 140–1, 147
Parsloe, P. 134, 147, 151
Parsons, R. 56
Pateman, C. 125
Payne, M. 70, 123, 127, 133
Peace, S. 89
Phelan, J. 88, 90
Philpott, T. 82
Piaget, J. 157
Pithers, D. 84
Plant, R. 14, 126, 128, 131–2, 159
Plato, 65
Plekhanov, G. V. 78
Polsky, H. W. 25
Pugh, G. 88

Rack, P. 178
Ragg, N. 63, 79, 143
Rawls, J. 65, 74, 144–5, 146, 147, 160, 185, 186, 187, 193
Rayfield, M. 88
Rees, S. 117, 153
Reeve, A. 19
Reid, W. 100
Rescher, N. 17
Reynolds, B. 115
Rhodes, M. L. 27, 76, 79, 111, 148, 157, 159, 160, 161, 167, 169
Robson, W. A. 105

Rogers, A. 178
Rorty, R. 76
Rowe, J. 28, 174
Rutter, M. 25

Salmon, J. W. 62
Sang, B. 119
Schleifer, M. 132
Sedgewick, P. 175
Seebohm, F. 100, 111
Seyd, R. 55, 59
Shaw, P. D. 65
Shue, H. 184
Siegler, M. 71
Simmons, S. 92
Simpkin, M. 61, 85, 92, 99, 152
Sinclair, I. 88
Sinclair, R. 119
Skinner, P. 119
Smart, J. J. C. 95, 96
Stacey, M. 64
Stalley, R. 2, 4
Stanley, J. S. 118
Stark, E. 63
Stein, M. 118
Stevenson, O. 147, 151
Subotsky, F. 76
Szasz, T. 176

Taylor, C. 75
Telfer, E. 27, 65, 67, 77, 159
Thomas, S. 118
Thompson, I. 67
Thorpe, D. 35
Tillich, P. 160
Timms, N. 1, 4, 19, 40, 73, 83, 84, 85, 100, 101, 121
Titmuss, R. 58, 131
Tizard, B. 33
Townsend, P. 62
Tutt, N. 36
Tyne, A. 118

Utting, W. B. 189

Vernon, J. 119, 172
Vickery, A. 148

Wallace, A. 117
Warburton, R. W. 123
Ward, L. 82
Ward, M. 93
Wardle, M. 59

Ware, A. 19
Warnock, M. 76
Warren, C. 87, 88
Watson, D. 2, 4, 131
Weale, A. 101, 106, 147, 187, 194, 195
Weiss, G. 74
Whitbeck, C. 66
White, K. 83
Whitmore, R. 148
Wicks, M. 7, 181
Wiggins, D. 76
Wilkes, R. 36, 37
Willcocks, D. 89

Williams, B. 75, 76, 94
Willmott, P. 91
Wimperis, V. 31
Wittgenstein, L. 85
Wolfensberger, W. 118
Wolins, M. 82
Wollheim, R. 12, 15
Wynn, B. M. 31

Young, K. 50
Young, L. 30
Younghusband, E. 103

SUBJECT INDEX

acceptance 14–15
access to records 114, 118, 120–3; as a
  control device 124
accountability: and locally based work
  57; in multi-disciplinary teams 64,
  70; and participation 104, 111; and
  recording 126–7
advocacy 191; client advocacy 119,
  126
approved social workers 68, 175; and
  training 177
autonomy 64, 70, 73–5, 76

Barclay Report (1982) 87, 108, 117
Beckford Report (1985) 142, 164
behaviourism 25
Beveridge report (1942) 180
black people: treatment under the
  Mental Health Act 178; the black
  experience 22; and social work
  37–9
Bonnington Report (1984) 87
British Association of Social Workers
  (BASW); code of ethics 2, 37, 39,
  100, 122, 153; and participation 98,
  118; and recording 120, 122–3,
  126–7, 128, 134
British Medical Association (BMA) 63,
  64, 76
bureaucracies 148–9
bureaucratisation: and mental health
  178; of personal life 76

care orders 137; due to social risk 164
care proceedings 163, 165
carers: Association of 118;
  responsibilities and rights of 51–4,

58, 79; and self determination 142;
  women as 53–4
case studies: Miss Ernest and Sam 34–
  7; Naseem and Miss Hasty 37–9;
  Miss Sad, Miss Small and Jane
  27–34
Central Council for Education and
  Training in social work (CCETSW)
  15, and residential work 82; and
  values 2, 4, 13, 15
Certificate of Social Service (CSS) 150
Charity Organisation 100
child abuse: and discretion 136–7; and
  media pressure on social workers 8;
  and risk 162; and teamwork 67, 72
Child Care Act (1980) 30
child care law 163
Child Poverty Action Group (CPAG)
  118
children and young persons:
  competence of 170–1; compulsory
  removal from home 170–4;
  consequences of removal from
  home 172; protection of 170
Children and Young Persons Act
  (1969) 137
children's homes 90, 92
Chronically Sick and Disabled Persons
  Act (1970) 191
Church of England Board for Social
  Responsibility (1986) 58
citizenship 17, 21–3; social citizenship
  180, 194
civil liberties 178, 179, 184
clients: and accountability 104; and
  bureaucracies 148–9; and conflicts
  of interest 140–2; in family centres

91–3; and locally based work 48–9; relationship with social workers 2–3, 103; in residential care 89–90
collaborative work and value conflict 67–8
Colwell inquiry (1974) 56, 136
community care 25, 53, 67, 168; and participation 107–8
community involvement: in health care 71; and participation 111–12
community social work 91; and participation 104; and resource centres 87, 116
competency 189–90; and children and young people 170–1; parental competence 171
compulsory admission 66, 142
compulsory removal from home 155–79; and children and young people 170–4; the legal context 165–7; and mentally ill 174–9; and old people 168–70; as protection 156; and risk 162–5
computers and data protection 121–2
confidentiality 14, 27, 56–60; and health care 64, 70, 71–3; utilitarian justification of 72
consent 74–5
consumers 118–19, 140–1; and access to information 122; consumerism 7, 117; consumerist model and health care 74
contract 23, 25, 183; contractarianism 80
control 58; and locally based work 54–5; in residential care 89–90
court reports 140
creative justice 160, 174, 179
cultural relativism 167; and child rearing 171
custodial care: ineffectiveness of 172–3

Data Protection Act (1984) 122
decision making: and clients 114–34; development in social work 115–20; ethical and philosophical questions about 124–33; factors affecting 26–7, 31–4, 40; the moral aspect of 24–5; participation in 125; and political intervention 150–1; and responsibility of social worker 135; after Seebohm 136; and value systems 138–49

Determination of Needs Act (1941) 52
Directors of Social Services: Association of 137
discretion 135–54; exercise of 138–40; limitations of 137–8
distributive justice 160
duty 20

Economic Affairs, Institute of 180, 181
Elderly Persons Support Unit (EPSU) 89
Environment, Department of 117
equality 105–6; of access 193

family centres 87–9; holistic approach to 92–3; origins of 88–9
family obligations 53
fraternity 13
Freud: influence on social work training 18

guardianship 168; of neonates 68

Health and Social Security, Department of (DHSS) 88
health: concept of 64–7; definition of 78
Hippocratic Oath 72, 76
holism 62, 66
holistic health care 61–81
home helps and wardens 48
humanism 27

illegitimacy 30–2
individual: needs of 93–7; primacy of 24; respect for 14
individualism 13
informal care: and locally based work 45–6, 51, 52; and women 53–4
institutional care: outcomes of 25, 30
interdependence and locally based work 58
intermediate treatment 34–7

Kincora 82

learning theory 18
liberalism 27
Lindop Committee (1978) 121
Local Authority Social Services Act (1971) 135
locally based work 45–60;

development of 45–8; and preventative work 55–6

Magistrates Association 137
managerialism 135–54; impact on discretion 137
Marxist theory 145–6; influence on social work training 18; and medicine 64, 67
medical profession: challenges to 61–3; and social work 63–4, 67–8
Mental Health Act (1959) 166
Mental Health Act (1983) 142, 155, 165, 168; section 136 and treatment of black people 178
Mental Health Act Commission 167, 191
Mental Health Review Tribunals 166
mental illness 67, concept of 175; and risk 176
mentally handicapped 162; and residential care 87
mentally ill 162; and the legal context 166; and risk to others 163
MIND 118
moral: and decision making 25–7, 96–7; definition of 12, development 157–62; dilemmas 11, 20–1; and a feminist perspective 157–62; judgement 20; and rights 182–4
Moslem society 38
multidisciplinary teams 61, 70, 72–3

National Assistance Act (1948) 155; section 47 165, 168–9
National Association for Mental Health 118
National Association of Social Workers (NASW) 2, 153
National Association of Young People in Care (NAYPIC) 87, 118
National Children's Bureau 118
National Schizophrenia Fellowship 118
natural rights: and private social work 184–5, 189–92
normalisation 118, 130, 141, 143
Nye Bevan Lodge 82

old people: and physical abuse 162; and removal from home 168–70
open records 114–34, 120–4; and arbitrary power 128–9

parental competence 170
parental drug addiction 68
parental rights 33, 37
participation 7, 98–113, 115, 117; BASW report on 118; in case conferences 119, 129; in decision making 119; and the effectiveness argument 124; in family centres 88; in locally based work 49–50; in residential units 83, 90–3
partnership practice 60
patch based social work 49; and confidentiality 56–7
paternalism 98–113; and medical ethics 73–4; and participation 109–13; and records 121
parents' rights 61–2, 74
Place of Safety Orders 165
pluralism 39, 75
Police Court Mission 100
Poor Law (1930) 52
poverty: and single parent families 33–4
preventative work: and locally based work 55–6
priorities 147–8
private residential care: efficiency of 189; growth of 181–2; moral opposition to 188–9
privatization: in social work 180–97, and morality 182–8
procedural fairness 194–6
professional ethical codes 26
professionalism 78, 153; and locally based work 57
proportional justice 141–2, 160, 179

reciprocity 49, 58, 78, 79, 91
recording 120–3; and BASW 123; and styles of work 123, 126–7
records 114, 118; access to 120–4
religious and cultural tolerance 37
residential care: and children 83–4, 86–7; and closure 138; and elderly 84; and needs of the individual 93; and relationship between staff and residents 83–4; and social needs of residents 89–90; and values 82–4
residential social work 82–97
respect: for the individual 14; for persons 99–101
resource centres 86–9; and the needs of the individual 93–7

responsibilities 51; of the family 51–4; sharing of 80

risk: environmental 164–5; emotional and social 162–4; evaluation of 142, 156, 162–5; and mental illness 176–7; physical risk 162; and risk to others 163–4

Seebohm Report (1968) 47, 136

self determination 13; constraints on 140–9, 151; and effectiveness 124; and liberty 14, 18, 19; limit of 24; and statutory obligation 33, 37, 38, 39, 73–5, 115–16, 126–8; and suicide 177

sexual abuse 162

shared decision making 114–34; development of conceptions of 115–20; and arbitrary power 128–9

single mothers: case study 27–34

Skeffington Report (1969) 51, 117

Social Affairs, Institute of 180, 181

Social Affairs Unit 181

Social Care Association 2; code of ethics 82

social citizenship 180, 181, 194

social control 155

social justice 33

social skills training 25

Spencer Report (1978) 164

Statement of National Objectives for Probation 36

statutory obligation 33, 36–7

statutory work 26

suicide 177

supervision 139

surrogate parenthood 68

system: and values 15–17

task centred casework 118, 130; and participation 104

unmarried mothers 26

utilitarianism 35, 77, 95–7, 143–6, 152, 185; 'restricted' utilitarianism 95–7; rule utilitarian 95–6

value conflicts: in collaborative work 67–8

value judgements 3–4, 37

value systems: differences between men and women 158; and social workers 13

value terms: differences between social work and medicine 61–81

values: definition of 4–5, 15–16, 18; importance of 1–4; and residential care 82–6

volunteers 51

vulnerability 190–1

wardship 165

whole person approach 48–9

workload management 148

Younger Committee (1972) 121